HOW TO
WIN SOULS
INFLUENCE PEOPLE

HOW TO
WIN SOULS
& INFLUENCE PEOPLE

RAY COMFORT

Bridge-Logos *Publishers*

North Brunswick, New Jersey 08902 USA

How to Win Souls and Influence People
by Ray Comfort
Copyright © 1999 by Bridge-Logos Publishers
Library of Congress Catalog Card Number: 99-067198
International Standard Book Number: 0-88270-788-4

Published by:
Bridge-Logos *Publishers*
1300 Airport Road, Suite E
North Brunswick, NJ 08902
http://www.bridgelogos.com

BV 4520. C 635

Dedicated: To my friends Stephen T. Smith and Jason Drake . . . good soldiers of Jesus Christ.

"The enemy is behind us.
The enemy is in front of us.
The enemy is to the right and
the left of us.
They can't get away this time!"
General Douglas MacArthur

CONTENTS

CHAPTER ONE

STATIONED AT THE GATES

*"Others save with fear, pulling them out of the
fire . . . " (Jude 23).*

I was feeling quite pleased with myself. For the
first time in months I didn't feel "wrung out." Often I
would return from weekend meetings absolutely
exhausted. Sue, my wife, would meet me at the airport,
drive me home and put me into bed. But this weekend
had been quite different. I was the speaker at a camp.
The organizers had not been to the *Squeeze the Preacher*
school, and had let me off with an amazing three
meetings in the whole weekend. Now the camp was over
and I was being shown my lodging for Sunday night.

After seeing my room, I made my way to an
upstairs living room. The view was magnificent.
Through the large window I gazed at the harbor below
and watched as the sun seemed to dance on the still
water. I sat down in a soft armchair and took a look
around. A footstool, the view, a large television, a stereo
. . . and now the hostess entered the room with a cup of
hot chocolate and a plate full of fresh home baking.
This place was made for Comfort. Ease consumed me.
I reached out to take one of the offered goodies when
suddenly, much to my shock and the surprise of the

1

woman, I jumped out of my seat like a terrified cat on a blistering hot tin roof. I then turned around to see a yellow and black bee crawling around the seat of the armchair. *I had been squarely stung on the hindmost part!*

I was in too much pain to be embarrassed. As I jumped about the room, my only consolation was the thought, *"There's got to be a sermon in this . . ."* Some years before, I had prayed a most dangerous prayer. I asked God to cause things to happen in my life which I could use as sermon illustrations. At this point in time I regretted having made that request.

It wasn't long until I saw the application. I am convinced that God wants the complacent Laodicean Church to rise up on its feet. For too long we have sat in ease and comfort. We have sat back in affluence and said, "I am rich, and have need of nothing," and if it takes the sting of God's chastening hand to cause the Church to stand upright, may it come quickly. Charles Spurgeon said, "God save us from living in comfort while sinners are sinking into Hell!" Whitefield said, "The Christian world is in a deep sleep; nothing but a loud shout can awaken them out of it!" Catherine Booth, the gentle co-founder of the Salvation Army, regarding church buildings said, "A barracks is meant to be a place where real soldiers were to be fed and equipped for war, not a place to settle down in or as a comfortable snuggery in which to enjoy ourselves. I hope that if ever they, our soldiers, do settle down God will burn their barracks over their heads!"

The Withered Hand

In Luke Chapter 6, the religious leaders were seeking an accusation against Jesus. We pick up the story in verse 6:

"On another Sabbath He went into the Synagogue and was teaching, and a man was there whose right hand was withered. The Pharisees and the teachers of the Law were looking for a reason to accuse Jesus, so they watched Him closely to see if He would heal on the Sabbath. But Jesus knew what they were thinking and said to the man with the withered hand, 'Get up and stand in front of everyone.' So he got up and stood there. Then Jesus said to them, 'I ask you, which is lawful on the Sabbath: to do good or to do evil, to save life or to destroy it?'

"He looked around at them all, and then said to the man, 'Stretch out your hand.' He did so and his hand was completely restored. But they were furious and began to discuss with one another what they might do to Jesus."

Some years ago, the *Dallas Morning News* reported that 68% of professing Christians outside of the "Bible Belt" didn't see reaching out to the lost as being the number one priority of the Church. This was in line with what the Barna Research Group found. In a survey, they discovered that among American adults who said they were "born again," 75% couldn't even define the Great Commission. Also around that time another survey, this one in *Christianity Today* (a major evangelistic magazine), found that only 1% of their readership said that they had witnessed to someone "recently." That meant that 99% of their readership couldn't say that they were "hot" or "cold" when it came to concern for the fate of the ungodly. They were just "lukewarm." In one year, over 3,000 churches from a mainline denomination *didn't report even one soul saved in that whole year*. Oswald J. Smith said, "Oh my friends, we are loaded with countless church activities, while the real work of the Church, that of evangelizing and winning the lost is almost entirely neglected."

The "right hand" of the Body of Christ is withered. The hand, which is supposed to be moved with and by compassion, is not pulling sinners from the fire, hating even the garments spotted by the flesh (see Jude 22-23). We have lost sight of our commission. The agenda, the plan of attack, the *reason* for the battle has been lost under a dark cloud of apathy. The right hand of the Body of Christ hangs limp at its side. We need to hear the voice of Jesus: "Arise, stand forth in the midst and stretch forth your hand." When we stand forth in the midst and stretch forth our hand we will begin to see that glorious, spotless, victorious Church for which Jesus is coming back. This is the fiery Church we see in the *Book of Acts*—a far cry from what we see in the Church of today. Take a fresh look at Acts. Every corner the Church turned, it preached the Gospel. It could not but speak that which it had seen and heard.

We have become like a frog in a bowl of water. The water has slowly been frozen, and the frog, not able to detect the drop in temperature, has remained in the water until it is trapped in ice. The professing Church has become snared in the ice-cold grip of contemporary traditionalism. It involves itself in everything but the purpose for which it was established—to reach out to the lost with the Gospel of Salvation. It has neglected the Great Commission. It calls Jesus Lord, but has left Him standing at its door, and is in danger of being spewed out of His mouth.

Fight the Good Fight of Faith

When Paul wrote to Timothy, he used military terms— "Fight the good fight of faith," "Endure hardness as a good soldier," etc. He wanted to remind Timothy that he was involved in a battle, and a great conflict. We shouldn't be surprised if the world fires hostilities at us. We are a friend of God and therefore an enemy of the world. It is time for the trumpet to give a certain sound so that the Church will prepare itself for battle. Either we take hold of shield and buckler and fight with the weapons God has issued, or we wither and die.

The Armory of Inspiration

I love the structure of the Salvation Army, with its barracks, soldiers, uniforms and its generals. General Booth formed that army of fiery believers so that they should never forget that they were involved in spiritual conflict. Satan has not declared peace with the Church, yet the Church acts as if he has. Men of God such as C.H. Spurgeon never lost sight of the spirit of militancy. In reference to inspired preaching he said, "Surely there is no weapon so powerful as that which is taken from the armory of inspiration."

There will be no peace on this earth until the Prince of Peace comes in power and great glory at the sound of the last trumpet, blown by the very cavalry of Calvary.

Like A Mighty Tortoise

Over the years, I have asked churches, "How many of you can say before God that you have witnessed verbally to more than 12 people over the past 12 months? That is, at least every 30 days or so somebody who is sitting in the shadow of death has heard the Gospel of everlasting life from your lips?" I have found that only 8-12 percent will raise their hands. Where is the zeal? Jesus said, "But you shall receive *power* when the Holy Spirit comes on you; *and you shall be my witnesses* in Jerusalem, and in all Judea and Samaria, and to the ends of the earth" (Acts 1:8, italics added). The Holy Spirit wasn't given without purpose in mind. He was given so that we might have power for the purpose of being witnesses of Christ. So many profess to possess the power, but where is the lifestyle that confirms what they profess to possess?

It would seem that the fear of battle has left many a soldier hiding in the barracks. They are afraid to let their light shine before men because they know that men hate the light. Yet, it is a natural principle that when light shines darkness flees. Darkness cannot overcome light. Try it. Switch on some darkness and see if the light leaves, then try it the other way around.

"Gross darkness" only covers this earth because the Church has not obeyed the admonition to "arise and shine." We often speak up when it comes to moral issues. We do scatter a little salt. But salt doesn't shine. Among other things, it merely preserves.

I was somewhere in the Midwest sitting with a friend at a respectable restaurant, waiting to be served. I went to the restroom and when I came back I remarked to my friend, "That's bad. They've got a pornographic poster outside the men's restrooms."

I suddenly felt like a hypocrite. I then walked over to a waiter and asked why the poster was on the wall. He stepped back defensively and said, "That wasn't *my* idea. It was the manager's. He's over there." I told him that I wanted to speak with the manager.

When the man approached me I said, "Is it the normal policy of this restaurant chain to have pornographic pictures on the wall?"

He looked at me inquiringly and said, "Is there a nude picture somewhere?"

I said, "No. I mean that one on the wall." I pointed to the poster of a beautiful woman wearing an excuse for a bikini, and said, "That's designed to stir up lust. That is just what it's going to do with some young guy, and before you know it some lady is raped in *your* parking lot." He went wide-eyed. I thanked him for listening to me, and made my way back to my table.

When my steak was served up a few minutes later, I called the waiter over and joked that it was still alive. He smiled and said that it would be back in a few minutes, but this time cooked properly.

It was back a few minutes later. My plate was delivered to me by the manager himself. He was very humble, and even took a tract from me.

The incident was a lesson for me not to complain to Christians about the sins of the world, but to confront the world. We forget that salt must be shaken out of the shaker.

The Bible says that we are salt *and* light. Salt preserves, but it's the "light of the glorious Gospel of Christ" that will banish the darkness.

What Battle?

Some years ago a traditional church dropped "Onward Christian Soldiers" from their song index because it made reference to war. That's understandable for people who have never been born again. War is the last thing on their minds. They are "peacemakers" meeting in a building which they think is the "church." They are not born of the Spirit, so they live in a natural world. They are spiritually insensitive because they are spiritually dead. The world may think there is peace between man and God, but the Bible makes it clear that unregenerate man is an enemy of God in his mind through wicked works, that anyone who is a friend of the world is an enemy of God (see Colossians 1:21, Romans 5:10, Romans 8:7, James 4:4). Many within the Church have lost sight of this important truth, something evident by their passive lifestyle. We have become like the Dead Sea. It is dead because it has water flowing into it, but no outlet. The water has become so salty, a human being can't sink into it. Nothing lives in it, no one can penetrate it...just like the contemporary Church. If the average church made as much noise *about* God on Monday, as it makes *to* God on Sunday, we would certainly see revival.

Useless though it seems, the Dead Sea contains very valuable minerals, which are waiting to be harvested. So does the modern Church. It is a field which is white unto harvest, both for souls and for laborers.

Perhaps much of the Church needs to consider dropping "Onward Christian Soldiers" and replacing it with something more appropriate:

Backward Christian soldiers, fleeing from the fight
　With the Cross of Jesus nearly out of sight.
Christ our rightful master, stands against the foe
　But forward into battle, we are loathe to go.
Like a mighty tortoise moves the Church of God

Brothers we are treading where we've always trod.
We are much divided, many bodies we
Having many doctrines, not much charity.
Crowns and thorns may perish, kingdoms
rise and wane,
But the Church of Jesus hidden does remain.
Gates of Hell should never 'gainst the Church prevail
We have Christ's own promise, but think that it will fail.
Sit here then ye people, join our useless throng
Blend with ours your voices in a feeble song.
Blessings, ease and comfort, ask from Christ the King
With our modern thinking, we don't do a thing.
(Anonymous)

Are we hot for God? Can we say that we have witnessed to more than 12 people in the last 12 months? Do we have the testimony "to live means opportunities for Christ?" Is there a zeal to witness burning in our bones? It doesn't matter how much we pray, tithe, fellowship . . . Jesus said to "Go." Obedience is better than sacrifice. Sure, those things are basics of the Christian faith, but if we are not sharing that faith we are not fulfilling our commission. We are like survivors of the Titanic singing songs as we polish brass in the lifeboat, when there is room for many who are drowning around us. There is nothing wrong with polishing brass . . . *but not while people are drowning around us.* We are *commissioned* soldiers. True Christianity is not a pleasure-cruiser on its way to Heaven, but a battleship stationed at the very gates of Hell!

CHAPTER TWO

PRE BATTLE: STANDARD INVENTORY

"For the weapons of our warfare are not carnal, but mighty through God to the pulling down of strongholds" (2 Corinthians 10:4).

As I sat in the plush home not too far from Hollywood, the flesh on my face was almost pulled back by the volume of the video I was watching. Two days earlier I had asked Sue where I could find some good military terms "to stir the troops," as I penned the final words of this publication. Now I sat in the home of a man whose job it was to check the sound of the master copy of "Gettysburg," the great motion picture epic which so graphically depicted the American Civil War. My new friend, Michael Strong, had worked for many years with the Billy Graham Evangelistic Association on films such as "Hiding Place" and "Joni," and for some reason he wanted me to see the battle scene in Gettysburg. He was a good sound man. Sound was his business, and sound is what we had as troops rallied with a unified roar of admiration around their general like "a mighty man who shouts by reason of wine."

As the battle began, most of the infantrymen lay on the ground as cannons blasted the enemy, vibrating the room in which I was sitting and filling the battle scene with thick smoke. With less than a second between each blast, I sat wide-eyed as the sound of each cannon hit me between the ears.

To my surprise, there was no direct confrontation between the two armies. The cannons did all the preparatory work, sending terror into the heart of the enemy, *then* the soldiers pressed in to the heat of battle. My heart was stirred as I saw the spiritual principles set so vividly before me.

We live in an age when the Church roars with adoration for our Commander on Sunday, but hides from the heat of the battle on Monday. I am certain that this is because we have set aside the cannons God has given us to do the preparatory work in our battle. If you are issued with a feather duster and pushed into the heat of warfare, it would be quite understandable if you were fearful. However, if you are issued with ten great cannons, *those very weapons would give you courage.*[1] We will look briefly at this teaching later in this publication.

Welcome to the Army

One great key to success in an army is a unity of purpose, a merging into one mind. This is unusually achieved by *de-personalizing* the recruits—"You sloppy bunch! In the next six weeks we are going to make you boys into men . . . you'll wish you'd never been born! I'm

---

[1] If you are not familiar with these great cannons, it would be well worth your while to read our book, *Hell's Best Kept Secret* (Whitaker House). See the last pages of this book for details.

going to tell you *how* to think, *when* to think, and *what* to think!" etc. Curly locks of hair are callously clipped from cringing craniums. The reason for this is that when an army is on the front lines, the commander doesn't want his troops spending time on the vanities of life. He doesn't want his men wasting time in front of the mirror. He wants one body of men to do what he wants when he wants. His life and the life of his men may depend on it.

God has made His own ways of getting new recruits into line (I think I prefer the army's way). As a new Christian, I went into what is commonly called a "wilderness experience." It was a most dreadful, miserable, depressing experience, but in retrospect it was a necessary part of my primary training. God wants to shake the "world" out of new converts. They have enlisted in the Army of God for active service. The quicker they respond, the quicker they will be trained . . . the quicker they will find themselves promoted in rank, and relocated to where the action is.

The Navy Way

When the U.S. Navy trains rescue pilots, they place so much psychological pressure on recruits, that 50% drop out. They want the best, so those who enlist are pushed to the limits by being dropped out of helicopters into freezing water. In the water, a man simulates a drowning, and when his rescuer reaches him, he deliberately panics, grabbing the would-be rescuer and pulling him under. The trainee must take charge of the situation or be disqualified from the course. He must take control, not only of the circumstances, but also of his own fears.

Christianity isn't for wimps. God put the heat of tribulation on Jesus in the desert (see Luke 4:1)— "though He was a Son, yet He learned obedience by the things that He suffered . . . " (Hebrews 5:8). How much more will you and I be tried if we want to walk in the footsteps of the Savior? If we want to rescue humanity from the fires of Hell, we must take control, both of our own fears and of the demonic restraints placed in front of us.

The time has come when every able soldier is needed in the front line of battle. He who will not overcome will be overcome. As a great man once said, "We must keep our fears to ourselves and share our courage with others."

We need to know what our weapons are, and we need to have expertise in their use so that we might be effective in penetrating enemy territory. Ephesians 6:10-18 lists some of our basic inventories, where seven standard items are listed:

1. The Belt of Truth
2. The Breastplate of Righteousness
3. Feet fitted with the Gospel of Peace
4. The Shield of Faith
5. The Helmet of Salvation
6. The Sword of the Spirit
7. The Power of Prevailing Prayer

It was James the First who said that armor was a wonderful invention. Not only did it stop anyone from harming the wearer, but it also stopped the wearer from doing any harm to anybody else. Not so with the armor of God. It is effective in both defense and offense. For it to be such, we must make sure we are continually wearing the "*whole* armour of God."

First, we are told to have our loins "girt about with truth." This is a reference to the belt worn by soldiers around the time this Scripture was written. Their clothing wasn't like ours. It was often loose. To be free from being hindered by this loose clothing, a soldier would "gird up his waist" or fasten the clothing to his belt.

The application of this is very plain. If we allow any untruth to be resident within our minds or to be uttered from our lips, it will eventually trip us, causing us to stumble or to be our downfall.

So our first preparation for battle is to determine to speak the truth, the whole truth, and nothing but the truth . . . from the heart, *without compromise.* That means we are to be honest with ourselves and others. David tells us that truth should be our shield. He says, "I have chosen the way of truth," speaking of a willful resolution. Solomon exhorts us to "buy the truth and sell it not." In other words, give your all for the truth and don't make concessions at any price.

If you want to see how we deceive ourselves with lies, try this way of sharing your faith. Ask an unsaved person if he has kept the Ten Commandments. Most will say, "Yeah, pretty much." Then say, "Let's go through them and see how you do. Have you ever told a lie?" The usual answer is, "One or two." Then ask, "What does that make you?" and watch human nature do verbal contortions rather than face the truth. They will say, "I'm not a liar. Everyone tells white lies. I'm only *human.* I bet *you've* told lies! They're just 'white' lies."

The Ten Commandments are like a mirror, and the picture we see reflected in the Law is not a pretty one. However, when we become Christians, we *face* the truth. *We are sinners.* Our hearts are desperately wicked.

We are easily deceived by our own conceit. We know that we can look in the mirror of the Law, walk away and "forget what manner of persons we are" (see James 1:24). We can lie to ourselves, therefore we must continually search our hearts under the spotlight of the fear of God and the light of the Word of Truth.

If this is to be our attitude to truth in general, how much more should it be our attitude to the truth of the Gospel, where the eternal welfare of men's souls are at stake. We are to be "valiant for the truth," following the One who has the "law of truth in His mouth," who is "full of grace and truth," who is "the way, the truth, and the life."

It's interesting to note the relationship John the Baptist had to Elijah. Jesus said that John came in the spirit and power of Elijah (Luke 1:15). There are also similarities between John and the Church. As with John, the true Christian:

1. Preaches in the "wilderness" of this world.
2. Rebukes even the sin of kings.
3. Has a diet of locusts (plague of the Law) and honey (the sweetness of the Gospel).
4. Is burning and shining light.
5. Prepares the way of the Lord.
6. Is uncompromising in regard to sin.
7. Preaches future punishment.
8. Is filled with the Spirit.
9. Is bold.
10. Is humble of heart.

It goes without saying then that there will be similarities between Elijah and the Church. It was said of Elijah that he was "a hairy man, girt with a girdle of leather about his loins" (see 2 Kings 1:8). John, like Elijah, wore "[2] camel's hair, and a leathern girdle about his loins." As we have seen, we are commanded to have our "loins girt about with truth." Why was Elijah hounded like a dog? Simply because he preached uncompromising truth. He would not bow the knee to Baal. Why was John the Baptist thrown in prison and eventually lose his life? Simply because he preached uncompromising truth. He refused to bend his message to accommodate a King's infidelity.

In Acts 21, a man named Agabus took Paul's girdle, bound his own hands and feet and said, "Thus says the Holy Spirit, 'So shall the Jews at Jerusalem bind the man who owns this belt, and deliver him into the hands of the Gentiles'" (verse 11). It was appropriate that Agabus used Paul's girdle because he was to be persecuted simply because he preached uncompromising truth. He refused to compromise the fact that a man is not justified by the works of the Law, but only by faith in Jesus Christ.

Jesus warned Peter that he would pay the ultimate price for his faith. He said that when he was young he girded himself, and because of this he was able to walk wherever he wanted. Then he said that when Peter was old, another would gird him and carry him where he didn't wish to go (see John 21:18).

When we are gird about with truth, the world will hate us. If we would just say that Jesus isn't the only way to God, or that you can sin and love God, or that the Bible is only one revelation of God to man, then we would have the world's smile. The unyielding truth may cause us to have to pay the ultimate price for our faith.

---

[2] Elijah may have also worn camel's hair. " . . . the 'mantle' worn by Elijah appears to have been the skin of a sheep or some other animal with the wool left on." *Unger's Bible Dictionary*

Like Peter, when we were young and lacked the understanding as to what produced true salvation, we had a choice. However, because we know the truth, we have no choice. We cannot but speak that which we have seen and heard.

Those who have been born of the Spirit of truth, "cannot do anything against the truth, but only for the truth" . . . "having your loins girt about with truth."

Holy Boldness

The second item which we are commanded to put on as soldiers of the Lord, is the "breastplate of righteousness." In 1 Thessalonians 5:8, Paul says, "Let us who are of the day be sober, putting on the breastplate of faith and love . . . " Here we are reminded that we are enlisted in the Army of the God of love. Righteousness by itself is no defense against the enemy. The Pharisees had a form of righteousness, yet were still sons of the devil (see John 8:44). Without love we are nothing (see 1 Corinthians 13:13). Charles Spurgeon said, "Love should give wings to the feet of service, and strength to the arms of labor."

Righteousness must be linked with faith and love (see Hebrews 11:6). It is this righteousness that shows whose side we are on:

"In this the children of God are manifest, and the children of the devil: whosoever doeth not righteousness is not of God, neither he that loveth not his brother" (1 John 3:10).

If we have been born of the God of righteousness we will live in righteousness.

"Righteousness" according to *Vine's expository Dictionary of New Testament Words* is the "character or quality of being right or just. It was formerly spelled 'rightwiseness,' which clearly expresses the meaning."

It is said of Jesus in Isaiah Chapter 59, "For He put on righteousness as a breastplate, and a helmet of salvation upon His head; and He put on the garments of vengeance for clothing, and was clad with zeal as a cloak."

Jesus Christ, the Lord of Righteousness loves righteousness. He has vehement fervor for justice. The soldier who has been taught and trained by the same Spirit that raised Christ from the dead will not only *have* righteousness, but will *do* righteousness. He should love what is right and hate what is wrong. The child of God longs for a new earth "wherein dwells righteousness." He "hungers and thirsts for righteousness." If we haven't that testimony, then we haven't seen an answer to the cry "Create in me a clean heart O God, renew a *right* spirit in me," or perhaps that has never been our plea. . . .

The breastplate keeps the heart clean, for out of the heart come the issues of life. How could we approach the King with soiled garments? Righteousness breeds holy boldness! If we had an audience with an earthly king, we would groom every hair on our heads. We would go over our clothes with a fine-toothed comb, and go over our teeth with a fine-bristled brush. We would check the mirror with the eye of a prosecuting attorney, looking for the finest of flaws. We would shine our shoes until they mirrored our face. The king's position *commands* such respect. How much more then should we cleanse our hearts and minds daily through the water of the Word, so that we might have a bold confidence before the King of Righteousness.

Do We Hear His Voice?

How loudly does the sergeant major of our conscience need to shout to bring us to attention? If we move out of order, do we hear his voice? A good soldier won't even wait for the voice of a sergeant major to call him into line. If by chance he gets out of step with what he knows he should be, he does immediate correction.

Have we debts unpaid? Then do all you can to pay them. Do we honor our parents? If they are still living, do them good. Give them your time, your money, your soul. This is acceptable to God (see 1 Timothy 5:4). Have we unforgiveness in our hearts? Then forgive or you will not be forgiven. Do we lack love? Then we must get on our knees and ask God to pour His love through us, or we have no biblical grounds to think we are saved. Are we easily irritated? Do we obey traffic laws; do we love and pray with our spouse; do we read God's Word daily; do we pay all our taxes; is our thoughtlife pure—do we daily confess our sins and ask for cleansing when necessary . . . are we zealous for God? These questions are merely soul-searchers to see if we have the things that accompany salvation. This is the profile of the *normal* Christian. If we lack these things, better we realize it now, rather than on Judgment Day.

Is God speaking to you about something right now? Don't let my words distract you. Stop reading this book and resolve to do what you have failed to do, and undo what you should not have done. If we confess our sins, He is faithful and just to forgive our sins and to cleanse us from all unrighteousness. If you leave that thing undone, you will give a foothold to the enemy. It will leave a gaping hole in your armor. Repent now, while there is time.

There is no such thing as small sin. To steal one cent is to be a thief in the sight of God. There is no mention that the theft of Judas was even noticed by the other disciples. Perhaps he just took a little here and there, but it only takes a small hole in the hull to sink an ocean liner. Then all that is needed is time.

Our Creator is righteousness itself. Righteousness can no more be separated from His nature, than the ink can be from this book. We must strive to always have a conscience which is void of offence to both God and man, not only for our own sakes but for the sake of the unsaved.

I desperately want God to use me to reach the lost. *If I am not a straight-shooter with a pistol, He won't let me near the cannon.*

Keep it Clean

One very valuable thing I learned as a new Christian was that the Scriptures say that we are to lay aside uncleanness of any sort. This means we are to lay aside the human tendency to have a perverted delight for that which is licentious or impure. We have a *delight* for impurity—unclean, gutter humor. A few moments of "adult humor" proves that to be true. As children of God we are to lay that aside. Being involved in itinerant ministry I am able to fellowship with literally thousands of Christians. How grieved I am when I hear Christians, who are otherwise spiritual, dishonor their testimony by allowing themselves to delight in unclean humor. If we wouldn't say it in prayer, then we shouldn't say it at all.

If we understand that humanity has a delight for impurity, then we can move away from it when we see it lift its grimy head. This should cut down the amount of "comedy" entertainment we listen to. Not only is most modern comedy unclean, but it employs recorded laughing that will have you laughing contagiously.

Satan wants to stain your robe. Wash it constantly in the Blood of the Lamb . . . " and having on the breastplate of righteousness."

Even the Lowliest Part

The next part of our apparel is often not seen as being a necessary part of armor. Paul goes on to say, "And having your feet shod with the preparation of the Gospel of peace."

Soldiers who have a fight within their spirit, a keenness, and a smell for the battle, make the best fighters. They are prepared within their heart: "The heart of the wise teaches his mouth, and adds learning to his lips." Their boots are on. Their bayonets are fixed. One word from the Commander and they are into the thick of the battle.

The Christian soldier has studied how to be effective as a witness of the Gospel. He knows that he who wins souls is wise. He has ordered his priorities, and knows that there is no higher calling than to lead a sinner to Christ. Like Philip, he will leave a revival to lead a sinner to the Savior. He "must" go through Samaria to speak to one woman at a well. He seeks that which the Son of Man came to seek . . . that which is lost. He knows what pleases Headquarters—that Heaven rejoices when one sinner repents.

The Scriptures say, "How beautiful are the feet of them that preach the Gospel of peace . . . " Do you know what that means? It means that if you will obey the Great Commission to go into all the world and preach the Gospel, it so pleases God that He considers even your feet to be beautiful. If you can, slip off one of your shoes right now and have an objective look at your bare foot. With all vanity aside, you must admit that your foot is a little unbecoming. The small toe looks like a reject jelly bean, yet God says that if you preach His glorious Gospel, He considers that lowly, unattractive (even ugly) foot to be beautiful.

Some years ago, I was on a plane on my way to preach the Gospel. It was called the "Champagne flight." The weather was hot and I was wearing open footwear. As the stewardess was walking down the aisle, she suddenly slipped and spilt the bubbly liquid over my feet. A moment later she returned and wiped them dry with a towel. As she was doing so, I remember thinking, "Wow, what VIP treatment God gives those who preach His Gospel—*I've just had my feet washed with champagne!*"

Join the Society of Beautiful Feet. Have your feet *always* shod with the preparation of the Gospel of Peace. Always be prepared to give an answer for the reason of the hope that is within you. Effective warfare means taking the *full* armor of God . . . having "your feet shod with the preparation of the Gospel of peace."

CHAPTER THREE

FIGHT THE GOOD FIGHT
OF FAITH

*"Whatsoever is born of God overcomes the world.
And this is the victory that has overcome the world—
our faith" (1 John 5:4).*

In late November of 1995, 20-year old U.S. Marine Lance Corporal Zachary Mayo tossed and turned on his bed, as his ship sailed through the warm waters of the Arabian Sea. In the early hours of a Saturday morning he had finally had enough tossing. He made his way to the deck and looked at the vast ocean before him. Suddenly, the boat rolled, the wind shifted, and like an enemy's hand in the darkness, a door knocked him off balance and into the sea. Despite his cries for help, nobody knew that Lance Corporal Zachary Mayo had fallen overboard.

It was a long 36 hours before he was rescued from the shark-infested waters by Pakistani fishermen. What was it (besides the grace of God), that kept him afloat and alive for so long? *It was his Marine training.* As he began to tread water in the dark Arabian night, he removed his military overalls, tied the two legs in a knot, then forced air into them by swinging them over his head, fashioning them into a make-shift life preserver. Like every recruit, Mayo spent four days in a pool of water, where he learned basic survival skills.

Sin is an enemy which has knocked humanity into the sea of death and damnation. The Bible is a book of survival skills. It tells us how we can live.

The Life Preserver

This next piece of armor is worthy of close inspection . . . this is a life preserver. The Scriptures say, "*Above all* taking the shield of faith." This part of defense is fundamentally, ultra-vitally essential. This is that which extinguishes all the "flaming arrows of the evil one." In other words, if you don't use this portion of your armor you will be wounded, perhaps fatally, by the flaming arrows of the enemy.

Faith is spiritually what oxygen is naturally. If the life of the flesh is in the blood, the life of the blood is in the oxygen. Without faith, the Christian gasps, writhes, and then dies. We know that without faith it is impossible to please God. Without faith, the sharks will devour us. With faith, it is not only possible to please Him, but to float above the infested waters of this world. It is also possible to move mountains, subdue kingdoms, wrought righteousness, obtain promises, and stop the mouths of lions.

God has even given us an honor roll of soldiers who have gone before us in battle. Hebrews Chapter 11 lists those who through faith did exploits for their God, and were afterward promoted to Headquarters. They exercised faith in attack and in defense, proving its worth. It's now up to us to follow their example.

These soldiers of the Cross found that faith in God gave them the ability to be "strong in the Lord and in the power of His might," to be "more than conquerors," because they knew that God was for them, that He always caused them to triumph . . . through faith.

It's all very well to speak in such glorious terms of faith, but how can *we*, in everyday life, live *practically* in this realm? To illustrate the principles of faith, let me share something interesting with you: For many years, I had the privilege of preaching the Gospel almost daily in an open city square. In one sense I was fulfilled in my ministry, and yet I had a great longing to reach more with the Gospel. In 1982, doors began to open for me to do just that. Requests began to come from churches saying, "Come and stir up our people to evangelism." Yet, I was horrified to find that not only did few Christians share their faith, but I found that 95%-100% of the congregations in our "Gospel outreach" services were made up of Christians. It seemed that much seed was being sown in the barn.

Then I heard that in 1982, $2,000,000,000 was spent on Christian television. I was impressed by the amount, until I found that those programs were being watched by only 4% of the viewing public. It would seem that most of the programs were being watched by Christians. This is called "inreach." The Church was "preaching to the converted," an idiom used by the world to express futility. Sad though it may be, few of the unsaved tune into Christian television. Of course, many Christian programs drum up support by speaking of a "potential" audience of multi-millions, but that merely means that there is a possibility that that many *could* actually be watching. In reality, sinners love the darkness and hate the light, neither will they tune into the light, lest their deeds be exposed. *Men and women don't want to surrender*. The Bible says that there are "none that seek after God." They are going to fight until they are *forced* to lay down their arms.

Add to that fact that no matter how comfortable we make our buildings in an effort to attract the unsaved to church, we have to go a long way to compete with the warmth and comfort of their own living room. There, they get coffee, cookies, with a good movie and some heart-palpitating sex and violence.

Secular, not Christian television is the medium to reach the lost. But how do we get the Word of Truth through the secular authorities, when the Bible tells us that they "suppress the truth in unrighteousness?" If a program even hints of sin, righteousness or judgment, and was somehow purchased by the world for broadcast, it would no doubt be slotted into the wee hours of the morning.

A Commercial Break

It was when I was considering these thoughts that I had an idea: Imagine you are an average unsaved person, enjoying your favorite sexually explicit and violent television program, when there's a commercial break. Suddenly, a man appears holding a Bible and you hear the words:

"The Bible is the world's all-time best seller, yet many don't read it because they don't understand it. Let me give you an example: This is the King James Version: *God commendeth all men everywhere to repent, because He hath appointed a day, in which He will judge the world in righteousness.* Now listen to how the *Good News* version puts the same verse: *God commands all men everywhere to turn from their evil ways, for He has fixed a day in which He will judge the whole world with justice.* Why not call into your local Christian bookstore and view the large range of Bibles ... you'll be amazed at the variety."

You watch a few more commercials, then back to the program, but now with the truth of Judgment Day fixed within your mind. This thirty second commercial has a threefold effect. First and foremost, it gets the Word of God, spoken twice (with a close-up shot of the wording for those who turn the sound off during commercials) in the hearts and homes of millions of viewers (remember, God's Word will not return void). Second, it promotes the Word of God (two versions). Third, it promotes Christian bookstores (most of whom advertise in church columns and Christian magazines, thus many arc unknown to the general public).

I was so excited about the concept, I hardly slept for three or four nights. I submitted the scripts of the commercials to the advertising department of the local television network, and to my delight they said they were OK. as advertisements. *I could hardly believe it.* They gave me permission to quote, "God commands all men everywhere to repent, etc.;" " ... You must be born again ... ;" "The fool has said in his heart there is no God;" "Jesus said, I am the way, the truth, and the life; no man ... ;" "God commended His love toward us in that while we were yet sinners, Christ died for us;" "The wages of sin is death, but the gift of God is eternal life through Jesus Christ our Lord." *They saw the quoting of Scripture in the commercials as merely a comparing of translations, to promote Bible versions!*

Years earlier, I heard about a hardened sailor merely hearing Scripture as he stood outside a meeting, and was soundly converted. The same Word of God cut me to the heart on the night of my conversion, and here we had an opportunity to use this mighty weapon right in the very midst of the enemy.

Seven Seas

It was on a Friday morning that I wrote in my diary to contact "Seven Seas Television," a Christian organization who could advise me as to how I should go about making the commercials. I would find their address on the Tuesday when I returned from a series of meetings in another city. I wasn't even sure of the city in which Seven Seas was stationed, but I would make that a priority for Tuesday.

After a seminar the following day, when I shared the vision of the commercials with the people with whom I was staying, they told me that they knew a television producer who knew the Lord. I said that I would love to spend some time with him to get his thoughts on the commercials. He was duly contacted, and I was delighted to find that he had already decided to come to my meeting the following morning.

After the service, I met the gentleman and shared the concept of the commercials. He loved the idea. He gave me some helpful advice, then handed me his card saying that if he could be of any help, not to hesitate to contact him. I stared in unbelief at the card—"Ian Ralston, producer, *Seven Seas Television.*" Standing in front of me was the very man I had wanted to contact on the Tuesday after my return. I neither knew the name nor the address, yet God had brought him to me. I felt sure that God was with me in the venture.

Where Was The Enemy?

The next move was to raise the necessary finances. A package of twelve commercials reaching a viewing audience of around 3,600,000 would cost $7,200. It was around that time I found out that a Christian friend had just started a job with a local secular television station. On inquiry, I found that Greg's job happened to be in the advertising department. Greg was ecstatic, and was even convinced that God had him in television for such a time as this.

I sent out literature to 350 churches, 90 bookstores and a number of individuals whom I knew had a desire to see the Kingdom of God furthered in the nation. The response was very encouraging. Thousands of dollars began to roll in. Opening the mail was a most uplifting experience. One Bible distributor did express a concern that the commercials gave an impression that we were demeaning the King James Version. I wrote back and told him that we were using that in every one of the twelve commercials, and that I was hoping that other Christians would see what we were actually doing. If we didn't structure the commercials to look as though we were comparing versions, there would be no way we would be allowed to quote Scripture. He was satisfied and showed his support by sending a large check. Almost everywhere I turned, I received nothing but encouragement.

All the money for the production and for the screening of the commercials rolled in. I felt that I was at last doing something substantial for the Kingdom of God. I was going to have the privilege of firing the cannon of the Word of God right into the heart of the enemy. Over previous months, I had become disheartened that the Church was always on the defense. It seemed I was forever being asked to sign petitions. We were putting all our energies into holding ground, and little into taking any. Now it was just a matter of aiming the cannon and waiting for the right time to light the fuse. Everything was set. The commercials were made using a well-known Christian newsreader who was delighted to do them free of charge. A Christian organization had produced them at a 50% discount—everything flowed. In fact, things were going so well, I was wondering where the enemy was. I was suspicious, but I wasn't complaining.

Enemy Sighted

I was relaxing at home when Greg appeared unannounced and grim-faced—"The top guy in television said that he did not approve those Scriptures . . . he's lying. I remember his words, Ray. Pharaoh has raised his ugly head!" Twice Greg had sought written confirmation of the commercials and nothing had come through. We talked for a few minutes and then decided to have a time of prayer. As we prayed, different Scriptures came to mind: "The battle is not yours but the Lord's," "If God be for us who can be against us." This was just another trivial fiery furnace, a little lion's den, a pint-sized Red Sea. The Lord would make the way for us to go through, and all we had to do was to "Stand still and see the salvation of God."

The combat had begun. The battleground was in my mind. I was determined to hold my ground. I held the shield of faith high. Suddenly, a fiery dart struck my mind—"What if God doesn't help you? What if the television people see what you are up to? If they have seen that you are preaching the Word of God there is no way they are going to let it through. How naive, to think that secular television would allow the Bible to be read on television!"

My mind flooded with the weight of other thoughts. I would have to return all the money. I would end up $2000 in debt because I spent it on production costs. All that work down the drain. So much for the offensive . . . back to the petitions.

I would think, "What's going on, I shouldn't be thinking like this!" The enemy was draining me of courage. He was wanting to totally discourage me into retreat.

The thoughts that had invaded my mind were merely imaginations based upon the belief that God was going to let me down. Paul exhorts us with the words,

"For though we walk in the flesh, we do not war after the flesh: (for the weapons of our warfare are not carnal, but mighty through God to the pulling down of strongholds; casting down imaginations, and every high thing that exalteth itself against the knowledge of God, and bringing into captivity every thought to the obedience of Christ" (2 Corinthians 10:3-5).

I took myself in hand and began obeying the command to have faith in God. I cast down the imaginations and determined within that I would trust the Lord no matter how grim it looked. *Nothing is too hard for God.* I would look to His ability and not the situation. I took hold of the two-edged Sword and thrust it in the face of the enemy: "If God be for me, nothing can be against me, for with God nothing shall be impossible."

I remembered the disciples' reaction to the workings of the enemy. Peter and John were forbidden by the religious authorities to speak any more in the name of Jesus. They took that matter to prayer and the Bible tells us that after they prayed, the place where they were meeting was shaken, and they were all filled with the Holy Spirit and spoke the Word of God boldly.

These soldiers did not allow the propaganda of the enemy to have an ear-hold. They did not look to the situation, but to the transcending ability of their God. They picked up the shield of faith and extinguished all the flaming arrows of the evil one. This was what I had to do if I wanted God's approval, and if I wanted to defend myself against the onslaughts of the enemy.

Faith will trust God in the lion's den with the beasts biting at our face, or at the edge of the Red Sea with Pharaoh biting at our heels. The mind says there is no escape, but faith says, "Stand still (don't panic) and see the salvation of God." It has been well said, faith is dead to doubt, deaf to discouragement, blind to the impossible, and knows nothing but success in God. Spurgeon said, "Faith may swim, where reason may only paddle." It is the victory that overcomes the world, with all its trials and discouragement. Faith in God gave Jesus such peace of mind that He slept during a raging storm while the disciples who had lost their faith, were filled with fear. After Peter was converted, he slept the night before Herod was about to execute him. The Bible promises, "You will keep him in perfect peace, whose mind is stayed on You, *because he trusts in You*" (Isaiah 26:3, italics added).

I had not kept my mind stayed on God. I had lowered my shield of faith and allowed the flaming arrows to strike me.

The battle raged for about 24 hours before God brought deliverance. Greg received a long-distance call from the top man in television advertising. He had viewed the advertisements and said, "Those commercials look OK. to me."

Some time later I had the unspeakably joyful experience of seeing the commercials screened right in the middle of prime time television. I was so ecstatic I actually did a somersault across the living room.

Doubting Castle

I had been through an experience similar to that of "Christian" and "Hopeful" so graphically illustrated in the great classic, *Pilgrim's Progress*. Both Christian and Hopeful left the King's Highway and fell asleep in the grounds of Doubting Castle. Giant Despair woke them and asked what they were doing on his grounds. They said that they were pilgrims who had lost their way. Giant Despair, being stronger than both of them, drove them into Doubting Castle and thrust them into a dungeon which is described as being "very dark, nasty and stinking."

For four long days and nights they lay there until Giant Despair's wife, Diffidence (lack of self-confidence) counseled her husband to beat them without mercy. Giant Despair was obedient to his sweet wife and beat them, then told them that they should kill themselves (nice guy).

Christian and Hopeful actually considered the suggestion, but the fear of God stopped them.

The next evening, the big fellow returned and became furious because they hadn't taken his advice. Mrs. Despair then told him to show Christian and Hopeful a few skeletons they had in their closet. The hen-pecked hulk then took them down to the castle-yard and showed them the bones and skulls of those he had already dispatched, and said, "These were pilgrims who trespassed on my grounds and I tore them to pieces." The giant then made no bones about the fact that he would do the same to them within 10 days. Hopeful and Christian decided to pray—good idea.

After about six hours of prayer, Christian cried, *"What a fool I am, thus to live in this stinking dungeon when I may as well walk out in liberty. I have a key in my bosom called 'promise.' That will, I am persuaded, open any lock in Doubting Castle."* Christian then pulled out the key, unlocked the door and they escaped . . . no doubt the wiser.

What a wonderful allegory of those who doubt the promises of God. How perfectly it described my own experience. The second my mind doubted the promises of God's help, Giant Despair would appear and begin to beat me without mercy. What a fool I was to lie in such a dark, nasty and stinking dungeon! The moment I took out the key of promise, I found release.

" . . . take up the shield of faith, with which you can extinguish all the flaming arrows of the evil one" (Ephesians 6:16).

CHAPTER FOUR

PRAISE THE LORD AND PASS THE AMMUNITION

"When I cry unto thee, then shall mine enemies turn back; This I know; For God is for me"
(Psalm 56:9).

No armor would be complete if provision is not made for the most vulnerable part of the body, the head. Once again, Paul admonishes us to "take" the helmet. If we will not take it and put it on, we will suffer the consequences. The helmet speaks of guarding the mind, using particularly the knowledge of God's coming deliverance. This use of the helmet is made clear in 1 Thessalonians 5:8, " . . . and for a helmet, the hope of salvation." The word "hope" comes from a Greek word *elpis*, which means more than the contemporary definition of the word hope. It means a "confident expectation." David's hope in God was clearly evident in the opening scripture of this chapter. He knew that God was for him, and that the Lord would fight on his behalf. David was wearing his head-gear.

The Christian's hope is ultimately the Second Coming of Christ. He lives with the knowledge that Jesus will appear in unutterable power and splendor.

The Captain of our Salvation will burst through the heavens to do final battle with, and triumph over the enemies of the Gospel. What a fearful Day for those who will not take heed to the call for surrender. Their proud, stubborn hearts will not allow them to lay down their weapons, lift up their hearts and cry, "All to Jesus, I surrender, all to Him I freely give."

As in any war, we may lose the occasional skirmish, but as Christians we have the knowledge burning within our hearts, that we have already won the war. This is the bold confidence of those who follow the One to whom all nations are as a "drop in a bucket." We have the key of promise that never fails to unlock any door the enemy may put in front of us. We know that the scripture given to Adam must be fulfilled— that God, "shall bruise Satan under your feet." Scripture cannot be broken—it must come to pass, therefore we need never to lose courage.

In the opening verse of Isaiah Chapter 42, the prophet speaks of the office of the Messiah. In verse 4, we are told that Jesus was never discouraged. It also tells us why: "He shall not fail nor be discouraged . . ." Jesus never lost His courage *because He knew that He would not fail!* How could He when the Father was with Him? There lies the key to not only the courage of the Son of God, but of Stephen, and every other hero of the Cross who laughed in the face of the enemy's greatest weapon, death.

Our brethren were valiant in battle because they knew that they could not fail. They had bolted down the helmet of salvation. They knew that death could not touch them—*it could only graduate them.* It was merely a doormat on which they wiped their feet as they entered the joy of Heaven.

The Christian's righteousness has been given to him by God. That's why we can have boldness even on the Day of Wrath. That's why we can have strong confidence in God. That's why we can have God fighting for us rather than against us. We know that He who is within us is greater than he who is in the world. Our eyes have been opened so that we can see who God is, and that one person who is on His side is an infinite majority.

Imagine for a moment that you are in the front line of battle. The enemy is falling before you like flies. Courage fills your heart as you fire your weapon above the heads of a retreating enemy. You laugh in victory.

Suddenly, your laughter stops in your throat. Eight hundred enemy tanks, in one great arm of attack, rise over the hill in front of you. They don't break rank. They move as one mighty wall of metal toward you. Nothing will halt them. The ground shakes beneath your feet; your knees do the same. What then do you do? *You run!* What happened? You lost courage, *because you lost sight of the victory!*

We have Him with us who could turn 800 billion enemy tanks into fine powder with the flutter of an eyelash. Never, never lose sight of the victory! Don't let the lies of enemy propaganda penetrate your mind. Remember the command, "Fear not; for I am with you; be not dismayed; for I am thy God; I will strengthen thee; yea, I will uphold thee with the right hand of My righteousness."

To be discouraged is to dishonor God. If He is with us we must never lose courage. Remember that Satan is just a creation of Almighty God. Never forget that:

A blind, anemic, weak-kneed flea on crutches would have a greater chance of defeating a herd of a thousand wild stampeding elephants, than the enemy has of defeating God!

You Have Nothing To Do

Over the years, I would often feel the weight of discouragement fall upon me when I didn't see fruit for my labors. Months would go by with many hearing the preaching, yet not a soul would be saved. But we shouldn't let any situation quench our zeal. A hen will scratch harder when worms are scarce. If souls are scarce, pray more, witness more, and you will get your worms . . . if you "faint not." They that sow in tears *shall* reap in joy. John Wesley said to his preachers, "You have nothing to do but to win souls; therefore spend and be spent in this work."

Now and then I hear from people who have responsible positions in church because they heard the preaching years before. God is the One who produces fruit. We merely plant the seed.

We plant in a hope that will not be disappointed . . . "Take the helmet of salvation."

The Sword Of The Spirit

C. H. Spurgeon said, "We must thrust the sword of the Spirit into the hearts of men." The enemy has particular loathing for this part of our armor. This is the weapon he wants kept in its sheath. He doesn't want Christians to see the point of the sword of the Lord.

The sword was to the soldier of Paul's day, what ammunition is to the soldier today. The Scriptures say, "And take . . . the sword of the Spirit, which is the Word of God." This is the mighty weapon which God has issued to all who enlist for service. The Word of God is quick and powerful, and sharper than any two-edged sword. It effectively cuts into the heart of all who oppose its gleaming blade. I have heard demons scream through the mouth of an unconscious girl when this weapon was used. When Satan attacked the Son of God in the wilderness, Jesus did not react carnally. He picked up the glistening razor-edge of the Word of God and said, "It is written . . . " He used the two-edged sword, and it was effective.

Look at how Christian utilized his sword in that great classic publication, *Pilgrim's Progress:*

"Then Apollyon, (a name for Satan meaning *destroyer)* espying his opportunity, began to gather up close to Christian, and wrestling with him, gave him a dreadful fall; and with that Christian's sword fell out of his hand. Then said Apollyon, I am sure of thee now. And with that he had almost pressed him to death, so that Christian began to despair of life. But, as God would have it, as Apollyon was setting his last blow, thereby to make a full end of this good man, Christian nimbly reached out his hand for his sword, and caught it, saying, Rejoice not against me O mine enemy! When I fall I shall arise! and with that gave him a deadly thrust, which made him give back, as one that had received his mortal wound. Christian perceiving that, made at him again, saying, *Nay, in all things we are more than conquerors through Him that loved us.* And with that, Apollyon spread forth his dragon wings, and sped him away, so that Christian saw him no more."

The book of Revelation describes the glorified Jesus by saying, " . . . and out of His mouth went a sharp two-edged sword." Soldier of Christ, throw away your sheath, it is not part of your armor. Strap the two-edged sword firmly in your hand. The way to keep the sword on hand is to have it in your mouth. In Jeremiah Chapter 1, God told the prophet not to speak words of fear. God then put His words in the mouth of Jeremiah, and in Chapter 5 we are given a development report of his transformation: " . . . thus says the Lord God of Hosts: 'Because you speak this word, behold, I will make My words in your mouth fire, and this people wood, and it shall devour them.'" God wants us to *speak* His word. In Genesis Chapter 1, God did not *think* "Let there be light," He *spoke* the Word. When Jesus stood before the tomb of Lazarus, He did not *think*, "Lazarus, come forth," He spoke the Word. He said, "My words are spirit, they are life." He said, "Marvel not at this; but the hour is coming when all that are in their graves shall hear His *voice*."

There is power to create, in the Word of God. When the light of the Word is spoken, the darkness of the enemy must vanish. An elderly Presbyterian minister told me that in the First World War, soldiers would come to him in tears, gripped by fear before a battle. He would read Psalm 91 to them and watch the fear vanish. Look at the wording: "He who dwells in the secret place of the Most High shall abide under the shadow of the Almighty. I will *say* of the Lord, 'He is my refuge and my fortress; my God, in Him will I trust.'"

Hebrews 13:6 says the same thing: "So that we may boldly *say*: The Lord is my helper; I will not fear. What can man do to me?" If the enemy's strategy is to put a blockade in your path, speak to it: "Have faith in God. For assuredly, I say to you, whosoever *says* to this mountain, 'Be removed and cast into the sea,' and does not doubt in his heart, but believes that those things he *says* will come to pass, he will have whatever he *says*." (Mark 11:22-23)

The adversary may have you in a place where there seems to be no hope. Like David, you feel that the enemy is about to swallow you up. Then speak the Word boldly in the face of the devil, grip the sword, flash it about like livid lightning, then thrust it at the enemy—"And take . . . the sword of the Spirit, which is the Word of God."

Last But Not Least

The last of the weapons which accompany the armor of God, mentioned in Ephesians Chapter 6, is the power of prayer. This is referred to in the KJV as "all prayer." Prayer is the line of communication we have with Headquarters. It is by that line that we send for supplies for the troops—ammunition, food, medical aid, etc. This is why it is essential to keep the communication line open, free from interference, and from Satanic static. Sin interferes with earth-to-Heaven communication.

Prayer is our lifeline to God, and it is evident that He is calling His Church to prayer. It is the kind of prayer that will storm the very gates of Hell in the Spirit realm. We need world-wide revival in the Church that will boil over into the world! We need to call the things that "are not, as though they were," to look at the things that are not seen; and to follow in the footsteps of Abraham, who "staggered not at the promise of God, but was strong in faith, giving glory to God, being fully persuaded that what God had promised, He was able to perform." Revival is God's will. He is not willing that any perish; He wants *all* to "come to a knowledge of the truth." Therefore we can confidently pursue God for men, then in urgent zeal, pursue men for God.

Prayer was the ignition to every revival fire in history. Prayer was the key to the doorway of ministry, for every preacher used by God in the past. For the soldier of Christ, true prayer should be a way of life, not just a call for help in the heat of battle. This message is made very clear in scripture:

> Ephesians 6:18: "Praying always . . . ,"
> Colossians 4:2: "Continue in prayer . . . ,"
> 1 Thess. 5:17: "Pray without ceasing,"
> Romans 12:12: "Continuing steadfast in prayer."

Hudson Taylor, the great missionary, said:

> "The prayer power has never been tried to its full capacity. If we want to see mighty works of Divine power and grace wrought in the place of weakness, failure and disappointment, let us answer God's standing challenge, 'Call to me, and I will answer you, and show you great and mighty things, which you do not know.'"

It has been said that he who is a stranger to prayer, will also be a stranger to power. We need to seek God to break the hard hearts of Hell-bound sinners. Hardly a day goes by when I don't beseech God for wisdom. I *need* the wisdom of God. The Scriptures say, "He that begets wisdom loves his own soul." If you have wisdom from above, you *will* seek to save souls. If you have wisdom you will never say or do anything wrong. If you have wisdom, you will see all the traps set by the enemy, you will encourage other Christians with insights from the Word, and you will cut sinners to the heart with the wisdom of God.

We need such an anointing[3] on our preaching that men will weep in a sense of their own sinfulness. That can only come through prayer.

---

[3] By the "anointing," I am not meaning "power" ministries. There are many who preach with a great show, and speak of the anointing often, but rarely mention the holiness of God, the Law, righteousness, holiness, judgment, repentance and Christ crucified.

God loves His children coming to Him in the intimate communion of prayer. The Scriptures tell us, "The prayer of the upright is His delight."

Let us never face a day in battle until we have faced the Father in prayer. John Bunyan said, "Prayer is a shield to the soul, a delight to God, and a scourge to Satan." Someone once said that Satan trembles when he sees the feeblest Christian on his knees. How utterly convicting are the words of Martin Luther: "I have so much to do (today) that I should spend the first three hours in prayer." Martin was a monk, and therefore had the time to spend in prayer, but we can see the principle of what he was saying—"Seek first the Kingdom of God."

Look at the context of this Scripture:

"If Satan has risen up against himself, and is divided, he cannot stand, but has an end. No one can enter a strong man's house and spoil his goods, unless he first binds the strong man, and then he will plunder his house" (Mark 3:26-27).

Jesus is talking about the enemy. He is speaking about the one who has taken sinners "captive, to do his will."

We are stronger than the adversary because our strength is not our own: "*The Lord* is my strength and my shield . . . Be strong *in the Lord* and in the power of *His* might." When we submit to God and resist the devil, he *will* flee from us. He retreats.

Within the very cartridge of prayer are the explosive forces of faith:

1. The name of Jesus.
2. The blood of Christ.
3. The sword of the Spirit.
4. The power of a confident affirmation.

Look at the spirit of victory behind these words from Psalm 149, which summarize what I have been trying to say:

"Let the saints be joyful in glory; Let them sing aloud on their beds. Let the high praises of God be in their mouth, and a two-edged sword in their hand, to execute vengeance on the nations and punishments on the peoples; to bind their kings with chains, to execute on them the written Judgment—*this honor have all His saints.* Praise the Lord" (italics added).

Sharpen the Ax

A man was once cutting a tree stump with an obviously blunt axe. He was only bruising the bark, as sweat poured from his beaded brow. Someone suggested he stop for a moment and sharpen the axe, to which he replied, "No way, I'm too busy chopping the tree to stop for anything." If he would only stop for a moment and sharpen the axe, he would slice through the tree with far greater ease.

Stop each day, and "sharpen the ax" through prayer. Seek first the Kingdom of God and you will slice through that day with far greater ease.

"And pray in the Spirit on all occasions with all kinds of prayers and requests. With this in mind, be alert and always keep on praying for all the saints" (Ephesians 6:18).

CHAPTER FIVE

DISCHARGING THE TROOPS

" . . . I cannot hold my peace, because you have heard, O my soul, the sound of the trumpet, the alarm of war" (Jeremiah 4:19).

A pastor once shared something that he said was of deep concern to him. For about nine months his fellowship had run an entertainment club to make contact with local teenagers. Rock music was part of the draw-card. Over the months, a few contacts had been made, but there had been little fruit. He asked for our thoughts. We told him that it was good that he was wanting to reach out, but the real question was, what is God's attitude toward the use of heavy rock music to draw young people to Christ? Does the end justify the means? Could we justify the use of alcoholic beverages as a means of reaching out to the ungodly. How do we reach out to the world?

I recalled how a few days earlier, Sue and I had witnessed to a number of teenagers. They said they hated God. Their language was filthy. One hated his father and longed to kill him, while another had a genuine desire to murder someone "slowly with a knife." The pastor in whose home we were staying added to my disquiet by telling us that his counter-culture neighbors had named their child "Lucifer."

I was grieved at such a thought. How lost, how rebellious could a generation get? I immediately went to my room and began crying out to God, asking how this generation could be reached. Suddenly, a still small voice seemed to say, "Go next door and meet them." I said, "No Lord . . . You're not capturing the spirit of my prayer." The impression became so strong, I decided to go next door. I took a copy of my first book, *My Friends are Dying,* (a book about the drug culture), to give to them.

As I walked up the driveway I heard, "*Ray!*" There stood a long-haired man I had never seen before, holding a bottle of beer and pointing his finger at me. He said, "Ray . . . I just finished reading your book, *My Friends are Dying* three days ago!"

I was invited into the home and introduced to a number of residents. I told them that I had been praying next door, and felt that God had wanted me to come and talk to them. As I sat in that filthy, smoke-infested, stinking room, surrounded by drugs, alcohol and blaring music, it dawned on me that if we cared, we would push aside our fears and boldly befriend this lost generation.

Holiness is not separation from *sinners*, but from *sin*. I made five friends that afternoon, and I didn't have to attract them, they attracted me. Like Jesus, we should be the friend of sinners, yet remain untainted by the things of this world.

Without Reserve

If there is one thing the Salvation Army had under the leadership of General Booth, it was a burning zeal for holiness and evangelism. They would stop at nothing to take the Gospel to the lost. Some of their ways may even have seemed rather radical and unorthodox, yet God blessed their endeavors because their passion for souls was seasoned with holiness.

Holiness is a word the enemy fears because it goes hand in hand with the word "power." Jesus was "declared to be the Son of God with power, according to the Spirit of Holiness . . . " Holiness signifies "(a) Separation to God, and (b) The resultant state, the conduct befitting those so separated" (*Vine's Expository Dictionary*).

This was the message preached by those early soldiers. They preached the great truth "without holiness, no man shall see the Lord." They proclaimed the uncompromising Gospel which declares, "Let everyone who names the name of Christ, depart from iniquity."

Look at what happened to the tribe of Ephraim when they lacked holiness—"The children of Ephraim, being armed and carrying bows, turned back in the day of battle. They did not keep the covenant of God; they refused to walk in His Law, and forgot His works and His wonders that He had shown them." To walk in His Law means to walk in the steps of Jesus . . . in that same Spirit of Holiness. Leonard Ravenhill said, "Let no man think of fighting Hell's legions if he is still fighting an internal warfare. Carnage without will sicken him if he has carnality within. It is the man who has surrendered to the Lord who will never surrender to his enemies."

The Apostle Paul never laid down his arms for a moment. He had a zeal that drove him to witness of his faith in Christ, even while in bonds. Can you imagine the boldness needed to witness to Roman guards, to men who were hardened to cruelty? Yet Paul begged, "Pray for me, that utterance may be given to me, that I may open my mouth boldly to make known the mystery of the Gospel, for which I am an ambassador in chains; that in it I may speak boldly, as I ought to speak." Instead of the attitude, "Oh no, here I am chained to two guards," his was, "Thank you Lord, I have two guards chained to me." He looked for an opportunity to witness, because the zeal of God's house had eaten him up. He had surrendered to the will of His Creator.

Paul's enthusiasm for the Kingdom of God remained steadfast because it was fed by the Spirit of Holiness. He was separated from the world to the God of holiness. This is the difference between the contemporary Church and the fiery and militant army of the Church of the book of Acts. The tanks of evangelism of the Army of God have become rusted to a standstill by the influence of the world. What is needed is an unprecedented outpouring of the oil of God's Holy Spirit to get mobile and into action, and that power will come when the Church becomes holy.

When God spoke to Gideon regarding his army to fight the Midianites, He said, "Now therefore, proclaim in the hearing of the people, saying, 'Whoever is fearful and afraid, let him turn and depart at once from Mount Gilead.'" Then 22,000 of the people returned, and 10,000 remained. God wants dead men in His army. He wants those who are not afraid because they are already dead to themselves and alive to God. They are the ones who overcome the devil, because they "love not their lives unto death." They are already crucified with Christ. They are not conformed to the world because they have presented their bodies as a living sacrifice, holy and acceptable to God . . . their reasonable service.

George Mueller said,

"There was a day when I died, utterly died, died to George Mueller, his opinions, preferences, tastes, and will—died to the world, its approval or censure—died to the approval or blame even of my brethren and friends—and since then I have only to show myself approved to God."

Caleb was another who had given all to the Lord. He knew that there was no place for retirement this side of Heaven. At the age of 85 he said, "As yet I am as strong this day as I was on the day that Moses sent me; just as my strength was then, so now is my strength for war, both for going out and for coming in."

Faith does not wrinkle with the skin. Look at his faith-filled words, "Now therefore, give me this mountain of which the Lord spoke in that day; for you heard in that day how the Anakims were there, and that the cities were great and fortified. It may be that the Lord will be with me, and I shall be able to drive them out as the Lord said." Remember, he was 85 years old.

There is no such thing as an honorable discharge in the Army of God. The only "Heavenly-rest" is our promotion to Headquarters, and until that time we must work while we have the opportunity and the inclination. I often think of the words to the famous song "American Pie." In the middle of the song they are repeated—"This could be the day that I die . . . this could be the day that I die." The Christian must remember that this could be his last day on earth . . . one day he will be right. There is a time to rest, but there is a special rest for those who give all to the Lord. We enter that rest the moment we lay down our self-will and sanctify ourselves wholly for His purposes.

Equipped For Battle

If there is one thing that equips the Christian for battle, it is to be filled with the Spirit. It took Peter from being a man who could not testify of his faith in Jesus to a little girl, to a fearless soldier of Christ who saw 3,000 saved under his bold proclamation at Pentecost. He told the murderers of the Messiah that they needed to repent. No less-welcomed message could have been preached, yet Peter was able to because he was filled to overflowing with the Spirit of God, who is a consuming fire. Ask God to fill you and keep you filled (see Ephesians 5:18). Evidence of being filled with the Spirit is love. That is pure fuel that fires the vehicle of evangelism.

Getting the Point of a Tack

It is time for the Church to arise in new-found courage and not only to *defend* ourselves, but to *attack* the enemy. I don't mean to get distracted in a tangent of social work, but to be salt *and* light. Salt to stop the rot, and light to show the way to the salvation of God. To speak up about abortion and other important moral issues yet not to preach the Gospel, is to point to the wound, yet not supply the cure.

The enemy knows the signs of revival. He has seen them in past centuries. He will do all in his power to clothe the Church with a shroud of apathy to blind them as to what can happen when the Church is on fire.

When Job found himself covered in sore boils he had two "comforters" feed him nothing but lies. In the background waited Elihu. As he listened he said, "For I am full of the matter; the Spirit within me constrains me. Behold, my belly is like wine which has no vent. It is ready to burst, like new wine skins!"

When we look at the lies being fed to the Job of this world, as he sits in despair, covered in sore boils from the crown of his head to the sole of its foot, do we have Elihu's declaration? Is there a holy anger building within us as the father of lies deceives this sick world? Can we say, "For I am full of the matter?" Does the Spirit of Truth live in us; are we filled with Him to a point where we cry, "The Spirit within me constrains me, pushes me on; the love of Christ burns within me! Behold my spirit is like wine which has no vent; it is ready to burst like new wine skins?" We cannot hold our peace. God has said,

"You are my battle ax and weapons of war . . . Make bright the arrows, gather the shields . . . set up the standard upon the walls of Babylon, make the watch strong, set up the watchmen, prepare the ambushes . . . attack, attack!"

If you are a sleeping saint, Satan will gladly rock your cradle. Oh, for a strong-sounding trumpet blast in the ear of those who would sleep, "Awake, awake, put on strength, O Zion . . . " If we sleep on our own domain, it won't be long before we are asleep on enemy territory. He will take what we don't defend.

We haven't moved, it's just that the ground we are on has become occupied. Some of our churches are so dead, the only thing keeping many awake is the sound of snoring. Would to God that more church buildings would be struck by lightning, as in England in 1984.

Soldier, what are you doing for the Kingdom of God? Are you waiting for a "word from God?" Then here it is—"Go" (Mark 16:15). What are you waiting for? Go somewhere, do something, say something to somebody somewhere, somehow. One day you will be dead, and then it will be too late. While you can think, speak, move your hands and feet, do something for God. Are you content to sit in the barracks while the battle rages? Form a platoon. Give out tracts everywhere, speak for your God. Do something before the dust of apathy covers you.

There is no neutral ground. You are either gathering or you are scattering for the Kingdom of God. We have been given our battle orders through the Word of God. He who reads them cannot but hear the "sound of the trumpet, the alarm of war." As a 12-year old Christian, I figured out that I had sat under the sound of 1,800 sermons. Work out how many sermons you have listened to, and then ask how many should you take in before you give out. How much training do we need? Many have become so fat in God they have rocked themselves to sleep trying to get out of the pews.

We must run to the battle. Our aim is not to kill, but to make alive. Men have rushed into battle merely to obtain dirt. They gave their lives to get back a hill in Vietnam, Korea or Israel, a hill which may be returned to the enemy through peace negotiations twenty years later. Their costly efforts proved to be futile. Our labor is not in vain.

We have to shake off the shackles of the fear of man. I often feel a flush of heat come to my face as I step into enemy territory to give out tracts or to preach. I don't find it easy, but the Bible says that, "the righteous are as bold as a lion." I am righteous in Christ, therefore I am as bold as a lion.

Sowing and Reeping Ministry

Think of the fate of those the enemy has "taken captive by him to do his will." While many of our brothers and sisters are content with "youth night," take a team and do a bar drop. Fill pits of darkness with the light of the Gospel. I find that I can put literature in a bar and be out of the door in about two minutes...in one door, out of the other before they know what's going on.

Sure, you heart may tremble with fear, but if a hero wasn't fearful, he's not a hero. Courage is to triumph over fear, not to be free from it. When I drop literature in a bar, half of me hates being there in the smoke, the smell of booze and the foul language, and the other half cries with compassion. I ignore the "What if I get caught?" thoughts. I don't take any weak soldiers who couldn't handle it. Those in this category can stay home and intercede.

We can so easily lose sight of the fact that we are called to be fishers of men. I once ministered at a meeting where the pastor had broken free from tradition and decided to have his meeting outside at the local botanical gardens. As the meeting began, I noticed two, obvious non-Christians, watching intently. I approached them and found out that one of them was a fisherman. We spoke about his work for a while, then he asked about the meeting. He wasn't at all interested and both of them began to walk away. I called after them, "Hey, I'm a fisherman too." At that, they immediately swung around and came back. They said, "And all the time we were going on about fishing, and you're an expert!" I said, "Yup . . . I've been fishing for over 12 years (and I've just got a bite)."

On the Right Track

A short time after that incident, our family was on a train for six hours. I felt that this was a good opportunity to spread some literature around.

I waited for about three hours until I felt that the literature would provide a relief from boredom. As the guard walked past into the last carriage to take the tickets, I took courage, and got up from the seat with a pile of our papers in hand to cover the forward carriages.

However, the last car of the train proved to be empty and the guard came back about five seconds after I got up. I quickly sat back down on another seat, with a pile of papers in hand and gazed out the window.

After he went, I handed out dozens of papers. As I sat down I wondered why I felt so nervous in the first place. People were glad to have something to read.

On our return trip, I was determined to do the same thing. We were in a carriage with about 40 tourists, so I waited until I felt the time was right, ignored the hot flush and gave out the papers. Almost everyone took them. One lady was a Christian and came and sat with us for a time. I could hear the people talking about the paper. About an hour later, the Christian lady who had sat with us, returned to her seat, took out a mouth organ, and played, "How Great Thou Art." Then the train stopped for no apparent reason. A woman down the back gently began to sing, "It's no secret what God can do . . . what He's done for others, He will do for you . . . "

I am sure hearts were touched. God only knows what a work was done for eternity with that simple act of giving out Christian literature.

They Were Hiding

In the eighties, I would often go frog and tadpole hunting with my children. On one occasion, I had made a dragnet which I would throw into the pond, being careful to avoid weeds which sat in the center. A normal haul was five or six tadpoles and perhaps a small frog or two. After some time, I accidentally threw the net right onto a large piece of weed and pulled it to the shore. I was a little dismayed that this was going to be a rather messy haul, but to our delight, that one haul netted 86 tadpoles. I had been avoiding their place of habitation.

Most Christians stay clear of bars and other weedy places, yet that is where the fish gather. Throw your net into the dregs of humanity and you will gloat at the results. The unsaved flock to bars, not church buildings. We have as much chance of getting sinners to visit church buildings, as we have of criminals visiting a police station. If we were policemen and business was down, we could chrome-plate the bars, put in carpet and air conditioning, with a notice on the front of our jail saying, "Tonight—7.00 p.m.—all welcome," but few criminals would visit the police station. If business is down we have to go and apprehend lawbreakers, and the same applies to evangelism. Our light shines most in the dark places.

Organize a combat battalion and go into the field of the world. Why stay as Private Barracks, when you can be a Field Marshall. Promotion does not come from the east or the west, but from the Lord. If you prove fearless and faithful, you will be honored with promotion. Pull out the pin of self-will, then place yourself as an evangelistic hand-grenade into the hand of God.

I Do Feel Bad

I was recently sitting in a plane when a woman sat next to me. She turned out to be a bar-owner from England. We spoke of natural things, then spiritual. I prayed that God would prepare the heart of the person who would sit by me, and He certainly did. The woman listened with both ears. I took her through the Commandments one by one, explaining our true state before God, as reflected in the mirror of His Law. Then I asked if she saw herself as a sinner in the sight of God. Her words were, "I do feel bad . . . after talking to you." Then we went through the Cross and I had the joy of praying with her. I am convinced that she was soundly converted because there were no lights dimmed, no organ-playing, nor twisting of the emotions. This was just a poor sinner asking God for mercy 32,000 feet above the ground.

As we came in to land she said, "It is so ironic. I have had to travel 12,000 miles to be shown the right way. *I feel like a different person since we left the ground.*" I hope she never comes down. There is no greater joy than to have God save someone through you.

However, when it comes to doing something for the Kingdom of God, some people stop at nothing. They have joy *unspeakable.*

Door-to-Door

I guess one of the hardest types of evangelism is "door to door." I feel conscious that the cults have so imposed on people's privacy, they have stolen our thunder. I had this thought in mind once when a woman opened her door to me. I said, in a sincere tone, "Hello, I'm not a Jehovah's Witness," and she said, *"Well I am!"*

Despite the knock-backs, door-knocking is very rewarding. My son-in-law (whose name is Emeal Zwayne . . . his friends call him "EZ") has (to date), knocked on amost over 700 doors around his area. He begins by saying that he is from a local church, asking if there is any way they can be of help in the area of yard work, plumbing, painting, etc. He also says that there is no charge for the work,and no donations would be accepted. He then mentions a questionnaire and asks if they would like to do it. The first question is, "Do you believe in the existence of God or a Supreme Being?" The second is, "The Bible teaches that there is a coming Day of Judgment when God will give everlasting life or everlasting punishment to humanity. Do you think it would be important for a person to know what they need to do to receive everlasting life?" Then the final question is, "Do you think you would know the answer to that question, and if so, what would you say it was?" That often leads to further discussion.

If you have knocked on a few doors, you will know that you will get the usual, "We've got our own religion, thank-you." You will also get the occasional door slam, and the faith-testing dog, but you will make valuable contacts, meet some lonely old saints who need encouragement, place seed in hearts, literature in homes, and reap if you faint not.

CHAPTER SIX

KNOWING OUR BATTLE ORDERS

*"Therefore do not be unwise, but understand what
the will of the Lord is"
(Ephesians 5:17).*

What a disaster it would be to have troops in the heat of battle, unclear about their mission! How can any soldier apply himself to combat if he isn't sure what his orders are? Our directive is crystal clear. The charge to assault the enemy and bring back those who will desert sin and the world, rings in the ears of those who are truly born of the Spirit. They hear His voice, and run to do His will.

In 1967, before my conversion, I worked in a bank. Each morning, it was my task to deliver checks from one bank to another. One day, I noticed a crowd of about 150 people packed around the entrance of a department store. The store was having a massive sale, and as a draw-card, they had some incredible bargains displayed in the window. One of the reduced items was a jacket, with a give-away price tag of only $2. As far as I was concerned that jacket was made for Comfort. I wanted it, but there was no way I could get it with so many people waiting at the entrance of the store.

After my deliveries, I made my way back to the store. I waited until about 20 seconds before 9.00 a.m., stood at the back of the crowd and said with a loud, authoritative voice, "Excuse me!" People at the back looked around, saw my black briefcase, and concluded the obvious. This was the man whose job it was to open the door and let everyone into the store. It was in their interest to get me to the front of the crowd as quickly as possible.

As I said, "Excuse me . . . stand back please, excuse me," people began saying, "Let him through please," and they opened up like the Red Sea. The timing was perfect. When I approached the door, a gentleman on the other side turned a key, and suddenly the dam of human bodies burst, pushing me into the store and straight to the goal of my jacket, which I purchased for $2.

How much do you want to break out of the comfort of the barracks and fight on the front line? If you desire it above all else, then set your sights on it, and don't let anything deter you from that goal. Set your face "as a flint toward Jerusalem." You have a large crowd to push through, and some won't move out of the way as quickly as others. Self-will will be your biggest obstacle. He will take some prodding with your case. Directly behind him is his best friend, the never satisfied and overweight Self-indulgence. He is more interested in eating a donut than he is in moving out of your way. Just beside him is Laziness, and his two bedfellows, Apathy and Hard-heart. Pride will stand arrogantly in front of you, and will persist in keeping his position. He will be wearing the disguise of the "fear of man," so he may be hard to recognize.

Condemnation, Doubt and Discouragement will

whisper lies in your ear to try and take your eyes off your goal. They can be dealt with through faith in God's promises. Watch them though, because they will be wanting to return the moment you push them aside.

Then you have to maneuver past the attractive subtleties of Legitimate Pleasure, Entertainment and Leisure. They will want you to stop and talk for a while.

The fundamental principle to getting each hindrance to move back, is the authority you and I have in Christ. What I did to get that jacket was deceitful. I let those people think that I was someone I wasn't. But, if you are in Christ, you are a son or daughter of the Most High God. The flesh, with all its appetites, is no longer a puppet for the devil. The strings were cut at Calvary. Jesus Christ gave you the right to boldly approach the Throne of Grace. God will open doors at just the right time for you to get your heart's desire.

It is your blood-bought right to break out of the barracks of mediocrity, obscurity, mundane and defeatist Christianity, and live on the cutting edge of the will of the Living God. Let's look at how you can do that.

Whose Idea Was it?

A young man sat in my office with a very troubled expression on his face. He had been seeking God's will for his life and had come to a point of total frustration. He didn't know what on earth God wanted him to do. So, I shared a simple key to unlocking the will of God, something which had been a guiding principle by which I lived since I was converted at the age of 22. I had been apprehensive about sharing the key with anyone, but the young man so appreciated what I told him, I decided to begin teaching it from the pulpit, and to my surprise, it was also appreciated in the pew.

I reminded him of the incident where David slew Goliath, and asked him whose idea it was for the youth to fight the giant. He thought for a moment, and then said, "David's." He was right. If you take the time to study 1 Samuel Chapter 17, you will see that there is no record of him seeking God for His will in this instance. How could this be? The Scriptures say, "Acknowledge Him in all your ways and He will direct your paths." Shouldn't David have acknowledged the Lord in some way? No doubt, he did pray as he faced his enemy, but there is no record of David asking God as to whether or not he should attack the giant Philistine.

The reason for this is clear. The Bible tells us in Proverbs 10:32 "The lips of the righteous know what is acceptable." There are certain things in life that we know are not acceptable. If you saw an elderly lady fall to the ground, do you ask God whether or not you should help her up? Certain things should be obvious to the godly. David took one look at the situation, and saw that such a thing was completely unacceptable—that this "uncircumcised Philistine" should defy the armies of the Living God.

David could draw that conclusion because he had a relationship with God. His senses were "exercised to discern both good and evil." He knew the Lord, and "they that know their God shall do exploits."

Doing Your Own Thing

The thought that may come to mind, is that the Christian must be careful not to move into the area of what is commonly called "presumption." There is an incident in Scripture where Israel presumed God was with them, when He wasn't, and the result was great tragedy. However, the issue is clarified the moment one understands the difference between faith and presumption. Take for instance my faith in my wife. Sue loves me and takes care of me. She keeps the house clean and tidy to a point where I am proud to have visitors. I have great faith in her. But presumption says, "You guys leave that mess there, the wife will clean it up . . . best housemaid I ever had!" The dictionary defines the word presumption as "an arrogant taking for granted, a liberty."

Love, respect and faith go hand in hand, and I trust that I never presume upon my wife. In the same way, each of us should love and fear God enough never to have an arrogant attitude of taking Him for granted. In fact, he who knows and fears his God would never take Him for granted—he will not venture into presumption. Yet, so many are so afraid of presumption they won't step out in faith. They are so scared of 'doing their own thing,' that they don't do anything for God.

It is interesting to note that the Apostle Paul rejoiced even when certain professing Christians *did their own thing* when preaching the Gospel. Look at his words: "Some, indeed, preach Christ out of contention, not sincerely, supposing to add affliction to my bonds; but the other, of love, knowing that I am set for the defense of the Gospel. What then? Notwithstanding, every way whether in pretence or in truth, Christ is preached; and in that I do rejoice, yea, and will rejoice" (Philippians 1:15-18).

For many years, I crossed swords with a man called "The Wizard." The man was a very eloquent speaker, who would dress up in all sorts of costumes to attract large crowds. His message varied from things of interest, to stupidity. He would provoke thought by saying how senseless it is that we pay doctors when we are sick. It is not in the interest of the medical profession for you to be healthy. If we are in good health, our doctors have no income, so there's no great incentive for them to work for our well-being. It would be far more sensible for us to pay our doctors $5 for every month we are well. Then they would have a reason to keep us in health.

We were both open-air speakers, and had a mutual understanding that I preached to the first lunch hour crowds in the local square, and he preached to the second. This happened almost daily for twelve years. Some days he would arrive while I was still speaking, and would suddenly burst from the crowd and verbally tear into me. I loved it. In fact, he was my best heckler. People thought I had great courage, but I knew that afterward we would go off together for a cup of tea. The wizard and myself were what I called, "friendly enemies."

This man was very anti-Christian. He would, much to the delight of the public, make an altar to the God of Israel and sacrifice a $10 bill by fire to God, in the name of the Father, the Son and the Holy Spirit. I was always surprised at God's patience with him. On a scale of evil, the wizard was a seven out of ten.

I also had another regular heckler, whose name was "Bernard." On a scale of ten, Bernard was a twenty-seven. He would say and do things in public that would make your hair curl. He was so anti-Christian, he made Saul of Tarsus seem like Mary Poppins. With cutting sarcasm and blazing contempt, he would say things like, "Jesus died for your sins. You have to repent because God has appointed a Day in which He will judge the world in righteousness." One day he was spitting out hatred with such intensity, he embarrassed himself by accidentally spitting out his false teeth. I almost choked with joy.

What should our attitude be toward such a man? We should grieve that he was so anti-Christian, but our grief should be for him, not for God—"Be not deceived, God is not mocked. Whatever a man sows, that will he also reap." It didn't worry me at all when he repeated scripture, because like Paul, I rejoice, even when Christ is preached with such an evil motive. The reason for this is that the quality is in the seed, not in the sower. A farmer can, with great proficiency, place his skillful hands in the sack of seed and scatter it on the soil. It will produce fruit if it falls on good soil. A simpleton can place his unskilled hands in the same sack and scatter the same seed, and it will also produce fruit, because the quality is in the seed and not in the sower. This is of great consolation to me. I know that God doesn't require my ability, just my availability to take the quality seed of His Word and scatter it on the soil of men's hearts.

Let me give you an example of this principle. Around the time Bernard was evilizing, a young man approached me and said, "I have been listening to the Gospel for some time, and I gave my life to Christ last Monday." I said how pleased I was, and asked him for details. The young man heard Bernard spewing out blasphemies in his usual anti-Christian, mocking fashion. After listening to him for some time, the man was so disgusted, he went somewhere quiet and gave his life to Jesus. The quality was in the seed of God's Word, and it found a place in his heart even when it was thrown down in ridicule.

Paul rejoiced that somebody, even out of a wrong motive, was scattering the seed of the Word of God, because anybody scattering the seed is better than nobody scattering seed. With these consoling thoughts in mind, to illustrate another important principle, I now want to share with you four small exploits that God allowed me to be involved in.

A few months after my conversion in 1972, I suddenly felt inspired to buy a bus to use for evangelism. This sudden flash of thought came when I was driving through "Aranui," a suburb of my home town. I placed an advertisement in the church column of a local newspaper to purchase a bus, and when nothing came of it I put the idea aside.

Two or three months later, I was driving through that same portion of Aranui, when I felt impressed to pray again for a bus. I could see it in my mind's eye. I would have scripture painted in quality sign-writing all around the bus. I would take out the seats and rearrange them around the walls, and lay plush carpet on the floor. It could be used for counseling, prayer, and for transporting Christians to preach the Gospel. When I arrived home, a friend called and read me a verse from the Book of Acts about turning "those who are in darkness to light." That night at a prayer meeting, another friend stuffed $200 into my shirt pocket (I liked that guy). The next day, God confirmed His Word with the kind of signs most of us enjoy, by supplying finances, from four different directions. It was about that time that I heard of a bus auction and went to it with faith, a friend, and finances.

As I waited for the first bus to be auctioned, I had a sense of anticipation as to what the Lord was going to do. It was just a matter of waiting, and clutching onto my grand total of $600. Unfortunately, the first of the three buses to be auctioned went for $1,790. I felt devastated, so I went for a long walk. It was then that God spoke to my heart with the words, "Lean not to your own understanding." The second bus sold for $1400, still well above our price range. We left the auction for a quick lunch, but upon our return, found that the auctioneers had changed, this one was fast and the auction had finished. I felt the air drain out of my lungs as we leaned against our lost bus and gave God thanks anyway.

We didn't say too much on the way home. Then, while driving back through Aranui, along the portion of road where I first prayed, I noticed a large bus parked in a field. We stopped the car, and I went next door to see if I could locate the owner.

I looked through the back door and saw a middle-aged man, who was fixing something on the floor at the end of a hallway. The bus belonged to him, so I asked if he was interested in selling it. He stood to his feet, scratched his head, and said, "That's really strange . . . *I was just thinking of selling it.*"

God gave me my bus for a grand total of $600, and it was twice the size I had envisioned. We tore out the old seats, carpeted it throughout, and put new seating around the walls. The destination on the front said "Heaven." We put Scriptures around the outside, and also painted a large picture of a man in a coffin on the back of the bus. Piled around him were masses of money, and the words, "What shall it profit a man, if he gains the whole world, and loses his own soul," underneath. We didn't get too many tailgaters.

It was a big bus. In fact, it was so big, I steered the thing while Sue worked the pedals. One day I was driving through the city and found that it was so big, I couldn't get it around a corner. I carefully checked the rear view mirrors, and backed up. It was then that I heard a sound I will never forget. It was a high pitched "Ne-ne-ne-ne-ne-ne!" with a "scrrrraaaaape" following it. I checked my mirrors again. Nothing there . . . and drove forward. Again I heard the mystifying "scrrrraaaaape" noise, so I pulled in around the corner to check what I thought was something dragging under the bus.

Suddenly, there was a feverish knock on the door. I opened it and saw a young man with a pale face. He had been parked directly behind the bus in a very small car, when a coffin with "What shall it profit a man if he gains the whole world and loses his soul," began heading toward him. He honked his car horn "Ne-ne-ne-ne-ne-ne!" as the bus scraped across the hood of his car taking the corpse, the coffin and the scripture right up to his windshield. I think God was speaking to that man. Over the years, the bus traveled thousands of miles, and was a means of taking the Gospel to many.

Locked Out

The second exploit was a tabloid Jesus Paper called "Living Waters." This 12-page newspaper had no income from advertising, no subscription fee and after the first issue, we never asked for financial support. We saw God supply finance for a total of 359,000 copies which were given away. On one occasion, I had ordered literature with only $5.75 in the bank. Some time later, we found a paper sack with over forty $20 bills in it, at our front door. The scripture which motivated us to get the bus and start the paper was solely, "Go into all the world and preach the Gospel to every creature."

The third exploit was the writing of our first book. I had previously published an eight-page paper called "My Friends Are Dying," and felt that there was an opening for the Gospel through a paperback with the same name. It was after I began writing the first chapter, that the verse was quickened, "Commit your works unto

Me and I will establish your thoughts." The first edition wasn't brilliantly written, but God blessed it anyway, and it sold between 15-20,000 copies, and now is in its ninth print. The scripture that motivated me to write the book was, "Go into all the world and preach the Gospel to every creature."

Three years after the book, we felt that a movie of the same name could also be an opportunity to share the Gospel, so we committed our ways to the Lord and He established our thoughts. Over a period of time, He supplied the necessary $24,000 to pay for the production costs. An amazing two thousand three hundred people showed up to the premiere. The theater was so packed, a thousand had to be locked out and an unscheduled second viewing held. Since that time, it has been screened hundreds of times, and seed has been sown in the hearts of many unsaved. God didn't tell me to get a bus, start a paper, write a book or make a movie—the sole motivation for those exploits was the same, "Go into all the world and preach the Gospel to every creature."

CHAPTER SEVEN

IN HARMONY WITH HEADQUARTERS

" . . . that thou mightest war a good warfare"
(1 Timothy 1:18).

When things don't work out as we think they should, we often quote Isaiah 55:8: "For My thoughts are not your thoughts, neither are your ways My ways, says the Lord." God's ways are above our ways, and often we have no idea why He allows certain things to happen. But the Scripture we so often lean on for consolation, is not directed at the godly. Here it is in context:

"Seek the Lord while He may be found, call upon Him while He is near. Let the wicked forsake his way, and the unrighteous man his thoughts. . . . For My thoughts are not your thoughts, neither are your ways My ways, says the Lord" (Isaiah 55:6-8).

God is directing Himself to the wicked and the unrighteous man. He is speaking to the unregenerate, those whose "carnal mind is at enmity" with Him, who "walk in the vanity of their mind, having the understanding darkened." Before we trust in the Savior, we are enemies of God in our minds through wicked works, and even our thoughts are an abomination to the Lord (Proverbs 15:26). Like a lost sheep, we have also "gone astray," we have "turned every one to his own way," and our ways are an abomination to the Lord (Proverbs 15:9).

Upon conversion, God puts His Law into our minds (Hebrews 8:10), giving us a new mind, the "mind of Christ," and renewing us in the "spirit" of our minds. He gives us a "new and living way" (Hebrews 10:20). Now God's ways are our ways and God's thoughts become our thoughts. We are led by the Spirit, walking "in His ways" (Psalm 119:3).

Once, our lives were dead in trespasses, governed by sin, selfishness, Satan, the soul and senses. But God made us alive in our spirit. Now we walk in the Spirit, have the mind of the Spirit, worship in the Spirit, and live in the Spirit. If we are walking in the Spirit, with our Adamic nature crucified, we can therefore be assured that the desires we now have are in line with God's desires. For example, before I was a Christian, it never entered my mind to start a Jesus paper, or get a bus and put Bible verses all around it—it would have been the last thing I would have been interested in. Now my desires are radically different.

I'm sure few of us have failed to underline Psalm 37:4 in our Bibles: "Delight yourself in the Lord, and He shall give you the desires of your heart." But what are our desires? What do we want most in life? Do we desire above all things to have a better paying job, a bigger house, thicker carpet, a superior car, and more money? Are we controlled by the lust of the flesh, the lust of the eyes and the pride of life? Or have we been transformed from the way of this world by "the renewing of (our) mind," that we may prove what is that good, and acceptable, and perfect will of God? Are our desires now in line with God's desires? Are we above all things "not willing that any should perish," that all men come to the knowledge of the truth? If that is our testimony, it is because we have the same Spirit in us as the Apostle Paul, who said, "For it is God who works in me both to will and to do of His good pleasure" (Philippians 2:13). Look at this verse in the *Amplified Bible*:

"(Not in your own strength) for it is God Who is all the while effectually at work in you—energizing and creating in you the power and desire--both to will and to work for His good pleasure and satisfaction and delight."

Scripture tells me that the reason I get desires to do exploits for God, is because He is in me "energizing and creating in me the power and desire to work for His pleasure." When I get aspirations to do things to reach the unsaved, it is because my desires have become His desires, and His desires have become my desires. I can pursue my aspirations, trusting that they are in the will of God, and therefore I can confidently expect Him to honor them. Remember, this is not presumption, "an arrogant taking for granted," but a pure, unadulterated desire to do the right thing by reaching out to the lost.

Let me ask you another question. Whose idea was it for Peter to walk on water? See if you can detect whose idea it was in these verses:

"Now in the fourth watch of the night Jesus went to them, walking on the sea. And when the disciples saw Him walking on the sea, they were troubled, saying, 'It is a ghost!' And they cried out for fear. But immediately Jesus spoke to them,

75

saying, 'Be of good cheer! It is I; do not be afraid.'
And Peter answered Him and said, 'Lord, if it is
you, command me to come to you on the water.' So
He said, 'Come.' And when Peter had come down
out of the boat, he walked on the water to go to
Jesus" (Matthew 14:25-29).

Peter said, "Lord, if it is you, command me to come
to you on the water." Peter had the concept, and Jesus
put His blessing on Peter's idea. Peter knew Jesus
intimately—he knew the mind of the Master. He knew
that his desire wasn't an impertinent presumption, but
just a longing to follow the Lord into the realm of the
supernatural. Jesus said, "If anyone serves me, let him
follow me; and where I am, there my servant will be
also. If anyone serves me, him my Father will honor"
(John 12:26).

This is why, when you and I do godly exploits, we
can trust that we are in the will of God and that He in
His goodness will honor them. This is the thought in
the words of Jesus in Mark 11:24 when He said,
"Whatever things you ask, when you pray, believe that
you receive them, and you will have them." The same
applies to John 15:7: "If you abide in Me, and My words
abide in you, you will ask what you desire, and it shall be
done for you." Or the often misinterpreted Mark 11:23:

"For assuredly, I say to you, whoever says to
this mountain, 'Be removed and be cast into the sea,'
and does not doubt in his heart, but believes that
those things he says will come to pass, he will have
whatever he says. Therefore I say to you, whatever
things you ask when you pray, believe that you
receive them, and you will have them."

Does this mean that we need merely speak the
words, "Mercedes Benz, diamond rings, fur coats," into

the air through believing prayer, and God will give them to us? I don't think so. If our covetous heart has been crucified with Christ, our desire won't be for more, bigger, better, but that none would perish. We seek first the Kingdom of God and His righteousness, and all these things will be added to us, if we need them. Scripture actually warns that a covetous prayer will not be answered:

"You ask and do not receive, because you ask amiss, that you may spend it on your pleasures" (James 4:3).

Where No Oxen Are

A verse that ministered to my heart for years is a strange little scripture in Proverbs 14:4. It is strange because on first seeing it, you wonder how it could inspire exploits for God. It merely says, "Where no oxen are, the trough is clean; but much increase comes by the strength of an ox."

Let me try to illustrate what this means to me: I proudly display a trough I have built out of high quality timber. When you ask when I will be putting oxen into it, I look disgusted, and reply that I would never put dirty oxen into my clean trough, as they would only mess it up.

The trough may be clean with no oxen, but it is useless without them. In the same way, many won't do a thing for the Kingdom of God because they are afraid of making a mess. They want to keep things neat, tidy and uncomplicated. They don't want to take risks, so they don't do a thing for the Kingdom of God.

It goes without saying that we shouldn't move until we get direction from God in certain major decisions. For some years, I desired to set up what I called the

77

Living Waters Free Christian Literature Distribution Ministries which, as the name suggests, is a ministry of providing free Gospel literature for the body of Christ world-wide. To finance this I wanted to establish a Christian bookstore and use the profits for the ministry. I suggested the thought to a number of godly men who said the idea was good, but the timing was wrong.

One day, one of those men felt a strong impression that the time was right. That evening we prayed about it after family devotions, asking God to confirm it to us. The same evening, Sue and I began our own Bible reading from Proverbs 11:21. We had been reading through a portion each night and the following verses so confirmed my desire, failure to step out in faith would have been blatant mistrust in God. Within days we had our own Christian bookstore opposite the local bar. The bar had a glass frontage and if drinking patrons looked toward our window they could see the words, "He who believes on Me shall never thirst—Jesus."

For that decision, which meant a change of vocation, we waited for direction, but the Great Commission doesn't leave any option. It is a command and therefore doesn't need a special word of confirmation. I don't have to seek God to confirm His directive to "preach the Word, in season and out of season." With such a clear admonition, we should be able to say as David said, "Once has God spoken, twice have I heard . . . " We shouldn't neglect prayer and waiting on the Lord—we should pray as we go.

The Original Greek

Here is a fascinating thing. The original Greek meaning of "Go into all the world and preach the Gospel to every creature" (Mark 16:15) opens up some

78

interesting thoughts. The word for "go" is very absorbing. It is *poreuomai*, meaning "go." The word "all" also carries with it gripping connotations. It is *hapas*, and actually means "all." And if that doesn't rivet you, look closely at the word "every." It is *pas*, and literally means "every." So when Jesus said, "Go into all the world and preach the Gospel to every creature," to be true and faithful to the original text, what He was actually saying was "Go into all the world and preach the Gospel to every creature." We are so fortunate to have access to knowledge like this.

Stunning Feet

Those who are obedient to the Great Commission will find that God will honor their desires:

"And whatever we ask we receive of Him, because we keep His commandments, and do those things that are pleasing in His sight" (1 John 3:22).

If anything is "pleasing in His sight," it is obedience to the Great Commission. Remember, God is so pleased with those who preach His Word and witness for the Gospel, that He sees even the lowliest part of us as beautiful—"How beautiful are the feet of them that preach the Gospel of peace." The Apostle Paul revealed the priority of his heart when he said, "To the weak, became I as weak, that I might gain the weak; I am made all things to all men, that I might by all means save some" (1 Corinthians 9:22).

Our bus, the paper, the book, and movie, were just concepts to reach the lost, and God in His goodness and His condescension, blessed them.

Those seeking a personal great commission need to go back to their relationship with Jesus and ask the question, "Do I know the heartbeat of my God?" Those who, like John, lay their head on the breast of Jesus will know the heartbeat of God. If we don't know His will, the Bible says we are unwise—"Therefore do not be unwise, but understand what the will of the Lord is" (Ephesians 5:17). Paul's prayer for the believer was that he would be "filled with the knowledge of His will" (Colossians 1:9). The very reason God came to this earth in the person of Jesus Christ, and suffered on the Cross, was for the salvation of the world. Has God lost His enthusiasm to see the lost saved? Has He changed His mind and is now willing that sinners perish? Is He now wanting worship without service? No, His will is that none perish, and that all come to repentance. To seek and save that which is lost is to flow in perfect harmony with the Father's will.

CHAPTER EIGHT

GAZING TOWARD HEADQUARTERS

"To him who knows to do good and does it not, to him it is sin" (James 4:17).

It was Charles Spurgeon who said,

"Brethren, do something, do something, do something! While societies and unions make constitutions, let us win souls. I pray you, be men of action all of you. Get to work and quit yourselves like men. Old Suvarov's idea of war in mine: 'Forward and strike! No theory! Attack! Form a column! Charge bayonets! Plunge into the center of the enemy! Our one aim is to win souls; and this we are not to talk about, but do in the power of God!'"

Watchman Nee, in his book, *The Spiritual Man* said:

"The passivity of the saint arises out of the non-use of his various talents. He has a mouth but refuses to talk because he hopes the Holy Spirit will talk through it. He has hands but will not engage them since he expects God to do it. He does not exercise any part of his person but waits for God to move him. He considers himself fully surrendered to God, so will no longer use any element of his being."

He continues by saying:

"They think their will must be canceled out and that they must become puppets. By falling into this state of inaction, the Christian now ceases from every activity. Indeed, he waits quietly all the time for some external force to activate him. And unless this force compels him to move he shall remain decidedly inert."

When Jesus ascended into Heaven, it must have been a glorious sight. The angels said to the disciples that "this same Jesus will come in like manner." He ascended in the same manner in which He will come! Therefore there must have been "clouds, power and great glory."

When the disciples were caught up in the glory of the ascension, the two angels appeared and brought them back to this world with the words, "Men of Galilee, why do you stand gazing up into Heaven?" The inference was, "Don't stand here gazing up into the heavens. God has granted everlasting life to sinful humanity. Go and wait for the power to take the Gospel to the world."

We haven't been saved to gaze up to Heaven, but to take the light to those who sit in the dark shadow of death. How can any person, who professes to have the love of God in them, sit in passivity while sinners die daily and go to Hell? Paul said, "Woe to me if I preach not the Gospel!"

A friend of mine couldn't get a clear word from God. He didn't know whether he should go to New Guinea with a team to both construct a church building and to evangelize. Then he heard about a man who was waiting on God for a long time. He waited and waited . . . then he died. So, my friend decided to go before he died. He had an incredible time.

Honors and Big Prizes

Elbert Hubbard once said: "The world bestows its big prizes, both in honors and money, for but one thing, and that is initiative. And what is initiative? I'll tell you: it is doing the right thing without being told!"

If you want people to appreciate you; if you want them to praise you, do the right thing without being told. If a friend drops into a seat, exhausted after a day's work, and you know he loves a hot drink when he is tired, make him one without being told. You will be praised. David did the "right thing" when he heard Goliath blaspheming. Peter did the right thing when he wanted to be with Jesus, and you and I do the right thing when we seek and save that which is lost.

With that thought in mind, look at the New Covenant (conversion) in Hebrews 8:10:

"I will put my laws within their mind, and write them on their hearts . . . "

The word "hearts" is *kardia* and means "the thoughts or feelings." Look at how the Living Bible paraphrases the verse:

"I will write My laws within their minds *so that they will know what I want them to do without My even telling them* . . . " (italics added).

Have you ever noticed how Luke begins his Gospel? Does he say that God told him to write it? No, he merely says, "It seemed good to me" to write it. Luke had a perfect understanding of the life and ministry of Jesus, so he put pen to paper, and God blessed his labor.

We need to "go to the ant, consider her ways, and be wise, which having no guide, overseer or ruler, provides her meat in the summer, and gathers her food in the harvest." In California, you don't need to go to the ant, the ant comes to you. Ants don't need to be continually motivated to work. They are full of initiative, in fact, in my conclusive studies of ants, I have never seen one taking a rest. The only still ant you will see is a dead ant. They are maniacs for work, and God points to them as our example.

Look at what Ernest Newman said:

"The great composer does not set to work because he is inspired, but becomes inspired because he is working. Beethoven, Wagner, Bach and Mozart settled down day after day to the job in hand with as much regularity as an accountant settles down each day with his figures. They didn't waste time waiting for inspiration."

The revealed will of God in Scripture should be our inspiration. If God has purchased the car, filled it with gas, paid the insurance, given us the license, sat us in the driver's seat, shown us our destination, started the engine, and told us to go, should He now have to push the car?

Peter used initiative in Acts Chapter 3 when he prayed for the lame man. He did the right thing without being told. He didn't have to pray and seek God's will, because he knew it already. He knew that Jesus "went about doing good, and healing those who were vexed by the devil." In verses 11 and 12 of the same chapter, we see that when the miracle of healing took place, "all the people ran together to them . . . and when Peter saw it, he answered the people . . . " A modern version says, "And when Peter *saw his opportunity* . . . (italics added)." Peter didn't pray and see if it was God's will to preach the Gospel to every creature, he saw an opportunity, and used his initiative and preached to them.

Do you remember the incident in Acts 16:6, where the disciples were heading for Asia, and God told them not to go there? What does that show us? It shows that the disciples didn't have a "word from the Lord" to evangelize in Asia. If they had prayed, "Lord, do you want us to preach the Gospel in Asia?" and God had directed them to go there, it means that He then changed His mind. Rather, the disciples merely obeyed the command to "Go into all the world, and preach the Gospel to every creature," and God in His faithfulness had directed their steps by saying, "Not Asia, at this time."

If there is one thing Satan seeks to kill, steal and destroy, it is man's initiative and creativity, especially in the area of evangelism. When people say to me, "You are very creative," I agree and say, "My Father is very creative. Look at Genesis Chapter 1." God is Creativity itself, and (I say it reverently), He is full of initiative. God took the initiative in the beginning when He spoke creation into being. When Adam fell, so did his direct contact with the Father, but now you and I have the mind of Christ. We have access to the incredibly infinite intellect of Almighty God, and we can let His creativity flow through us.

Left Foot of Fellowship

You may be asking the question as to what you can do in a practical way to reach people for the Kingdom of God. Here are a few suggestions: There are a number of evangelistic organizations you may like to join. I was in Gideons International for seven years, until I became a pastor, as they don't allow pastors to be involved, only lay people. It is such a blessing to be involved in an organization that gives away copies of God's Word. Then there is Youth With A Mission, Youth For Christ,

85

Campus Crusade For Christ, and many others you could become involved in. Perhaps you could invest in a small advertisement in the personal column of your local paper saying something like "Find reality, read John 8:31-32." Get a cost quote before you commit yourself. I wanted to buy a full page in the L.A. Times during the Gulf War in 1991. I thought it would be around $6,000, and figured I could probably raise that amount of money.

I called the Times and the gentleman gave me the cost: "A full page is $61,023." I thought he had slipped an extra number in by mistake. Wrong. I dropped that idea quickly.

Perhaps you could visit a hospital once a week, with the purpose of finding and befriending someone who doesn't normally have visitors. If you have a flare for drama, start a drama group. How about writing a tract? Don't say, "But I can't write," say, "I can do all things through Christ who strengthens me." Write out your testimony, and have a friend or two read it, and give their opinions. Then print out the edited copy, and have it typeset at your local printers. Remember to get quotes before you do anything, so that you won't get burned. When it is printed, keep copies in your wallet or purse to give to old friends or people you meet, with the words, "You may like to read this when you have a moment. I wrote it myself." Put copies into the envelope when paying bills.

Back in the late 70's, I had 40-50 children in our garage every Friday for a 20-minute "Good-time" Club. I remember praying that God would send me someone who could play a guitar to give the music a bit of a lift. One Friday evening, my brother-in-law walked into our living room knowing nothing of my prayer, and said, "For some reason I feel the Lord wants me to give you my guitar." I hadn't thought of me. I was never able to play a guitar, but now I can do all things through Christ who strengthens me (I just have trouble convincing those within earshot).

You could easily start a club through your local church. When I decided to start mine, I just took a marker pen and wrote, "KIDS CLUB, FRIDAY 4 P.M., (ADDRESS), CANDY, PRIZES, STORIES AND SONGS," gave out photocopies at a school gate, and had a crowd of children eager to learn about the things of God. Nowadays, with all the allegations and accusations of child molestation, etc., it would be wise to have both male and female leaders. Start with a firm hand, sing some lively songs, tell a Bible story, teach a memory verse, give out some candy, then tell the kids, "It's all over, see you next week." If the children don't say "Ohhhhhhh!" you've probably gone on too long and they may not be back the following week. I found 20 minutes was adequate for most.

Sometimes talented Christians don't feel right about using their gift of music or writing, etc., to reach the unsaved. It is often because of their own pride, that their conscience is condemning them, and not God. This happens regularly with counter-culture people who become Christians. Their conscience will not allow them to eat meat. After some time they come across a scripture such as 1 Timothy 4:3-4, which says that God has created all foods "to be received with thanksgiving by them who believe and know the truth. For every creature of God is good, and nothing is to be refused, if it is received with thanksgiving." Immediately their conscience is released by understanding the Word of God.

When we understand the emphasis which the Word of God places upon evangelism, we should humble ourselves, thank God for the gift He has given us, then use it for His glory. If you have got no apparent talents, visit an old folk's home, or ask your pastor if you can help in any way within the local church. Do something for God. Desire to do nothing, and God will give you the desires of your heart.

The Sparkle of Diamonds

An old Arab once told a poor man of the beauty of diamonds. He told him that if he possessed just a handful of sparklers, he would never want for anything ever again. He could have whatever he desired in life. From that time on, the poor man began to dream about diamonds. He spent every moment thinking about those glittering gems. Finally, he was so consumed by that dream, he left his home and began to search for his dream. Wherever he went he would dig for diamonds. Years passed, until that disappointed poor man flung himself into the sea and committed suicide.

The old Arab visited the poor man's home not knowing of his death. As he walked into the living room he noticed a rock on the mantle and said, "Where did you get that diamond . . . is the poor man back?" Those in the house said that it was just a rock they had found out in the back yard. The Arab picked it up in his trembling hand and said, "I know a diamond when I see one—where did you get it?" They rushed out to the back yard and began digging in its white sands, and found diamond, after diamond, after diamond. Thus began the Golconda Diamond Mines, which exceeded the Kimberley   Mines in value!

You don't need to chase around the world searching for the illusive and sparkling diamonds of the will of God; just begin to cultivate your own back yard. The Bible says, " . . . a good man shall be satisfied from himself." Start digging for those gems of creativity, and then do something for the Kingdom of God.

When John Wesley was asked what he would do with his life if he knew that he would die at midnight the next day. His answer was something like this: "I would just carry on with what I am doing. I will arise at 5:00 a.m. for prayer, then take a house meeting at 6.00 a.m. At 12 noon, I will be preaching at an open-air. At 3:00 p.m. I have another meeting in another town. At 6:00 p.m. I have a house meeting; at 10:00 p.m. I have a prayer meeting and at 12:00 midnight, I would go to be with my Lord."

If we knew we were to die at 12 o'clock tomorrow night, would we have to step up our evangelistic program, or could we in all good conscience carry on just as we are?

It would seem that there are only three types of people in this world—the jawbone, the wishbone and the backbone. The jawbone says he will do something, one day. He never puts his muscle where his mouth is. He prays about things, but never does them. His conscience stirs him to prayer, but the warmth of his comfort zone stifles his good intentions, because his own well-being is more important to him.

The wishbone gazes with starry eyes at his godly heroes and wishes he could be like them. His is a world of dreams. Like the wishbone, he is easily divided from his goals. He wishes he could preach, write, pray, sing and dance. Yet, no one ever did anything without doing something. An aspiration will only become a realization with perspiration. If he wants to see revival, he should stop wishing and start fishing, but his dreams are not fuel enough to motivate him.

In contrast, the backbone sees Goliath and runs toward him. He breaks out of the comfort zone of apathy, warmth, and security. He leaves the fat cat of indifference sleeping by the fire. He walks on water while others sit in the safety of the boat. He rushes headlong into battle. He uses what he has to do the will of His Heavenly Father. He knows His God, and does exploits.

CHAPTER NINE

DEVOTION TO THE CAUSE

"No man that wars entangles himself with the affairs of this life, that he may please him who has chosen him to be a soldier" (2 Timothy 2:4).

Sue and I were once trying to pry resistant nuts from their shells. They would crack open, but were very difficult to get out from the inside of their casings. Suddenly, a bright idea struck me. I put one in the microwave oven for ten seconds. Then, when I cracked the nut, no longer did it cling to the shell. It came out without the slightest resistance.

If there is one thing that will bring the timid Christian out of his shell, it is the heat of persecution. That's all that happened when God allowed Saul of Tarsus to put the early Church in the microwave. Persecution put the fear of God in the hearts of those who were exercised by it. The puritan author, William Gurnall, the author of, *The Christian in Complete Armour* (of which Spurgeon said, "Gurnall's work is peerless and priceless"), said:

> "We fear men so much, because we fear God so little. One fear causes another. When man's terror scares you, turn your thoughts to the wrath of God."

Here is something that will help you get rid of the fear of man and replace it with the fear of God: HE EXECUTES COWARDS, DESERTERS AND TRAITORS (Hebrews 10:26, Revelation 21:8). His Army is for men and women of faith. Our courage is fueled by faith in God. If we lack courage, it's only because we lack faith. If we lack faith, we insult the integrity of Almighty God.

Trials also can have the effect of bringing us to our knees and seeking God's will rather than our own. In South Korea, a baseball team called the "Dolphins" began a training program with a difference. They would climb a high mountain, remove their shirts and stand bare-chested in the freezing wind. Then they would dig holes in the ice, and subject their bodies to freezing cold water. They said that the practice made the team hardy, and also promoted team unity. They went from being a laughing-stock, to the top of the league. Now all the other teams have imitated their training program.

As much as we don't like the thought, blessings tend to take our eyes off God. Trials put them back on. Icy tribulation builds strength of character within the Christian, and the cold winds of persecution purify the Church by bringing a sense of unity and purpose.

We need not wait for God's chastening hand. Perhaps if we chasten ourselves, we will not need to be chastened. If we remove the unfruitful branches, the Gardener won't have to cut them off.

In 1963, the U.S. Government took the Ten Commandments off the walls of the schools and prayer from the classroom, and the nation is reaping a whirlwind of destruction. When there is no wall of absolute authority, anarchy comes in like a flood. When a generation has no fear of God before their eyes, then the laws which forbid murder have no influence. On any given day in the U.S., an estimated 100,000 guns and knives are smuggled into schools. Every year, hurricanes, floods, tornadoes, draughts and disease ravage the country. Each week in the U.S. 250 children are diagnosed with cancer. Every 12 months prostate cancer kills 34,000 men. There are 280,000 new cases of breast cancer each year. More than 40,000 American women die of ovarian cancer each year. Our nation is in a desperate state.

How on earth do we move the Hand of the God of Heaven? The answer is, and has always been two-fold. We must first get on our knees and beseech God to save this generation, then ask Him to use us to take the *means* of salvation to the unsaved. He has chosen the foolishness of preaching to save those who believe. He has entrusted us with the Word of reconciliation, and it is therefore up to us to break free from that which binds us.

On the Hot Front

Three front row infantrymen were Shadrach, Meshach and Abednego. The King told them to bow down to his idol, but rather than sin against God, they refused. They knew that the Law said,

"I am the Lord your God who brought you out of Egypt, out of the house of bondage. You shall have no other gods before Me. You shall not make for yourself a graven image, or any likeness of anything that is in heaven above, or that is in the earth beneath, or that is in the water under the earth; you shall not bow down to them nor serve them. For I am a jealous God, visiting the iniquity of the fathers on the children to the third and fourth generations of those that hate Me, but showing mercy to thousands, to those who love Me and keep My Commandments" (Exodus 20:1-6).

The three godly men loved God and therefore kept His Commandments. Their choices were to compromise and keep in good with the king, or obey God and be cast into the fiery furnace. They knew what was acceptable. Like David when he faced Goliath, they didn't need to seek the mind of the Lord in this matter. The Law had already given them knowledge of right from wrong. Look at what they said to the King when he threatened them with such a terrible death:

"O Nebuchadnezzar, we have no need to answer you in this matter. If that is the case, our God whom we serve is able to deliver us from the burning fiery furnace, and He will deliver us from your hand, O king. But if not, let it be known to you O king, that we do not serve your gods, nor will we worship the gold image which you have set up" (Daniel 3:16-18).

The warrior of Jesus Christ will not bow down to the golden image of mammon, with its promise of gratification, security and comfort. Even if the devil threatens to heat up the furnace of persecution and tribulation seven times, he will not bow down. He looks to the Word of God as his authority "denying ungodliness and worldly lusts."

He is a soldier of Christ and therefore thanks God that he has been counted worthy to suffer for the Name of the Savior. He is as Moses who broke free from the gratification of Egypt, "choosing rather to suffer affliction with the people of God than to enjoy the passing pleasures of sin."

Muscle grows through resistance. If you want to grow physically, get into a swimming pool and hold a five gallon container filled with water at head level. To stay afloat, you will have to kick for dear life. The key in this exercise is to have the lid off the container, face it down and let the water drain out as you kick. A great consolation is that you know that as time passes, as you tire, the weight is going to get lighter, and that knowledge will spur you on.

As you step into the waters of personal evangelism, the weight of apprehension may seem unbearable, but as you pour yourself out for the Gospel, you will have the knowledge that God will relieve you of the weight. Each time you exercise yourself in this, you will strengthen yourself spiritually.

Hive of Activity

I was sitting with a pastor in a restaurant in Nashville, when a waiter approached us with a meal, looked at the pastor and said, "Chicken fingers!" The pastor hardly noticed the insult, but I couldn't help but want to call the waiter something similar. Another waiter told us that he had bathed his cat that day. He said it took him an hour to get the fur off his tongue. Then the conversation swung to the waiter's physical features. He said that he thought that his nose was too big. Another brother at our table said that he thought his own nose was too big. Then the pastor's wife shared her concerns about a fear that her ears would get big as she grew older. The conversation reminded me about how we so often become overly concerned about things that don't matter in the light of eternity. I know a man who often looks into the mirror while he brushes his hair and says, "Lord, send revival, raise up laborers, save this nation." Then with great passion he cries, "And please Lord, please *don't let my hair fall out!*" It is easier to agonize about the immediate here and now, rather than about the eternal here-after.

Some time ago, after I finished speaking at a church in Minneapolis, the pastor of evangelism took hold of the microphone. He was an ex-cop, and his voice cracked with emotion as he spoke of an accident victim he once held in his arms. The critically injured man thrashed back and forth for a moment, sighed deeply, then passed into eternity. The pastor's voice was filled with emotion, because his own church had over a thousand members, and only five attended his evangelism class.

It was obvious that the army's hive of activity was in the barracks of everything but evangelism. He pleaded, saying, "What's wrong with you? *Don't you care that people in our city are going to Hell?* I can teach you to rid yourself of fear . . . " His was no proud boast. The prison doors of fear *can* be opened with very simple keys—a knowledge of God's will, ordered priorities, love that is not passive, gratitude for the Cross, and the use of the Law before Grace . . . just to name a few.

What *is* wrong with us? How can we not care that sinners are being swallowed by death? Why am I sometimes more concerned about losing my hair than I am that sinners are going to Hell? I grieve that my eyes are dry while I pray for and preach to the unsaved. I recently received the following challenging letter from an atheist I had been witnessing to via e-mail:

"If you're right, as you say you are, and you believe that, then how can you sleep at night? When you speak with me, you are speaking with someone who you believe is walking directly into eternal damnation, into an endless onslaught of horrendous pain which your loving god created, yet you stand by and do nothing. If you believed one bit that thousands every day were falling into an eternal and unchangeable fate, you should be running the streets mad with rage at their blindness. That's equivalent to standing on a street corner and watching every person that passes you walk blindly directly into the path of a bus and die, yet you stand idly by and do nothing. You're just twiddling your thumbs, happy in the knowledge that one day that "walk" signal will shine your way across the road. Imagine the horrors hell must have in store if the Bible is true. You're just going to allow that to happen and not care about saving anyone but yourself? If you're right then you're an uncaring, unemotional and purely selfish b-st-rd that has no right to talk about subjects such as love and caring."

The Voice of the Rescuer

On a warm spring day in New York, a fire broke out in a high-rise building. When firemen arrived, they saw a man on a ledge of the 12th floor. Smoke billowed out from the structure, blinding the terrified man and forcing him to the very edge. Death seemed to lick its merciless lips.

Quickly, a fireman was lowered from above by a rope, and rescued him before he was forced to jump to his death. The man said that it was a miracle that he was saved. He said that he was blind, but heard the voice of his rescuer, and from there clung to him for dear life.

How perfectly that sums up our salvation. We had climbed the stairs of the high-rise of sin. The Law of sin and death forced us onto the ledge of futility. We stood blind, fearful, helpless and hopeless . . . *until we heard the voice of our Savior.* We heard the joyful sound of the voice of the Son of God, as He reached down from the heavens with His holy hand and snatched us from death's dark door. *But there are still others on the ledge going through the terror we once experienced.* We cannot rest until we direct them into the hands of Jesus.

I thank God that He saved me while I was young, while I still have energy to reach out to the lost. I pray that God will make me to know the number of my days that I might "apply my heart to wisdom." It is the epitome of wisdom to spend every ounce of energy and every moment of every day seeking the salvation of souls.

CHAPTER TEN

THE THREE-FOLD BATTLE

"Let the redeemed of the Lord say so, whom He has
redeemed from the hand of the enemy"
(Psalm 107:2).

The moment we exercise repentance toward God and put our faith in the Savior, we step right into the middle of a threefold battle. We find that we are torn by the world, the flesh and the devil. The appetite of the flesh was fully satisfied with the pleasures of sin. Suddenly it is starved to the point of gnawing at the mind for want of food. It causes what the Scriptures call a "war in your members." Thoughts which once were acceptable, suddenly stir the alarm of conscience. Not long after my conversion, I became so concerned about the battle within my mind, I sought deliverance through prayer. I was a little disappointed that nothing happened. It wasn't a demon I was wrestling with, but the powerful aroma of my corrupt and sinful Adamic self. I was now a new creature in Christ Jesus, old things had passed away, and all things had become new. The old nature, like four days dead Lazarus stunk because it was dead in Christ, and now I had to bury it.

Just after our first child began to walk, he picked up a blanket and adopted it as his "cuddly." He would

99

take that blanket wherever he went. In the usual child-like manner, he would put two fingers and part of his blanket into his mouth and make sucking noises.

When it was washed and hung on the clothesline, he would stand beneath it and jump up to try and grab it. We felt that we had better try and break the habit before his wedding day, so we cut it in half and gave it to him. The next day, we secretly cut it in half again. Every few days, we would cut it in half, until it became so small it just disappeared.

That is what we are to do with the flesh. It is forever running around like a turkey with its head chopped off. It is dead, but it won't lie down without a little help from the whetted blade of the two-edged sword. The witless creature not only needs to have its head removed, it needs to be gutted, plucked, and its soft flesh carved on the wooden plate of Calvary's cross. That will put thanksgiving in our hearts.

The only access the enemy has to cause us to sin, is through the flesh. If we deal with it once and for all, the world will have no attraction for us, and the devil will have no foothold on us. It is vital to identify this Judas in our heart. That old nature is nothing more than a cowardly traitor who will cry "Master, Master," and then betray the Son of God with a kiss. We must so hang Judas by the neck until he "bursts asunder in the midst, and all his bowels gush out." If we do not deal with this enemy, he will quietly steal from us until he betrays us and the cause for which we stand.

The Lust Stand

I find that I am forever approached by young men, and occasionally young women, who hang their heads in shame, and confess that they have a "lust" problem.

The reaction is interesting when I say, "Who doesn't?" They are relieved to find that they are not alone in the battle against the "lust of the flesh, the lust of the eyes, and the pride of life." If you don't have any "problem" with lust, then you've got problems. You have more than likely surrendered to it.

Sexdrive is God-given. It can find satisfaction in marriage. But lust is more than a "drive." It is a vehicle that overtakes the driver. It straps the driver in, locks the doors and takes over the wheel. It steers him onto a fatal collision course with the Law of God. Lust is a spark in the eye that will start a fire in the heart if we don't put it out as soon as we detect its presence. In almost every case where scripture specifies distinctive sins, sexual sin is at the top of the list. Sin, especially sexual sin, draws us as a moth to a flame. Scripture speaks of being "hardened through the *deceitfulness* of sin." *The Amplified Bible* puts the same verse this way, " . . . hardened through the trickery which the delusive glamour of his sin may play on him." Sin has a delusive glamour to it. The old saying, "as miserable as sin" just isn't true. The person who said it probably also said, "Crime doesn't pay." Moses chose to suffer affliction with the people of God, rather than *enjoy* the pleasures of sin for a season. Sin is enjoyable. I have walked the streets of New York and have noticed that porn stores don't have to do too much advertising. All they need is a peep-hole for perverts.

The soldier of Christ must keep his heart with all diligence. Impure thoughts fill the room of the mind with lethal gas, and all it takes is an ember of opportunity to create a disaster. Sin holds a deep-rooted charm for our sin-full nature, but carries the sting of death with it. Lust is a landmine hidden in the dirt of the world. Keep out of the world or you will end up maimed by it. People in the world stomp around in dirt and wonder what hits them when things blow up in their face. Lust explodes into sin, and sin, when it's conceived brings death.

Let Lying Dogs Sleep

Two women from Southern California were about to cross the Mexican border to return to the U.S., when they saw what looked like a very small sick animal in the ditch beside their car. As they examined it in the darkness of the night, they saw that it was a tiny Chihuahua. Then and there they decided to take it back to the U.S. and nurse it back to health. However, because they were afraid that they were breaking the law, they put it in the trunk of their car, and drove across the border. Once they were in the U.S., they retrieved the animal and nursed it until they arrived home.

One of the women was so concerned for the ailing dog she actually took it to bed with her, and reached out at different intervals during the night to touch the tiny animal, and reassure it that she was still present.

The dog was so sick the next morning, she decided to take it to the veterinarian. That's when she found out that the animal wasn't a tiny sick dog. It was a Mexican water rat, dying of rabies.

The world, in the blackness of its ignorance thinks that sin is a puppy to be played with. It is the light of God's Law that enlightens the sinner to the fact that he is in bed with a deadly rat.

We were once "deceived, serving different lusts and pleasures," but now, if we are truly converted, our eyes have been opened. We see sin for the sugar-coated venom that it is.

Farewell Speech

I find that most we call erroneously "backsliders," hold on to a form of godliness. They pray. They may even find a fellowship to suit their sins, but they stop reading the Word. To open the Bible when there is sin in the heart is convicting. The two-edged sword cuts too close to the flesh.

Stephen gives us an interesting insight into the workings of a false convert in Acts Chapter 7. As this soldier of Christ gives his farewell speech to those who are about to promote him to Headquarters, he spoke of Israel's backsliding in the wilderness, saying,

"But our fathers refused to obey Him. Instead, they rejected him and in their hearts turned back to Egypt. They told Aaron, 'Make some gods who will lead the way for us. As for this fellow Moses who led us out of Egypt—we don't know what has happened to him.' That was the time they made an idol in the form of a calf. They brought sacrifices to it and held a celebration in honor of what their hands had made."

Here we not only have three stages of Israel's backsliding, but we also have three signs of a "backslider in heart"—the false convert. According to Bible typology, Egypt is a type of the world, and Moses is a type of Christ.

The first sign of false converts is "in their hearts" they turn back to Egypt. No one else may know—but they know, and God knows that deep within the heart is a yearning to go back to the world. Like Lot's wife, they are longingly looking back. The Scriptures warn that "fellowship with the world is enmity with God." It teaches that whoever "wants to be a friend of the world makes himself an enemy of God." Therefore those who profess to be in the Army of God, but have a desire to go back to the enemy of the world, are not on our side. How can they be if God's Word says they are the enemy of God?

Second, they said, "As for this Moses fellow who led us out of Egypt—we don't know what has become of him!" The backslider in heart loses the reality of his walk with Jesus—"As for this Jesus who led us out of the world—we don't know what has become of Him." They leave what they said was their first love. To say, "I love you Jesus" sounds trite to them, yet the Bible warns, "If any man loves not our Lord Jesus Christ, let him be cursed."

Third, they make for themselves an idol. They create a god in their own image. They shape a god to suit their own sins, then worship the work of their own hands. Their god becomes one who is void of reference to sin, righteousness and judgment. There is no need to flee from sin, because their god condones sin. Then it is only a matter of time until they slip down the slippery and sinful path they have chosen. He who loves the world may not be in the world, but the world is still in him. Of them, the proverbs are true: "A dog returns to its vomit," and "A sow that is washed goes back to her wallowing in the mud." The pig wallows in the mire to cool its flesh.

The Distinguishing Mark

What can be done to ensure that we are not part of the great company who fall away, or of the great mass who will cry "Lord, Lord?" How can we be sure that we won't be lined up as deserters and shot from Heaven into Hell? The answer is in Galatians 6:14:

"But God forbid that I should glory, except in the Cross of our Lord Jesus Christ, by whom the world is crucified unto me, and I unto the world."

A personal revelation of Jesus Christ on the Cross is the key. This truth is graphically illustrated in the following story: A father and son once went on a camping trip. When they arrived at the site, the father pitched the tent and said, "Son, see that river; it's full of crocodiles. If you want to do any fishing, fish off the wharf." The son reluctantly agreed that he would stay on the wharf.

After three days of fishing, the son began to think about the excitement of fishing amidst the crocodiles in the safety of a boat. So, that is what he did. He obtained a boat, and in a sense of bravado, rowed out into the river.

He had only been fishing for a short time when a crocodile came alongside the small boat and hit it with its tail. The terrified boy was thrown into the water. The father heard him scream, saw what had happened, and without hesitation dived into the crocodile-infested waters. He grabbed his beloved son and pulled him to the safety of the shore.

When the boy opened his eyes, he saw a grisly sight. A crocodile had wrapped its massive jaws around the father's legs, leaving him in bleeding shreds.

The following thought is unthinkable. Imagine if the son looked at his father lying in agony, bleeding to death, and said, "Dad, I really appreciate what you just did for me. But I found it exciting out there with the crocodiles—you wouldn't mind if I got another boat and went out again, would you?"

If the son could *think*, let alone *say* such a thing, the blind fool hasn't seen the sacrifice his father has just made for him!

If we have any, *even hidden desire*, to go back into the sinful excitement of the world, we haven't seen the sacrifice of the Father.

If that son has seen what his father has just done for him, a sense of horror will consume him at the cost, the extreme, the length, the expense his father has just gone to, to save him. He would pour contempt upon the very drops of water that still cling to his flesh.

The true Christian has seen that God in the person of Jesus Christ, without hesitation, dived into the very jaws of Hell to save him from the folly of sin. A sense of horror consumes him at the cost, the extreme, the length, and the expense his Father went to, to save him. He cries,

> "And when I think, that God His Son not sparing, sent Him to die, I scarce can take it in; that on that cross, my burdens gladly bearing, He bled and died to take away my sin."

The Christian pours contempt upon the sinful desires that still cling to his flesh. The true convert is crushed by a sense of his own foolishness and yet at the same time, he has inexpressible gratitude for the "unspeakable gift" of the Cross. He has seen Jesus Christ "evidently set forth and crucified." He says with Paul, "God forbid that I should glory, save in the Cross of our Lord Jesus Christ, by whom the world is crucified to me, and I to the world." After seeing the sacrifice of the Father, how could he ever go back to the exciting pleasures of sin? To do so, he would have to trample underfoot the blood of Jesus Christ. He would have to count the sacrifice of Calvary as nothing.

Instead, he willfully crucifies himself to the world, and the world to himself.

He whispers with the hymnist:

"When I survey the wondrous cross, on which the Prince of Glory died, my richest gain I count but loss, and pour contempt on all my pride."

As the songwriter says, "The Cross has become the Tree of Life for me." The world cannot attract him any longer. They that are Christ's have crucified their affections and lusts.

CHAPTER ELEVEN

VICTORY AMIDST DEFEAT

"He teaches my hand to war, so that a bow of bronze
is broken by my arms" (2 Samuel 22:35).

The army that does not train well, will not fight well. Soldiers are not only trained in the use of their weapons, but they are conditioned to become strong. Deliberate resistance is put in front of every soldier. He finds himself facing obstacle courses. He weaves his way through all types of difficulties, bunkers, hazards, hindrances, snags, tripwires, hurdles, hedges and barriers. He is made to run with great weights upon his shoulders, march for miles, arise at the crack of dawn, and stand for long periods of time. He is forced to go against the grain. The objective is to create a strong, disciplined, finely-tuned, well-regulated, and organized force of soldiers who will stop at nothing to achieve the objective. Wimps drop out.

Muscle comes through resistance. The strong, muscular, conquering hero didn't get that way through easy living. To attain such a physical state, he had to train hard. Through many years of running, weight training and self-discipline, he brought himself to the peak of condition. The more resistance he put against his muscles, the more they developed.

God wants to bring His soldiers to the peak of condition. He is refining us through resistance. He desires to build in us the muscles of a strong and good character. He doesn't want us to be caught up in the vanities of this futile life. He wants to teach us good judgment, self-discipline, perseverance, godliness and love. These are the rippling muscles that impress God. These are the virtues of His Divine Nature, the qualities that will cause the Army of God to be strong, delicately-tuned, and well-regulated to a point where we will obtain our objectives.

It was Leonard Ravenhill who said, "Every smart top brass military expert has arrived there *because* he wore the harness of discipline." The soldier who truly understands this principle, and the objective of his superiors, will gladly submit himself to the discipline of the army. The true soldier of Christ, who sees the objective of his Superior, will joyfully submit himself to the discipline and trials of the Christian walk. In the light of the objective, the yoke of Jesus is easy and the burden is light. He has not been *drafted* into the army of God, but he has *willingly submitted himself* to the yoke of Christ. He knows that whatever affliction, trial, or weight of resistance comes his way, comes only by the will of his Superior. God has allowed a particular trial, no matter how bad it may seem, for his good. He can fall into the great safety-net of Romans 8:28 when everything else fails. When no human hand can rescue him, he falls upon the sure and true promises of a faithful Creator. Paul says, "And we know that all things work together for good to those who love God, to those who are called according to His purpose."

Look at John Wesley's understanding of the disciplines of God:

"Receive every inward and outward trouble, every disappointment, pain, uneasiness, temptation, darkness and desolation with both hands, as to a true opportunity and blessed occasion of dying to self and entering into a fuller fellowship with thy self-denying suffering Savior."

Wesley knew that affliction works for, not against the Christian—"For our light affliction, which is but for a moment, *is working for us* a far more exceeding and eternal weight of glory" (2 Corinthians 4:17, NKJV, italics added). Remember that in tribulation every problem which comes our way can be a stepping stone, rather than a stumbling block. The Apostle Paul actually took pleasure in trials because he knew that they had the effect of bringing a closer commitment to the cause (see 2 Corinthians 12:10). Every scar on his flesh was a testimony of a deeper commitment to His Savior. Every stripe across his back with the whip, not only revealed a heart sold out to God, but it cut a fresh resolve in his soul to further die to this world and live for the next.

It has been rightly said that one distinguishing mark of an unregenerate man is ingratitude. The soldier of Christ will not entangle himself with the affairs of this world, because he is continually motivated to please God, by gratitude for the Cross. He has meat to eat that the world knows not of. The Cross gives him a merry heart, a "continual feast"—rations that keep him energized in the battle.

George Whitefield said, "I had a day in my life when I fully surrendered in consecration to the Lord and that day I said, 'I call Heaven and earth to witness that I give up myself entirely to be a martyr for Him who hung on the Cross for me. I have thrown myself blindfolded and without reserve into His mighty hands!'" The troopers of the Cross who have seen the commendation of the love of God, cannot help but fling themselves into the heat of the battle, constrained by the same irresistible force that drove Jesus to Calvary.

Trials not only have the effect of driving us closer to God, but they also show us our point of growth as Christians. The soldier who fails an obstacle course, needs more training.

If it wasn't for our trust in God—our knowledge that He knows what He is doing with our lives, we certainly would lose heart. It seems that the Christian life is one obstacle after another, yet we know that when we are tried we "shall come forth as gold." God is not only preparing a place for us, but He is also preparing us for that place.

An Unhelpful Friend

A man once noticed movement in a cocoon outside his bedroom window. It was obvious that a butterfly was struggling to get out, so he took a razor-blade, leaned out of the window and slit the side of the cocoon to help the poor creature. The butterfly struggled for the moment, then fell out onto the ground. It looked sickly and pale. After a little movement, it died. The man hadn't helped the butterfly, he had killed it. The very process of struggling in the cocoon should have pumped blood into the wings of the butterfly, giving it beauty, life and character. In the same way, all the trials and struggling which comes our way, are not to do us harm, but to do us good. They are bringing beauty and color to our character, which will be revealed the moment we break free from the cocoon of this life.

If we have faith in God we will be exceedingly joyful in all our tribulation. This rejoicing may be a "sacrifice of praise," almost a matter of gritting our teeth and saying, "I don't know what's going on. Everything is working against me, but I will rejoice anyway, and give God thanks because He has said that all things are working together for my good."

This is not easy to do, but the more difficult the situation, the more you will have to trust in the Lord with all your heart, and lean not to your own understanding. The athlete doesn't buckle under the pressure, he resists it and in so doing, strengthens his muscle.

One of My Fans

As I have mentioned earlier, for some time Sue and I had our own Christian bookstore. This was in the suburbs and proved ideal for my writing. Our busy day was Saturday, and during the week it was peaceful and quiet. God, in His faithfulness, had not only directed us into the ministry, but He had also confirmed my writing and speaking ministry in a wonderful way. Our family had been overseas for about four weeks, and when we returned, my pastor asked if I would share with the congregation where I thought God was taking my ministry. I began to seek the Lord, and all I could get was Psalm 45:1: "My heart is overflowing with a good theme . . . my tongue is the pen of a ready writer." I dismissed it as my own mind. If any scripture was appropriate, that one was. I wanted to use both my pen and my tongue.

On the following Sunday, I stood in front of the church, ready to share how I felt God was leading me to speak out and write for Him. The service opened in prayer, then went straight into worship. During a quiet time during the worship, someone spoke out the words, "My tongue is the pen of a ready writer." The person had no idea what I had in my mind, but God knew. This was my first service in this church for four weeks, and the very Scripture which had been on my heart all week had come out to confirm the direction I was taking. It was because of this clear leading, I had confidence that the bookstore was God's further provision for my writing ministry. It was ideal, so I expected smooth sailing.

After some time in the store, the premises next door became vacant. I prayed that a Christian would move in, and sure enough, within a week or so a young Christian gentleman moved next door to open a sandwich shop. The name of our store was Living Waters Book Store, and our window sign read, "Jesus said, he that believeth on Me, shall never thirst." My new neighbor in the sandwich store suggested, "Man shall not live by bread alone" for his window. We both decided to pray that a Christian butcher would move in next door and have, "Labor not for the meat that perishes" in his window.

We had launched into the perfect little evangelistic setup. As I expected, it was smooth sailing until one day my friend had a large fan installed and took the wind out of my sails. It effectively sucked out unwanted air on his side of the wall, but sent unbearable vibrations through our side. One could hardly hear the vibrations, but they could certainly be felt. They were the type of thing one can imagine would be used in torture. My neighbor kept the fan turned down to a minimum, but this hardly helped the situation. The most concentrated area of vibration was right at my writing desk.

I prayed about the situation repeatedly. I called in experts who told me that the fan was incorrectly mounted, so I had it mounted correctly. That cost me about $100. All this time I wanted to keep my attitude right toward my Christian brother. He was not in a position financially to help with any costs for improvement. Besides, even with the correct mounting, it didn't help. I moved my office to another area, but that didn't help much either.

Every morning it was the same. I would open the door and step into a vibrating, pulsating, shaking, throbbing, painful torture room. It would have the affect of tensing my throat muscles. One day it was particularly bad. When I arrived home, I was a wreck.

The next day I opened the door and entered the store. I jumped for joy, rejoiced, gave thanks and nearly burst into tears as I began another day in the torture chamber. I knew all the principles of trials being for our good, but I could stand it no longer; *it was driving me insane.* I felt so trapped. I felt utterly helpless, but there was nothing I could do. I was at the point of breaking down. If I stayed in that store for one more minute, I would lose my sanity! As far as I was concerned, it was God's business, so I would close up shop and go home. I had had enough. No more. I could no longer bear the pain.

I began writing a note to leave on the door, "We apologize for any inconven . . . " Suddenly the fan stopped. *At that exact moment* a woman stepped up to me and handed me $1,000 to help our ministry. The timing was incredible. I held onto that money and said, *"You know Lord, that noise isn't so bad after all."*

God knows exactly what we can take. He knows how to encourage us, and when to deliver us. He is strengthening and training us so that we can say, "It is God who arms me with strength . . . You enlarged my path under me; so that my feet did not slip. I have pursued my enemies and overtaken them . . . for You have armed me with strength for the battle."

If Moses Had a Boat

So often we blame the devil for adversity. We must remember that God is sovereign, and that if the enemy does come against us, it is by His permission. This does not mean that we are to live in fatalistic passivity. As I have stated in previous chapters, when Satan comes against us in any way, we are to submit to God, then resist the devil. It is in the trial that we are to exercise faith, patience and steadfast resistance to the wiles of the enemy, being fully confident that the trial will work together for our good.

David had the utmost confidence while enduring affliction: "It is good for me that I have been afflicted, that I may learn Your statutes. I know, O Lord, that Your judgments are right, and that in faithfulness, You have afflicted me." (Psalm 119:71,75).

Often, as in my situation, we are brought to a point of total helplessness, and therefore utter dependence on God. God brought Moses to a point where he had to "stand still and see the deliverance of God." *There was no alternative.* If Moses had had a boat (a large one), there would have been no miracle. Daniel was placed into that same position of helplessness. He didn't have a whip or a chair to fight off the beasts. His only means of escape was by way of the supernatural. It was either death or deliverance. We are to come to a point where we will say "we should not trust in ourselves, but in God, who raises the dead."

We spoke earlier of the soldier who failed to pass the obstacle course and needed more training. This is the test of whether we pass or fail—*the measure of faith we have in God will be evidenced by the amount of joy we have in tribulation.*

Look at this powerful scripture: "I am filled with comfort (that's my problem). I am exceedingly joyful in all our tribulation" (2 Corinthians 7:4). These were not just boastful, empty words from Paul. When he and Silas lay bleeding in a cold Philippian jail, they sang hymns to God. He tells us why he rejoiced in tribulation in Romans Chapter 5, "...but we also glory in tribulations, knowing that tribulation produces perseverance; and perseverance character; and character, hope" (NKJV). Therefore the question arises, "How on earth do we get that sort of faith?"

Respect for the Pilot

Some years ago, I was travelling by plane with a rather large lady sitting next to me. As we were about to land I noticed that the woman had a look of terror in her eyes. I leaned over and said that if she was afraid she could hold my hand. I had hardly finished speaking when her hand whipped across and held mine so tightly that it turned white. I remember thinking, "Great. She's still in fear and now I'm in pain."

Imagine if I said to that fear-filled female, "You don't need to be scared, I know the pilot of this plane. He's an incredible guy. He could land this plane blindfolded." Perhaps the woman would look at me and say, "Do you really know him?" Fear begins to leave her eyes. "Oh yes. I've known him for years. He has flown over 4,000 times and never even had one mishap, let alone a crash. Your fears are totally groundless." The more I speak of the ability of the pilot, the less fearful she becomes.

As I build respect for the pilot, can you see that *knowledge* allows her to choose faith, and reject fear?

Soldier, are you becoming a little fearful? Let's have some plane speaking for a few moments about the Captain of our Salvation. Let's build up our respect for the One who directs our path. Respect for Him is commonly called "the fear of the Lord." Proverbs 2:1-5 gives clues as to how we can obtain "fear of the Lord," which is "the beginning of wisdom":

"My son, if you receive my words, and treasure my Commandments within you, so that you incline your ear to wisdom, and apply your heart to understanding; yes, if you cry out for discernment, and lift up your voice for understanding, if you seek her as silver, and search for her as hidden treasures then you will understand the fear of the Lord, and find the knowledge of God."

When we understand the greatness, the integrity, the majesty, the power, the magnificence, the glory, the preeminence, the nobility, the splendor, the grandeur, the supremacy and the ability of our God, then we will begin to fear Him. I love storms with thunder and lightning. When the earth trembles and when the sky lights up and darkness flees at the speed of light, we see a tiny display of the power of our God. We are witnesses to the fact that creation displays the genius of the Creator. Look at this quote from the *Reader's Digest* and remember that it is not speaking about "Mother Nature," but of the handiwork of our God:

"In the order of the universe, the sun is an ordinary, typical medium-sized star. Yet its energy and violence almost defy imagination. It is a dense mass of glowing matter, a million times the volume of the earth and in a permanent state of nuclear activity. Every second, millions of tons of hydrogen are destroyed in explosions which start somewhere near the core, where the temperature is 13 million degrees Celsius. More energy than man has used since the dawn of civilization is radiated by this normal star in a second! The earth's entire oil, coal and wood reserves would fuel the sun's energy output to the earth alone for only a few days. Tongues of hydrogen flame leap from the sun's surface with the force of 1,000 million hydrogen bombs! They are forced up by the enormous thermonuclear explosion at the core of the sun where 564 million tons of hydrogen fuse each second to form helium. Matter at the core of the sun is so hot that a pinhead of it would give off enough heat to kill a man more than one hundred million miles away!"

That incredible sun is only a tiny part of the creation of our God. He is an infinitely greater Creator than any of us can begin to imagine. No wonder the Psalmist says, "Who can utter the mighty acts of the Lord? Who can show forth all His praise? Great is the Lord and greatly to be praised; and His greatness is unsearchable." The Prophet continues to give us light:

"All nations before Him are as nothing; and they are counted to Him less than nothing; and vanity. To whom then will you liken God or what likeness will you compare unto Him? To whom then will you liken Me, or shall I be equal? saith the Holy One. Lift up your eyes on high, and behold who hath created these things, that bringeth out their host by number: He calleth them all by names by the greatness of His might, for that He is strong in power: not one faileth. Why sayest thou, O Jacob, and speakest, O Israel, My way is hid from the Lord and my judgment is passed over from my God? Hast thou not known? hast thou not heard, that the everlasting God, the Lord, the Creator of the ends of the earth, fainteth not, neither is weary? there is no searching of His understanding" (Isaiah 40:17, 18; 25-28, KJV).

There are some thoughts about God which I have to dismiss from my mind because they are too mind-boggling for me to hold onto. Let me give you an example. When I look at you, I am limited to seeing you from the front. When you are facing me I can't see the back of your head. But the Bible tells us that the "eye of the Lord is in *every* place," so from what direction does God see you? You say, "From above, because He is in Heaven." But if His eye is omnipresent, He will not be limited to seeing you from one position. When God sees you, He sees you all at one time, from above, behind, in front, underneath, each side, inside and outside! *What then do you look like to God?* David said that God is in front of him and behind him. Then he says, "Such knowledge is too wonderful for me; it is high, I cannot attain it." The Bible says, "His ways are past finding."

While the unregenerate have the "understanding darkened," we can receive "spiritual understanding" (Colossians 1:9). This is why the Psalmist exhorts us to, "Sing praises *with understanding.*" How can we give God praise if we don't understand His infinite greatness? We, even as Christians, are still blind to the greatness of His power. We take so much for granted even in nature. How is it that the same soil and water produces the sweetness of an orange and the bitterness of a lemon? How can soil and water produce a beet and onion alongside each other? The substance of both come directly from the same water and soil.

We should pray, "Open my eyes that I might continually see the genius of Your mind displayed in creation." If we could walk in such a spirit of illumination, we would walk around awestruck! We would continually worship God. We would be filled with such faith, we would see no problem too great for our God. We would say, "Ah, Lord God! (as the revelation of His greatness astounds us), Behold You have made the heavens and the earth by Your great power and outstretched arm. There is nothing too hard for You!"

Such knowledge of His power and ability would cause us to have faith that produces joy, even at the edge of the Red Sea, even in the lion's *mouth*. We can look at the world with all its problems, sins and pains, and know that one small breath of Almighty God's Spirit, and our nation can be saved. If the mere tip of the finger of God is for us, nothing can be against us.

Be encouraged soldier, whatever trial you are going through at the present time, realize that it is God who is at work within you to will and do of His good pleasure. He is teaching your hands to war, so that a bow of bronze is broken by your arms. He has the ability and the wisdom to deliver you from it, or take you through it, so that when you have been tried you will come forth as gold.

Early in 1993, in Auckland New Zealand, a small group of people moved into an old jewelry factory to conduct their church services. After cleaning the building they were left with a pile of dust, which someone had the good sense to take to a gold refinery. *It yielded $8,500 in gold dust!* When the refinery asked if they could burn the carpet, the church group gave them a piece which was 12 feet square. It produced $3,500 worth of gold. They also vacuumed $350 worth of gold dust from the ceiling.

We are nothing but dust, but God is at work in us. He knows that there is hidden treasure. The heat will separate the dirt from that which is of great value. The fire of trials produces in us that which is precious in His sight. Charles Spurgeon said, "Let Satan do what he may, he only speeds on the cause which he desires to hinder."

There is no way the enemy can defeat those soldiers who trust in God. Their victory is their faith in Him. The soldier truly stands in a victorious spirit, who can say "You prepare a table before me in the presence of my enemies."

CHAPTER TWELVE

RUNNING ON WATER

*"Through Thee we will push down our enemies:
through thy name will we tread them under that rise
up against us" (Malachi 4:3).*

I had to drive about six miles each day to the heart of the city to preach the Gospel. My old car's mileage had been around the clock, and had a habit of boiling over regularly. We made inquiries about a better vehicle, but after hearing of the finances needed, we decided to resort to prayer. The only way we would get one, was if God provided it miraculously.

A few months later, we were having dinner with a Christian couple, when the husband leaned over and said, "We feel God has told us to give you our car." His wife nodded in approval. "We've been praying about it for months," he said earnestly. "I've never felt so excited about anything in all my life. We both have Scriptures on it . . . our only fear is that you won't take it." His fear was unfounded.

He then produced the ownership papers, the transfer fee and had me sign on the dotted line. I felt such a mixture of emotions—humbled by this couple's obedience to the Lord, amazement that God was concerned about my transport, and blown away by such a gift.

The car had a full-length, yellow, genuine sheepskin seat cover on the driver's side, which the couple said they felt God wanted them to leave in the car. I remember thinking that it would be nice to have one for the passenger side, but hadn't said anything about it to anyone. I was returning from my pre-breakfast bi-monthly run in the park one day, when I spotted something lying on the ground in front of me. It was a full-length, yellow, genuine sheep-skin car seat cover! I made inquiries as to the owner, but to no avail, and came to the conclusion that when God gives you your heart's desire, He does it right down to the last detail.

What are your desires in life? If you have sought first "the Kingdom of God and His righteousness," you can expect God to take care of you, right down to the last detail. The key is to serve Him with all your heart. A young man once asked Leonard Ravenhill what was the key to success as a Christian. He just said one word— "Obedience." Bill Gothard remembered that word, took it to heart, and God entrusted him with a massive world-wide ministry. The key to success is to do whatever you do, with all your heart.

Gilbert and Sullivan wrote a song which illustrates the principle of success perfectly:

"When I was a lad I served a term, as an office boy in an attorney's firm. I cleaned the windows, and I swept the floor, and I polished up the handle on the big front door. I polished that handle so carefully, that now I am the ruler of the Queen's navy."

Everyone who opened the door to the attorney's office saw the polished handle, and it soon brought the lad a promotion. The way to impress God is to polish up the handle of an obedient heart of servitude. The way up, is to start low.

You Will Know

On March 7, 1982, I began to earnestly seek God as to what He wanted to do with my life. When would I begin to see a fulfillment of different prophecies given to me, and when would God honor my deep desire to be used by Him? One day I was reading John Chapter 13, when verse 7 jumped out at me: "What I am doing you do not understand now, but you will know after this." From that moment on, I had a distinct impression that God wanted me to travel to Australia in September of that same year. So, with this conviction, I began saying to my friends and family, "God wants me in Australia in September." Different instances began to confirm my confidence. The Scripture came a second time, from a different source, "What I am doing you do not understand now . . . "

In July of the same year, I received a call from Australia asking if I would be willing to come for one month in September and teach 400 young people from around the world on the subject of evangelism. I said that the maximum period of time I would leave my family was 10 days, so the man said he would call me back in one hour. When the call came, I was told that his committee had decided to invite my whole family over. I said, "In that case I'll come for a month."

It was around that time, that I discovered the importance of the use of the Law in evangelism.

After returning from Australia, I had a dream in which I saw a shipwreck, half submerged in water, with people crying out for help around the sinking ship. I found myself running across the water toward them. I then climbed a huge rope net with the survivors. At the top of this net was a door, but the survivors were struggling to get through, because the door was small. There seemed to be confusion and congestion around the entrance. I leaned forward and submerged my hand into a wooden door which had no handle. Within the wood was a hidden handle which opened a larger door, and allowed people to get through without hindrance. Inside was a room in which survivors were eating and drinking hot soup, and were given blankets to warm themselves.

It became clear to me that the shipwreck was the world. The running on water spoke of the nature and the urgency of the Christian message. We are able to work "while it is yet day" under the supernatural power of our God. The net and the small door signified the way of salvation (see Matthew 13:47, John 10:7).

How easy twentieth century evangelism has made salvation seem—just "say this prayer," or "Give your heart to Jesus." Yet, we read these words in Luke 13:24: "*Strive* to enter in at the strait gate" (italics added). The word "strive" comes from a Greek word from which we derive our word "agonize." Spurgeon said of evangelism in his day:

"Possibly, much of the flimsy piety of the present day arises from the ease with which men attain to peace and joy in these evangelistic days. We would not judge modern converts, but we certainly prefer that form of spiritual exercise which leads the soul by the way of 'weeping-cross,' and makes it see its blackness before assuring it that it is 'clean every whit.' Too many think lightly of sin, and therefore think lightly of the Savior. He who had stood before his God, convicted and condemned, with the rope about his neck, is the man to weep for joy when he is pardoned, to hate the evil which has been forgiven him, and to live to the honor of the Redeemer by whose blood he has been cleansed."

A friend of mine had his noisy dog debarked. One of the saddest sights you can see is a dog barking frantically, with no noise coming out of its mouth.

Someone once saw my friend Garry at his gate with his dog. As the man approached the animal to pat it, it opened its mouth to bark at him. It was then that Garry said, "No bark!" The dog opened its mouth and did its thing, but as usual, no noise came out. The man was *very* impressed with what he saw as incredible obedience.

Some preachers are like Garry's dog. They look like preachers and they go through the motions of preaching, but the *bark* of the Gospel is never heard coming from their mouths. They speak of faith, healing, the anointing, prayer, praise, the promises, prosperity and power—everything *but* sin, righteousness and judgment to come.

It is because of this that church records world-wide are full of fruitless "decisions for Christ." Others don't fall away or backslide—neither do they slide forward. They just sit in church. They don't examine themselves to see "if they are in the faith." They have made their "decision," therefore conclude that they have entered through the door of salvation. Their confidence is not based upon the Word of God. It says if you are lukewarm you will be spewed out, if you are fruitless you will be cut down, if you are not gathering you are scattering, if you are not living in holiness, you will not see the Lord. If you even "look back" to the world you are not fit for the Kingdom.

Multitudes of professors of faith are standing at the top of that roped net, with no Spirit-witness assurance that they have passed through the door of salvation. The modern evangelistic message preaches a large, wide door of salvation, but upon close examination it is shown to be small . . . only a few of those crowds prove themselves to be soundly converted.

The concealed handle, represented the Law of God. Few preachers see the Law as an evangelistic tool. Scriptures such as "The Law of the Lord is perfect, converting the soul" mystify them. But those who have the good sense to use the Ten Commandments to bring the knowledge of sin, will find that the Law is indeed the handle that swings open the door of Grace to the sinner. He who enters through that door will know true broken contrition, and genuine repentance.

If the noose of God's Law is secured around the throat of the ungodly, if the bag is placed over his head, if he hears the trap-door creak beneath his trembling knees, if he sees he is condemned with no way of escape . . . then, when the pardon is produced, he will receive it with unspeakable joy.

The Law also produces contrition, by revealing the truth of what we are in the sight of God. Look at these verses:

"For if anyone is a hearer of the word and not a doer, he is like a man observing his natural face in a mirror; for he observes himself, goes away, and immediately forgets what kind of man he was. But he who looks into the perfect Law of Liberty and continues in it, and is not a forgetful hearer but a doer of the work, this one will be blessed in what he does" (James 1:23-25).

If we look into the mirror of the Law we see our true state. The image of what we are in truth leaves a deep impression upon our minds. We go away from the Law not forgetting what we are without the Savior's blood. The result is that we are "doers of the work."

The only way you and I can see ourselves in truth, is to look into a mirror. Yet, a mirror can only do its job and reflect truth if there is bright light. In Scripture, the Law of God is called both a mirror, and light (see James 1:23-25, 2:11-12, and Proverbs 6:23).

Many of today's converts aren't shown the mirror of the Law. We think that a long look at what they are in truth will be too painful for them. "All have sinned" is all they get. They are not left in the womb of conviction.

When the hearer comes under conviction that produces godly sorrow, then he appreciates the Savior and sups with Him in sweet communion. He passes through the door of sound conversion and "eats that which is good." He is "abundantly satisfied with the fatness of (God's) house," and "drinks of the river of (God's) pleasures." Instead of producing a lukewarm decision, such a way of salvation produces a fireball for the Kingdom of God. A hot coal from the throne of God touches his lips. He becomes ignited with the flame of God's Spirit. Another spiritual arsonist is recruited in the army of God, and thrust into battle to fight the good fight of faith.

I met a young man once who had spent some time in prison. He promised God that if He allowed him to be released, he would become a Christian, but when he was released, the man didn't keep his word.

Some time later, he was on a roof removing tree branches. Unfortunately, some builders had illegally left live power lines hidden among the trees. As he unwittingly gripped the wire, a massive electrical current burned its way into his body. He was immediately knocked unconscious, and his hands were incinerated beyond recognition, and had to be replaced with hooks.

It took some years for him to come to grips with what had happened, working through bitterness, a divorce, drugs and pain. Finally he found a place of genuine repentance with a total surrender of his will to the Lord, something evidenced by the joy in his eyes.

Sadly, the modern message of Christianity misleads the sinner into thinking that he is at liberty to bargain with God. It leaves the sinner without the fear of God in his heart. What a great deal of misery and pain would have been averted, if that man had been "convinced of the Law as a transgressor" (James 2:9), and that he could only fling himself at the mercy of the Judge, rather than offer some sort of negotiable obedience to God. I'm sure he would be first to admit, now that he understands his unregenerate state before God, that it would be far better to enter Heaven without hands, than go to Hell with them. Jesus said that if our best hand offends us, we should cut it off. That's a sobering testimony regarding the serious nature of sin, something the ungodly cannot understand until the Law shows them sin in its true light.

Satan wants to keep that handle of the Law of God concealed. He is quite happy to see lukewarm, unrepentant "conversions." They are no threat to his kingdom, because they are still children of darkness.

Most of the unregenerate have little thought of eternity until they are confronted by death. On May 18, 1993, a woman in Costa Mesa, Southern California saw a man steal her vehicle. When she followed him in another car, he stopped, walked back to her and said, "If you keep following me, I'll kill you." She persisted in following him, so he kept his word and shot her five times.

Amazingly, the woman lived to tell her story. As each bullet pelted her body, she cried out, "Oh my God, if I die . . . please take me to Heaven."

God's Law does more than confront a sinner with the issues of eternity. It makes them cry, "Oh my God, when I die . . . I'm going to Hell." I believe that is a great key to getting the depth of burden Spurgeon had for the lost. Look at his own testimony to the influence of the Law upon his salvation:

"Wherever I went, the Law had a demand upon my thoughts, upon my words, upon my rising, upon my resting. What I did, and what I did not do, all came under the cognizance of the Law; and then I found that this Law so surrounded me that I was always running against it, I was always breaking it. It seemed as if I was a sinner, and nothing else but a sinner. If I opened my mouth I spoke amiss. If I sat still, there was sin in my silence. I remember that, when the Spirit of God was thus dealing with me, I used to feel myself to be a sinner even when I was in the house of God. I thought that, when I sang, I was mocking the Lord with a solemn sound upon a false tongue; and if I prayed, I feared that I was sinning in my prayers, insulting Him by uttering confessions which I did not feel, and asking for mercy with a faith that was not true at all, but only another form of unbelief. Oh yes, some of us know what it is to be given into custody of the Law!

"Then the Law, as interpreted by Christ, said, 'Whosoever looketh on a woman to lust after her hath committed adultery with her already in his heart.' The Law said, 'Thou shalt not steal,' and I said, 'Well, I never stole anything;' but then I found that even the desire to possess what was not my own was guilt. Then the Law informed me that I was cursed unless I continued in all things that were written in the book of the Law to do them. So I saw that I was 'shut up.'"

131

Spurgeon tasted the bitterness of the Law, and so appreciated the sweetness of the Gospel of Grace. Such experience produces a broken spirit. His Adamic nature was crucified by the Law, on the Cross of Calvary. It is fitting that Jewish tradition says that the tablets of the Law were similar to tombstones: "This depiction of rectangular tablets with rounded tops resembling both the shape of typical old Jewish tombstones . . . and boundary markers" (*The Torah*, p. 538, W. Gunther, Union of Hebrew American Congregations). The function of the Law is to give boundaries to humanity. Each of us has transgressed those boundaries, and therefore the Law brought death to us.

Martin Luther said, "The true and proper function of the Law is to accuse and to kill; but the function of the Gospel is to make alive."

This is why we should never preach Grace, until we have thoroughly prepared the ground of the heart with the Law. Martin Luther also said,

"We can not understand or desire to hear the Gospel that Christ's saving work redeems from sin unless we have stood under the Law. Apart from the Law, we cannot recognize the greatness of what Christ does for us and to us. The Gospel is thus directly related to the Law. The proclamation of the Law is the indispensable and necessary supposition for the preaching of the Gospel" (*The Theology of Martin Luther*, p. 258).

I was once speaking to a man named Duane. Duane would not admit that he was a sinner. When I asked him if he had lied, he said that he had. I asked what that made him. When he hesitated, I said, "A liar?" He shook his head and said, "No, I'm not a liar." I looked to his friend who was standing next to us, by asking him, "If Duane has told a lie, what is he?" He turned to him and said, "A sinner, man!" Duane said, "I'm not a sinner!" His friend said, "We have all broken every one of those Commandments." I reminded Duane that he had blasphemed earlier, and told him to be honest with himself, which caused him to say that he was going to go to church. After a few minutes of reasoning with him about the Law, he said, "You've made a little sense today." He then smiled and said, "You do feel better after you admit the truth, and be true to yourself."

It was L.O. Thompson, a respected Bible teacher of the last century who said, "The attempt to keep the Law in its spirit will lead to the revelation of self, and disclose both a disinclination and an inability; and, when this is the case, the Law becomes a schoolmaster to lead us to Christ."

Smitten by the Law

In Acts Chapter 12, we are told that Peter was put in prison by Herod. He was sleeping between two soldiers and bound with chains. Suddenly, there was a light in the darkened prison. *But the light wasn't enough to awaken Peter.* Even with the brilliant light shining, he snoozed on. It was then that the angel of the Lord "struck Peter on the side and raised him up" (verse 7). His chains fell off, he was told to gird himself, tie on his sandals, put on his garment and follow the angel.

The word used in the Greek to describe how the angel struck Peter means "to sting as a scorpion." Being struck in such a way while asleep probably hurt and frightened Peter, but it woke him up from his plight of sure death (see Acts 12:2-4).

The sinner is asleep in the prison of sin (see Ephesians 5:14). He lives in a dreamworld. He is bound in chains of his own personal iniquity (see John 8:34). Death and Hell restrain him (see Revelation 1:18), but even the light of the glorious Gospel does not awaken him (see 2 Corinthians 4:3-4). Almost everyone in the United States knows that Jesus Christ died for their sins. We celebrate His birth, His death and resurrection, but even with the Gospel light, their understanding is still darkened.

John Wesley in speaking of the "smiting" power of God's Law said that there is only "one in an age (who) has been awakened . . . by hearing that 'God was in Christ, reconciling the world unto himself.' But it is the ordinary method of the Spirit of God to convict sinners by the Law."

Charles Finney said:

"This Law, then, should be arrayed in all its majesty against selfishness and enmity of the sinner. All men know that they have sinned, but all are not convicted of the guilt and ill desert of sin. But without this they cannot understand or appreciate the Gospel method of salvation."

He continued, "Away with this milk-and-water preaching of a love of Christ that has no holiness or moral discrimination in it. Away with preaching a love of God that is not angry with sinners every day."

John Wesley also said:

" . . . the very first end of the Law, namely, the convicting men of sin; the awakening those who are still asleep on the brink of Hell . . . the ordinary method of God is, to convict sinners by the Law, and that only. The Gospel is not the means which God hath ordained, or which our Lord Himself used, for this end."

It seems that John Wesley had those in his day who refused to preach the Law to bring the knowledge of sin. It also seems that they justified their method by saying that they preached "Christ and Him crucified." So Wesley points to Paul's method of preaching Christ crucified:

" . . . when Felix sent for Paul, on purpose that he might 'hear him concerning the faith in Christ;' instead of preaching Christ in your sense (which would probably have caused the Governor, either to mock or to contradict and blaspheme,) 'he reasoned of righteousness, temperance, and judgment to come,' till Felix (hardened as he was) 'trembled,' (Acts 24:24-25). Go thou and tread in his steps. Preach Christ to the careless sinner, by reasoning 'of righteousness, temperance, and judgment to come!'"

Bible teacher Rolfe Barnard said, "The preaching of the Gospel is but sounding brass and tinkling cymbals if it falls into the ear of the best man out of Hell who has not been awakened to his awful condition by the thunderings of the Law . . . "

It is only when the sinner is smitten by the Law of God that he will rise up and escape (see Romans 7:7-13). It is the Law that awakens him so that he can see the light of the glorious Gospel of Christ (see Galatians 3:24). It is then that his chains will fall off (see John 8:31-32), he will gird the loins of his mind (see 1 Peter 1:13), tie on his Gospel shoes (see Ephesians 6:15), put on his garment (see Luke 22:36) and follow Jesus (see Matthew 4:19).

Perhaps the many who sit passively within the Body of Christ still chained—bound by the fear of man, are that way because they have never been smitten by the Law in the first place.

135

CHAPTER THIRTEEN

STANDARD BATTLE PROCEDURE

"Blessed be the Lord my rock, who trains my hands
for war, and my fingers for battle"
(Psalm 144:1).

God is calling for each soldier in His army to become personally involved in the battle, to win this world for Christ. No longer can we rely solely upon great preachers to do our fighting for us. Billy Graham said, "Mass crusades, to which I have committed my life will never finish the job; but one to one will."

The answer to the dilemma of how to reach the unsaved is for each of us to do battle right in our workplace, to rub shoulders with those held captive by the enemy.

I am often asked if I was specifically "called" to preach the Gospel. I have been called, along with every other Christian. If we are following Jesus, it should be because He has called us to be "fishers of men." If we are not preaching the Word in season and out of season, it is probably because we are following at too great a distance. We can neither see His example nor hear His voice. Those who follow close to the Master will know His voice. They will obey it and be true and faithful witnesses.

I was a two-year old Christian. I had spoken in open air a couple of times, but I had decided to go to the city square to preach. As I stood in the area which had been designated for public speaking, a Christian came up to me and began to chat. He had no idea what I was about to do. As we both looked at about 20-30 people sitting on steps, he casually said, "Hardly worth preaching the Gospel to this bunch!" I knew where that came from and took no notice.

If you are going to do anything for the Kingdom of God, be ready for unexpected discouragement. This may come through a Christian brother or sister—the place least expected. Satan spoke directly through Peter in an attempt to stop Jesus doing the will of the Father. It was David's elder brother who tried to discourage him from slaying Goliath.

A zealous Christian told me of a conversation he had with his own mother which totally discouraged him from seeking the lost. She was his own flesh and blood, and he listened to her speak nothing but discouragement for over an hour. She told him of his foolishness in wanting to preach when he hadn't even been through seminary. Who was he to go around telling people about their need of Christ, when he wasn't even trained to be a minister! Words of death went right into his heart and stole his courage. He lost his zeal, his direction, and his desire to do anything for the Kingdom of God. It was only when he gave himself to prayer that he realized Satan's subtlety. He will stop at nothing to get you back into the barracks of your local church building. He wants you worshiping God and ignoring His will. He will use any mouthpiece available, and there are plenty of willing lips. Jesus said, "Watch!" He said, "What I say to you, I say to all, watch."

Satan will often withhold an attack until you are in a place of vulnerability. He will not strike when you are full of faith and power, but when you are tired, fasting, or carrying a problem on your shoulders. I have lost count of the times I have finished open-air preaching and have been approached by a Christian brother or sister. They will say things like, "You're doing a good job, but do you think that you are really doing any good?" They will tell me how it would be better if I just did one to one or that I really should be just living the Christian life rather than confronting people about their sin. Satan has no mercy. He will stomp on you when you are down, and dig his grimy heel into the back of your neck. *Don't listen to his lies!* Satan hates you and has a rotten plan for your life. Your downfall is his delight. So, keep your shield held high and "watch."

I love the word en*courage*ment. Robert Louis Stevenson said, "Keep your fears to yourself but share your courage with others." This was so clearly illustrated in the lives of Joshua and Caleb. They had positive, hopeful, valiant, courageous, optimistic spirits. This is also called "faith."

If we can't say something positive, we shouldn't say anything. The children of Israel were told not to speak as they walked around the walls of Jericho. What they were doing was foolish. They were opening themselves to the ridicule of the enemy. It would have been hard to say anything positive, but when they did say something, it brought the downfall of the enemy, not their brethren.

Enemy Propaganda

The devil is the progenitor of falsehood. He is a compulsive liar. He is the master of deception. One of his biggest lies it to tell Christians that to witness for Christ is difficult.

Fear of man is compromising with the enemy. To say that we are unable to witness is to say that God's promise of help is empty. If I say, "I can't," when God's Word says, "I can do *all* things through Christ who strengthens me," and I choose the former, I am choosing a lie rather than the truth.

Ecclesiastical Locomotive

I make no apology for the length of this huge quote from a sermon by the turn of the twentieth-century soldier, Billy Sunday:

"I believe that lack of efficient personal work[4] is one of the failures of the Church today. The people of the Church are like squirrels in a cage. Lots of activity, but accomplishing nothing. It doesn't require a Christian life to sell oyster soup or run a bazaar or a rummage sale.

"Many churches report no new members on confession of faith. Why these meager results with this tremendous expenditure of energy and money? Why are so few people coming into the Kingdom? I will tell you—there is not a definite effort put forth to persuade a definite person to receive a definite Savior at a definite time, and that definite time is now.

"I tell you the Church of the future must have personal work and prayer. The trouble with some churches is that they think the preacher is a sort of

---

[4]Personal evangelism.

ecclesiastical locomotive, who will snort and puff and pull the whole bunch through to glory.

"Personal work is the simplest and most effective form of work we can engage in. Andrew wins Peter. Peter wins three thousand at Pentecost. A man went into a boot and shoe store and talked to the clerk about Jesus Christ. He won the clerk to Christ. Do you know who that young man was? It was Dwight L. Moody, and he went out and won multitudes to Christ. The name of the man who won him was Kimball, and Kimball will get as much reward as Moody. Kimball worked to win Moody and Moody worked and won a multitude. Andrew wins Peter and Peter wins 3,000 at Pentecost. That is the way God works. Charles G. Finney, after learning the name of any man or woman, would invariably ask: 'Are you a Christian?' There is no one here who has not drag enough to win somebody to Christ.

"Personal work is a difficult form of work, more difficult than preaching, singing, attending conventions, giving your goods to feed the poor. The devil will let you have an easy time until God asks you to do personal work. It is all right when you sit in the choir, but just as soon as you get out and work for God, the devil will be on your back and you will see all the flimsy excuses you can offer for not working for the Lord. If you want to play into the hands of the devil, begin to offer your excuses.

"There are many people who want to win somebody for Jesus and they are waiting to be told how to do it. I believe there are hundreds and thousands of people who are willing to work and who know something must be done, but they are waiting for help; I mean men and women of ordinary ability. Many people are sick and tired and *disgusted with just professing religion; they ar*e tired of trotting to church and trotting home again. They sit in a pew and listen to a sermon; they are tired of that, not speaking to anybody and not engaging in personal work; they are getting tired of it and the church is dying because of it. People should wake up and win souls for Jesus Christ.

"I want to say to the deacons, stewards, vestrymen, prudential committees, that they should work, and the place to begin is at your own home. Sit down and write the names of five or ten friends, and many of them members of your own church and two or three of those not members of any church; yet you mingle with these people in the club, in business, in your home in a friendly way. You meet them every week, some of them every day, and you never speak to them on the subject of religion; you never bring it to their attention at all; you should be up and doing something for God and God's truth. There are always opportunities for a Christian to work for God. There is always a chance to speak to someone about God. Where you find one that won't care, you'll find 1,000 that will.

"If it is beneath your dignity to do personal work then you are above your Master. If you are not willing to do what He did, then don't call Him your Lord. The servant is not greater than the owner of the house. The chauffeur is not greater than the owner of the automobile. The servant on the railroad is not greater than the owners of the road.

"Certainly they are not greater than our Lord Jesus Christ.

"It requires an effort to win souls to Christ. There is no harder work and none brings greater results than winning souls.

"You will need courage. It is hard to do personal work and the devil will try to oppose you. You'll seek excuses to try and get out of it. Many people who attend the meetings regularly now will begin to stay at home when asked to do personal work. It will surprise you to know some lie to get out of doing personal work.

"Personal work is the department of the Church efficient to deal with the individual and not the masses. It is analogous to the sharp shooter in an army so dreaded by the opposing forces. The sharpshooter picks out the pivotal individual instead of shooting at the mass. The preacher shoots with a siege gun at long range. You can go to the individual and dispose of his difficulties. I shoot out there two or three hundred feet and you sit right beside people" (from *"Billy" Sunday* by William T. Ellis).

Front Lines

I was once asked to take a three day crusade at a university. I was told by a member of the committee that the Christian Union had a "good name" in the university. I soon found out why. They preferred that we didn't use our literature, which exposed the demonic aspect of heavy rock music, touched on the abortion issue, as well as stated the scriptural stance on homosexuality. I was told that homosexuality was a "touchy issue." I unwillingly submitted myself to their authority and had the three days of meetings. At the end of the third day, I asked the crowd of about 200 people how many knew the Lord, and found that almost all of them were Christians. I left that meeting determined never again to submit myself to committees who fear man more than they fear God.

A month earlier I was at another university, and this time there was no committee[5]. A group of Christians had given out our literature, and by the time I appeared, the students were so angered, they were tearing down posters advertising my visit.

Just before I was due to go into the main hall, I was shown a letter written by the local chaplain. He stated that as university chaplain, he wanted it to be known that he had nothing to do with the invitation for me to speak at the university. He also said that he thought that I would turn people away from "true Christianity." Then he listed a number of points of contention. My immediate thought was that no one would turn up to the meeting. When I tried to find a "closet" to encourage myself in God, I couldn't even find one.

I was then called for, and ushered into the auditorium. To my delight, there were about 500 students packed into the room. For the next forty minutes I had the joy of preaching sin, righteousness and judgment. Over the years I thought I'd seen an anti-Christian spirit, but I hadn't seen anything compared to that day. They had a unified spirit of hatred. If there had been stones handy, I am sure I would have followed closely on the heels of Stephen. There were homosexuals, lesbians, pro-abortionists, dope-freaks, all

[5]The spelling of "committee" seems to optimize it's superfluity—two m's, two t's and two e's. I would have spelt it "comity." For God so loved the world that He didn't send a committee.

soaked in the most blasphemous, foul language imaginable. Here were our future doctors, lawyers and politicians. One long-haired man, who was sitting on the front row stood up, and said something offensive. He was about to lead an exodus away from this fanatical preacher. He raised both of his fists with his fingers pointing to the sky, then he pointed both fists toward to the door in a gesture of "follow me." He left alone.

The next day at least 800 students (and one chaplain) packed into the hall. I had another opportunity to preach God's Word. That opportunity was there because the Christians had the guts to make an uncompromising stand for the Gospel. They shook off the shackles of fear of rejection. They knew that sinners must be confronted with sin before they will repent. They were only concerned about having a "good name" in Heaven.

How weak and fickle much of our preaching is, compared to men of the past who knew how to use the weapon of the Law. Charles Spurgeon said:

> "Sometimes we are inclined to think that a very great portion of modern revivalism has been more a curse than a blessing, because it has led thousands to a kind of peace before they have known their misery; restoring the prodigal to the Father's house, and never making him say, 'Father, I have sinned.' How can he be healed who is not sick? or he be satisfied with the Bread of Life who is not hungry? The old-fashioned sense of sin is despised and consequently a religion is run up before the foundations are dug out. Everything in this age is shallow. Deep sea fishing is almost an extinct business so far as men's souls are concerned. The consequence is that men leap into religion and then

leap out again. Unhumbled they came to the Church, unhumbled they remain in it, and unhumbled they go from it."

Jesus said the enemy is the one who sows tares among the wheat (Matthew 13:25). With today's Gospel, he doesn't need to. Modern evangelism does that for him.

With God's help, we are to convince the sinner that he is destitute. He is without God (Ephesians 2:12), without Christ (Ephesians 2:12), without hope (Ephesians 2:12), without strength (Romans 5:6), and without excuse (Romans 1:20). We neither condemn nor condone, but we are seeking to convict then convert. To do this, we present the essence of the Law of God.

Reason of Sin, Righteousness, and Judgment

I sat down and looked around the scene. Three people were talking together and I didn't feel comfortable approaching them with the Gospel. As a passerby passed by, one of the three asked, "Got a light?" and held up a cigarette. The person passing by didn't have a light. The would-be cigarette smoker glanced at me, but for some reason decided to bypass me. Another passerby passed by match-less. When the young man glanced at me, I said, "I've got a light!" I then called him over. As he held out his cigarette, I said, "Let me show you this first," and gave him a tract, then spent some time giving this man light for his darkened soul. As I did so, I did some sleight-of-hand, which attracted another four men. They asked if I would do an encore. I did, then witnessed to them using the Law to bring light to them. One of them said, "That's really neat. I have never had anyone take the time to sit down and explain this to me." His reaction was typical because "the Commandment is a lamp, and the Law is light" (Proverbs 6:23).

A quick study of scripture reveals that Paul "reasoned" with Felix. He did not tell him that Jesus loved him. He reasoned of sin, righteousness, and judgment. Paul preached future punishment by the Law, and Felix "trembled." Failure to preach future punishment is to enlist potential deserters into the ranks of the Army of God. Before I march with a soldier behind me wielding a bayonet-fixed, loaded rifle, I would want to know that he was on my side. His decision to enlist would not convince me. His uniform would not convince me. Before I believe he is on our side, I want to know his heart. Does he love the country he is fighting for? Does he believe in the cause? Is he willing to die for it?

Listen to George Whitefield speak on this subject:

"I am glad you know when persons are justified. It is a lesson I have not yet learnt. There are so many stony-ground hearers, that receive the Word with joy, that I have determined to suspend my judgment till I know the tree by its fruits. . . . The way the Spirit of God takes us, is like the way we prepare the ground; do you think any farmer would have a crop of corn next year unless they plow now; and you may as well expect a crop of corn on unplowed ground, as a crop of grace, until the soul is convinced of its being undone without a Savior. That is the reason we have so many mushroom converts, so many people that are always happy! happy! happy! and never were miserable; Why? Because their stony ground is not plowed up; they have not got a conviction of the Law; they are stony-ground hearers; they hear the Word with joy, and in a time of temptation, which will soon come after a seeming or real conversion, they fall away. They serve Christ as the young man served the Jews that laid hold of him, who, when he found he was likely to be a prisoner for following Christ, left his garments, and so some people leave their profession. That makes me so cautious now, which I was not 30 years ago, of dubbing converts so soon. I love now, to wait a little, and see if people bring forth fruit; for there are so many blossoms which March winds you know blow away, that I cannot believe they are converts till I see fruit brought forth. It will do converts no harm to keep them a little back; it will never do a sincere soul any harm."

While we rejoice over "decisions," Heaven reserves its rejoicing for repentance (Luke 15:10).

Fear of Fear

Look at what motivated Christian to search for salvation in *Pilgrim's Progress*. It was fear of the judgment to come:

"In this plight, therefore, he went home, and restrained himself as long as he could, that his wife and children should not perceive his distress; but he could not be silent long, because this his trouble increased. Wherefore at length he brake his mind to his wife and children and thus he began to talk to them. O my dear wife, said he, and you the children of my bowels, I, your dear friend, am in myself undone by reason of a burden that lieth hard upon me; moreover, I am for certain informed that this our city will be burned with fire from heaven; in which fearful overthrow both myself, with thee my wife and you my sweet babes, shall miserably come to ruin, except (the which yet I see not) some way of escape can be found, whereby we may be delivered.

"I saw also that he looked this way, and that way, as if he would run; yet he stood still, because (as I perceived) he could not tell which way to go. I looked then, and saw a man named Evangelist coming to him, and asked, Wherefore dost thou cry?

"He answered, Sir, I perceive, by the book in my hand, that I am condemned to die, and after that come to judgment; and I find that I am not willing to do the first, nor able to do the second.

"Then said Evangelist, why are you not willing to die, since this life is attended with so many evils? The man answered, 'Because I fear that this burden that is upon my back will sink me lower than the grave, and I shall fall into Tophet. And, sir, if I be not fit to go to prison, I am not fit to go to judgment, and from thence to execution; and the thoughts of these things make me cry.'

"Then said Evangelist, if this be thy condition, why standest thou still? He answered, Because I know not whither to go. Then he gave him a parchment roll and there was written within, Flee from the wrath to come."

Never fear the thought that you are causing sinners to fear, by making reference to the Judgment. Judgment Day is the climax of the ages. It is an event that the very creation cries out for. It has done so from the blood of Abel to the last injustice of this age. God loves justice . . . and He will have it:

"Let the Heavens rejoice, and let the earth be glad; let the sea roar, and all its fullness; Let the field be joyful, and all that is in it. Then all the trees of the wood will rejoice before the Lord, for He is coming, *for He is coming to judge the earth*. He shall judge the world with righteousness, and the people with His truth" (Psalm 96:11-13, italics added).

Judgment is most "reasonable." A little reason can convince sinners that Judgment Day makes sense. Surely when God sees that 98% of all street crimes in New York never come to justice, He cares. Surely, the Creator of the sun, the moon, the stars, flowers, birds and trees has a sense of right and wrong. When God sees a man like Hitler slaughter millions of innocent people, is He stirred, or has He less sense of justice than sinful mankind? Is it only man who is good enough to care about justice and truth? Is he the only creature in the universe that has a court system that attempts to right wrong?

Preaching Judgment by the Law is a light that shines upon the dark, unregenerate mind. It is powerful because it is *reasonable*. It will cause him to tremble, as did Felix. We must warn them of the terror of that Day:

"God is a just Judge, and God is angry at the wicked every day. If he does not turn back, He will sharpen His Sword; He bends His bow and makes it ready" (Psalm 7:11-12).

God will bring every work to Judgment, including every secret thing, whether it is good or whether it is evil (Ecclesiastes 12:14). It is appointed to man, once to die, and after this the Judgment. Every idle word a man speaks, he will give an account thereof in the Day of Judgment. How can we say that we are free from their blood if we don't warn them of the reality of Eternal Justice! How can we expect to receive the commendation, "Well done, you good and faithful servant" if we don't serve God faithfully? We have such an awesome responsibility.

A lighthouse keeper gained a reputation as being a very kind man. He would give free fuel to ships that miscalculated the amount of fuel needed to reach the port to which they were heading. One night during a storm, lightning struck his lighthouse and put out his light. He immediately turned on his generator, but it soon ran out of fuel as he had given his reserves to passing ships. During the dark night, a ship struck rocks and many lives were lost.

At his trial, the judge knew of the lighthouse keeper's reputation as a kind man and wept as he gave sentence. He accused the lighthouse keeper of neglecting his primary responsibility—to keep the light shining.

The Church can so often get caught up in legitimate acts of kindness—standing for political righteousness, etc., but our primary task is to keep the light of the Gospel shining so that sinners can avoid the jagged-edged rocks of wrath and escape being eternally damned.

Someone sent me this poem, which says what I am trying to say:

> *My friend, I stand in judgment now,*
> *and feel that you're to blame somehow.*
> *On earth I walked with you by day,*
> *and never did you show the way.*
> *You knew the Savior in truth and glory,*
> *But never did you tell the story.*

My knowledge then was very dim.
You could have led me safe to Him.
Though we lived together, here on earth,
you never told me of the second birth.
And now I stand before eternal Hell,
because of Heaven's glory you did not tell!
(Anon)

The Hard Heart

John Newton, the converted slave trader wrote "Amazing Grace." He said, "My grand point in preaching, is to break the hard heart, and to heal the broken one." The Law breaks the hard heart and Grace heals the broken one. You can tell if someone is ready for Grace by the fact that their mouth will be stopped. They will not try to justify themselves. Instead, they will acknowledge their guilt. If they have no sense of their sinfulness to a point of repentance, and you are able to "get a decision," you will probably deliver a still-born.

The fruit of "Jesus loves you" evangelism was epitomized recently. While open-air preaching, I touched on the subject of homosexuality. At that point, a young lady verbally defended it. She was in her mid-twenties, very attractive, with long blond hair, tastefully made up, and impeccably dressed. However, I detected that the voice tone was slightly lower than one would have expected from such a lady. I asked, *"Are you a guy?"* The voice answered, "Transsexual." Then it said, "And I've asked Jesus into my heart, darling . . . and God loves me just the way I am."

How do you speak to such a deceived person? Simply by preaching the Law. The Law was made for homosexuals (1 Timothy 1:9-10). The Law shows him that he is condemned despite his lifestyle.

I had an angry lesbian heckle me while speaking in Santa Monica one Friday night, in front of a large crowd. I was so pleased to have the Law of God as a weapon. When she insisted that she was born with homosexual desires, I told her that I was too. I was born with a capacity to be a homosexual, to fornicate, commit adultery, to lie, and steal. I said that it was called "sin," and that we all had it in our nature. It defused her intent on making me seem like a "gay-basher." I could see the frustration on her face when she wasn't able to take the discourse in the direction she wanted. Instead of seeming the poor victim, she found herself in the public hot-seat of having sinned against God by breaking the Ten Commandments.

Probing the Conscience

I once had dinner at a restaurant with a couple who were in their 50's. While the man was chatting to me, I noticed that a two-inch hair was stuck on the outside of his glasses. It was stopping me having uninterrupted cyc-contact, and I surmised that it must have been blurring up his vision, so I said, "You have a hair stuck on the outside of your glasses."

As I spoke I leaned forward and grabbed it. It was then that I noticed that the hair was attached to something . . . *his eyebrow.* I said, "Oh . . . it's part of your eyebrow, let me just put it back . . . " As I tucked the hair into bed, I patted it gently and kind of brushed it a little, then carried on listening to him. The whole thing seemed to happen in slow motion. I have made up my mind that in future, if someone is talking to me and there's a cat sitting on their nose, I won't even mention it.

There are certain things in life we shouldn't touch. However, when it comes to the sinner's conscience, we must probe it thoroughly. A great preacher once said, "I would rather hear it said, 'That man said something in his message that made many of the people think less of him; he uttered most distasteful sentiments; he did nothing but drive at us with the Word of the Lord while he was preaching. His one aim was to bring us to repentance and faith in Christ.' That is the kind of man whom the Lord delights to bless." He also said, "Ministers who do not aim to cut deep are not worth their salt. God never sent a man who never troubles men's consciences."

As Simple as ABC

I felt annoyed that ABC had the gall to place a large billboard of a naked woman[6] in our neighborhood. I was so upset by the poster, I purchased a tall ladder, climbed the structure at 6:00 a.m. and stapled a blanket over the naked woman's body. Then I sent a release to the news media saying what I had done and why. I told them that I didn't want my wife or daughter raped and then murdered by some pervert who gets stirred up by ABC's lusty picture. Nor did I want any of the children— whose school was a few hundred yards down the road from the billboard, kidnapped and sexually assaulted.

You may not be aware of the fact that each year over 120,000 women report being raped, over 500,000 women are sexually assaulted, and there are more than 400,000 reports of verified sexual assaults filed with authorities each year by teachers and doctors (see *Time*, April 17, 1995).

It seems that these folks are so bent on making big bucks, they couldn't care less about what happens to

---

[6]She waslying on her stomach with a small towel on the back of her legs.

women and children in our society. Then they hide behind the anonymity of "ABC." If I had made copies of the same picture and merely *showed* it to young kids as they came out of school, I would be arrested as a sexual deviant. But they walked into our city and place a twenty-foot sexually explicit picture a few hundred yards from an elementary school, and no one could do a thing about it.

Only a simpleton or someone bent on destruction lights fires in a dry forest. Back in 1997, California had 67,000 registered sex offenders. The state has become a tinder-dry forest of sexual predators. ABC's billboard was a lit match. When a network screens something on television I consider to be 'adult' entertainment, I can change the channel, but when they come into a city and put a sexually explicit billboard a quarter of a mile from my home, there is little I can do.

I was encouraged by a phone call I received the same day I climbed the billboard. A father of four was so stirred into action when he heard of the incident, that he called his local transit authority. Then he registered a complaint about the same advertisement being displayed in bus shelters in his area. The manager said that years ago it wouldn't have worried him, but now that he had children, he could see the point, and assured the man that the posters would be removed. The father then went to the shelter, waved down two cars and asked if they thought the picture was appropriate to display by an elementary school. Both drivers said that such a picture was offensive, and they assured the man that they would also call the authorities and register a complaint. The posters were immediately removed.

Come and Hear The Good News

Imagine if your local police decided to offer amnesty for all lawbreakers. All criminal charges would be dropped against those who had broken the law, if within a certain period of time they would present their weapons at the police station. After the offer, there would be a massive bust in which every criminal would be rounded up and charged for their crimes.

How would they speak of the good news of the amnesty? They decide to put advertisements in the police column of the newspaper. Their reasoning is that lawbreakers read their column. They make the police station attractive. They have the prison bars chrome-plated. The cells are carpeted. Piped music played throughout the cells. Notices are then posted outside the station saying, "Come and hear the good news."

Of course, the police are not mindless enough to think that anyone is going to visit a police station when they are guilty of breaking the law. Yet this is the mentality of modern evangelism.

The police are more likely to share the good news in this manner:

THE PENALTY FOR POSSESSING ANY OF THE FOLLOWING WEAPONS IS A FIVE-YEAR IMPRISONMENT. If you surrender your weapon within seven days we will not lay charges. REMEMBER, FIVE LONG YEARS—don't be foolish, take advantage of this amnesty now!

The law officers preach future punishment to lawbreakers. It gets results. They are not alone. Fear is often used in advertising. In the late 90's the following was used in billboard advertising: "Diabetes—

amputation, blindness, death. It's *that* serious." That is a scare tactic. It's using fear, but is legitimate, because they are stating the truth.

I'm Glad You Asked

I once asked God to use me on a particular day for the extension of His Kingdom. I couldn't see how He could, as all I had planned was to stay at home all that day and proofread a new publication.

A neighbor had left her key with us, and asked if we could let a repair man into her home. He arrived as I was praying.

As we chatted, we moved from the natural to the spiritual. I casually asked if he had been born-again. He stunned me with the reply: "I'm glad you asked that!" He then went to his car and showed me a book he had been reading called "*Hungering After God*," which he borrowed from the public library. A few minutes later he accepted Jesus Christ as Lord and Savior.

Most of the time I am sowing in tears. This day God had heard my prayer and had let me reap in joy. Don't get discouraged if you seem to be continually sowing. This world has more young lawyers than it does Nathaniels. Perhaps this is because so few Christians are sowing the truth in tears. I have sat next to thousands of people on planes, and never once has anyone tried to witness to me. This is despite the fact after probing, I have found that many of these people were Christians.

Presenting the Case

On a recent flight to Dallas, I sat next to a defense attorney who didn't think God would punish sin. I reasoned with him about the fact that if a judge in Miami turned a blind eye to the crimes of the Mafia, he would be a corrupt judge. He should be therefore brought to justice himself. Between 1978 and 1988, there were 63,000 unsolved murders in the United States. That means there are at least 63,000 murderers walking around in America who have gotten off free, just within that time period. If God turns a blind eye to what they have done then God is corrupt by nature and should be brought to justice Himself.

After talking for some time, I said, "Let me present my case." He agreed, so I took him through three of the Commandments, which he acknowledged he had transgressed. He still tried to justify himself and cited a case he had been involved in the previous day. He said that the judge asked two teenage criminals if they were sorry for their crime. They said they were, so the judge was lenient with them. He then pointed out that if they weren't sorry, he would have given them a very stiff sentence. *The attorney actually built a case against himself.* I told him that he was a guilty criminal in God's sight, and that if he kept trying to justify himself, he would be found guilty and end up in Hell. If he would be sorry, repent and put his faith in Jesus, God could show him mercy because of the work of the Cross. I gave him a book, and we parted on very good terms.

After the Dallas flight, I waited in the back of another plane, watching as an endless stream of passengers poured on board. I could see one row of three seats halfway down. This was a potential Comfort bed. While I waited, I talked with the flight attendant, who happened to be a Christian. Suddenly, a tall man with snowy-white hair stood up and spoke to her. She walked down the plane, came back and spoke to him. He then walked down the aisle and stole my potential bed. When the flight attendant realized that she had given away my seats, she apologized. It didn't really worry me, because I surmised earlier that if I didn't get a seat, God wanted me to witness to someone next to my designated seat.

I made my way back to my designated seat and found that someone had taken it. I now had no seat. Suddenly, I saw one and sat down. The young man next to me was in his early twenties, and he didn't hesitate to begin a conversation. He was in the army, and said how he was tired of training. He wanted combat. When I asked him if he was afraid of getting killed, he said that he wasn't. When I asked him why, he merely said, "Because of God." When I asked if he was a Christian, he said, "I'm a Protestant." Further on in the conversation, he said how he had been on an earlier flight in a small plane and he was very scared. In fact, while telling me, he used the name of Jesus in blasphemy. I tucked that ammunition away for later on in the battle that God had so evidently placed me in.

When we touched on Christian things later on in the conversation, he admitted he had broken a number of the Commandments. When I told him he had blasphemed the name of Jesus, he was *very* concerned. He knew he had done that in the past, but had determined never to do it again.

After we had discussed the Law and the Cross, spoken of justification by faith alone, he said that he was without excuse. He said that he would be a fool not to get right with God. He also said that he had gained a great deal of understanding through our conversation.

Once again, I learned that day Who guides our steps. You may think that you are planning each step you take. You may think that you make the decisions . . . but if you have acknowledged the Commander in Chief, He will guide your steps. They are "ordered by the Lord."

The Church Needs More "Lerts"

Be alert. Stay aware of the enemy's tactic to sidetrack with "red herrings," or "rabbit trails." Occasionally sinners have a genuine difficulty with "Darwin's theory," "hypocrites in the Church," etc., but in most cases they are nothing but red herrings. We are called to be fishers of men, not herrings. Red herrings are the "hedges" Jesus told us to go to. Sinners make hedges, behind which they try to hide from God, as did Adam. The best way to get to a sinner out from behind a hedge, is to beat it with the rod of the Law. Flush him out so that he stands exposed before his Creator.

Get him to admit that he has lied, stolen and eyed with lust. If he says, "I don't believe in Judgment Day," just gently say, "That doesn't matter, you will still have to face God on Judgment Day, and you've admitted that you are a lying, thieving adulterer at heart. God gave you a conscience so that you would know right from wrong. You will be without excuse. If you stand on a railway track and don't believe in trains, your unbelief won't change reality."

I have had letters from people who now use the Law in witnessing, relieved that they no longer have to be experts in Darwin's theory, or in apologetics.

Never forget that we have an ally right in the heart of the enemy. It is the sinner's conscience. It will not fight against you. It is independent of the sinners will. Often, however, conscience has been tied hand and foot and its voice gagged. You have to cut the ropes with the sharp edge of the sword of God's Law and untie the gag. Don't be afraid to say things like "God gave you a conscience . . . you know right from wrong. Listen to the voice of your conscience . . . it will remind you of sins that you have committed." It will encourage you in battle when you hear its voice coming through. It is the work of the Law written on their hearts. It will bear witness with the Law of God (see Romans 2:15).

If you have preached the Word, it won't return void:

" . . . he who has My word, let him speak My word faithfully . . . is not My Word like a fire? says the Lord, and like a hammer that breaks the rock in pieces?" (Jeremiah 23:29)

Don't be intimidated by the enemy. If someone says that they are Roman Catholic, don't feel as though you have to convince them that the teachings of the Roman church are wrong. Instead, ignore the rabbit trail, and stay on the path of sin, righteousness and judgment. Your great weapon is the Law. The enemy will never surrender if you are distracted to the point of putting it down to speak of other things. Read the first few verses of Luke chapter 13 and see how Jesus never lowered this great weapon for a moment in the face of subtle distractions.

Look for your Divine directives. No battle is easy. If you go into a conflict armed with the Law, the enemy will discharge fiery darts of discouragement. Remember, if you don't have your shield of faith held high, they will find their mark.

Divine Directives

Early in 1994, I stepped onto a battlefield, targeting a man who was sitting by himself. I had my sights on him. When I fired a question at him, there was little reaction. He was dead to me. I relocated. I was aware that my aim was not yet on *God's* target. I shifted my sights to a woman who made my first target seem sociably hot. Again, I moved my sights. I sat next to another man whose head was horribly scarred, his eye was disfigured and his arm was in a sling. I discharged the Cannons of God's Law. With a wide eye, he confided that he was in a motorbike accident and his parents informed him that while he was in a coma (though he didn't recall it), he said that God had told him that He didn't want him to come to Him yet. He was *very* open and was obviously God's appointment for me at that time.

Never be afraid to aim the cannons at a sinner merely because he is wounded by the world. If we are compassionate, we won't want the person to go to Hell, on top of the sufferings he has already had in this life. Pray that his pains don't distract from what you want to say to him.

We often get accused by the world of pushing religion "down their throats." Don't give them religion. Give them the Ten Cannons. When they open their mouths in rebellion, light the fuse. Watch the Law shut the mouth of justification. Let them taste the fear of God. If such hard speech concerns you, tell me, which is better—fear of God in the Day of Grace, which will bring them to the Cross, or would it be better for the world to have no fear of God right up until the Day of Judgment, which will bring them to the Lake of Fire? Our Commander doesn't want *any* to perish. All we want to see is for sinners to hold up a white flag.

CHAPTER FOURTEEN

THE TEN-STAR GENERAL

" . . . looking to Jesus, the author and finisher of our faith" (Hebrews 12:2).

In previous chapters we have established that it is very clear from Scripture that God doesn't want sinners to perish. His will is for the world to be saved. It is also clear from Scripture that we should be seeking to fulfil the Great Commission. How then can we continually motivate ourselves to do so? That is what we will look at in this chapter.

I wonder if you are happy with your reaction to the word "evangelism?" Does it produce a feeling of guilt or joy? Do you run to your evangelistic responsibility as did Philip to the Ethiopian in Acts Chapter 8, or do you run from your evangelistic responsibility as did Jonah? The answer will more than likely be, "A little of both." The spirit is willing, but the flesh is weak. You can identify with me when I speak of fears I have, when I'm about to speak to someone about the Kingdom of God. Our heart wants to seek and save that which is lost, but our Adamic nature would far rather stay tucked in the bed of indifference. A major motivation comes from the knowledge that, if I *really care* about the person who sits next to me, I will make every effort to witness to him.

I remember sitting next to a man in his early twenties who wasn't at all open to the things of God. He wasn't antagonistic, just apathetic. My questions received minimal response. I could have easily pacified my conscience by saying that I had done all I could to reach out to him. As I was typing on my laptop computer, he looked at it and said, "I'm not reading what you are writing—my eyesight isn't good enough." Suddenly, I saw my opportunity and said, "This is an amazing computer. It can create huge type." I quickly typed out, "Unless you repent, you shall perish," and said, "Watch this." I put a 60-point font in front of the scripture, pushed a few buttons, and before the man's eyes appeared the huge sentence, "UNLESS YOU REPENT, YOU SHALL PERISH." He went very quiet. I told him they were the words of Jesus, and that if he as much as lusted after a woman, he had committed adultery in his heart. He looked at me and soberly said, "I'm going to Hell a thousand times over then." For the next few moments I had the opening to focus his eyes on eternity and his own eternal salvation.

If we love the world, we will weigh our motives for every argument, reason, excuse, rationalization, defense and justification we can find for silence. As soldiers are we being led by the Spirit of God, by love and concern, by the devil, or by our fearful and dispassionate mind?

In the Epistle of Paul to Philemon, he tells how he continually prays for Philemon, saying that he has heard of the "love and faith" which he has, both toward the Lord and toward his brethren. Then he says that the "sharing of your faith may become effective by the acknowledgement of every good thing which is in you in Christ Jesus" (verse 6). The Greek word for "effective" means "active, operative and powerful." Isn't that what we want? We want to be active, operative and powerful in our witness for the Gospel. The key to getting this is very clear. Both the love and faith Paul spoke of are not passive. Love is not dormant. If we have love for God and man, we will share our faith, because from those two fruits of the Spirit (love and faith) spring most of the other fruits. Love will produce goodness, gentleness and patience, while faith issues joy and peace.

The Key

In Philippians, Paul speaks of God exalting Jesus and giving Him a name which is above every name, and that "at the name of Jesus every knee should bow . . . and that every tongue should confess that Jesus Christ is Lord, to the glory of God the Father" (Philippians 2:10-11). Then he says that we should work out our salvation with "fear and trembling." How do we obtain those commanded virtues of fear and trembling? Simply by seeing Jesus Christ as "Lord." This same thought is brought out in Psalm 2:11-12. Yet, many Christians still see Jesus as the Man portrayed in the Gospels. To them He is still the man from Nazareth, limited to time and space. They still picture Him as the one who grew tired, hungry and thirsty.

If that is our image of the risen Son of God, whether it be in our mind or a picture on the wall, we must rid ourselves of it because it is hindering us from growing in God.

The Apostle Paul said that we "have known Christ after the flesh, yet now henceforth know we Him no more" (2 Corinthians 5:16). The word "flesh" is *sarx*, and means "human nature with its frailties." Look at the *Amplified Bible's* rendering of the verse: " . . . even though we did once estimate Christ from a human viewpoint and as a man, yet now (we have such knowledge of Him that) we know Him no longer (in terms of the flesh)."

Jesus is no longer "lower than the angels" that was for the "suffering of death." He is now "crowned with glory and honor." He is the Lord of Glory, "all power" has been given to Him. He has the glory that He had with the Father "before the world was." Isaiah saw Him in His pre-incarnate glory and said that he saw the Lord sitting upon a glorious throne, and that He was "high and lifted up and His train filled the temple . . . the seraphims cried, Holy, Holy, Holy is the Lord of Hosts . . . the posts of the doors moved at the voice of Him . . . then said I, Woe is me! For I am undone!" (Isaiah 6:3-5). John also saw Him in His glory and said that he saw "the Son of Man . . . and His eyes were as a flame of fire . . . and His voice as the sound of many waters . . . and His countenance was as the sun shines in His strength. And when I saw Him, I fell at His feet as dead" (Revelation 1:13-17).

This is what the Scriptures are saying when they speak of the sharing of our faith becoming effective by the acknowledgement of every good thing which is in you in Christ Jesus. The word "acknowledgement" means to understand every good thing we have in Christ. We have treasure in earthen vessels. *The very source of all life dwells in us.* We have Christ in us, the hope of glory. In Him dwells all the fullness of the Godhead bodily, and we are complete in Him. If we could comprehend what we have in the Savior, we would never lack joy, and we would never for a minute let apathy enter our hearts. We would radiate with love for God, for what He has given us in Christ.

Paul spoke from experience when he expressed the fact of not knowing Jesus "after the flesh." We are not told what knowledge he had of Him in His flesh, but he certainly knew Jesus in His glory. The blinding light from Heaven took away his eyesight. His fleshly eyes glimpsed light inaccessible. When he wrote to the Thessalonians, his mind wasn't clouded by a false image of the Son of God, because he knew Him as the "King of Kings and the Lord of Lords, who only has immortality, dwelling in light unapproachable." He wrote that the Thessalonians shouldn't be troubled because "the Lord Jesus shall be revealed from Heaven with His mighty angels, in flaming fire taking vengeance on them that know not God, and that obey not the Gospel of our Lord Jesus Christ: who shall be punished with everlasting destruction from the presence of the Lord, and from the glory of His power . . . " (2 Thessalonians 1:8-9).

As we see Jesus Christ as the Lord of Glory, we will not only work out our salvation with "fear and trembling," but the fear of God in us will begin to work for the salvation of those around us who are the heirs of eternal damnation.

This same vengeance with fire is spoken of by the prophet Isaiah in Chapter 66:

"For behold, the Lord will come with fire, and with His chariots like a whirlwind, to render His anger with fury, and His rebuke with flames of fire. For by fire and by His sword will the Lord plead with all flesh: and those slain by the sword shall be many" (verses 15-16).

A Christian friend once told me how his daughter jumped out of bed, and with a radiant face told how she had dreamed of the coming of the Lord. She said how she had heard the trumpet sounding and had seen Him in His Glory. Flames were leaping from house roofs, and those who were inside were fleeing in terror. But this little girl woke up radiant, because she was forgiven. She had nothing to fear. She was one of those who will "love His appearing." The Scriptures tell us that it "does not yet appear what we shall be, but we know that when He shall appear we shall be like Him for we shall see Him as He is" (1 John 3:2). The second the trumpet sounds, in one "twinkling of an eye," we shall be transformed into a body not subject to the terror that the ungodly will feel. We shall have boldness on that Great Day, but for those still in their sins, that Day will be a day of unspeakable terror. Paul says, "It is a fearful thing to fall into the hands of the living God . . . wherefore knowing the terror of the Lord we persuade men."

Each of us should be able to say with the hymn writer:

"Mine eyes have seen the glory of the coming of the Lord; He is trampling out the vintage where the grapes of wrath are stored; he has loosed the fateful lightning of His terrible swift Sword, His Truth is marching on."

What Must Our Sins be Like?

The prophet Isaiah tells us of our unregenerate state before God by saying that "we are all as an unclean thing, and all our righteousnesses are as filthy rags; and we all do fade as a leaf, and our iniquities, like the wind, have taken us away" (Isaiah 64:6). Note carefully that it is not our sins that are as filthy rags in His sight, but our righteousnesses. If that is the case, what must our sins be like in the perception of our Holy Creator? If that which is "highly esteemed" among men is an abomination in the sight of God, what must that look like which is detestable among men?

The Day of Vengeance is in God's heart, He will "tread them in His anger," and "trample them in fury." We only see a tiny fraction of the tip of the tip of the cold and hard iceberg of sin. Think of what makes up this world: The Mafia, prostitution, strip clubs, filthy movies, child pornography, rape, drug pushing, corruption, greed, lust, torture, hatred, cursing, blasphemy and murder. In fact, by the time you take to finish this chapter, in the U.S. alone, more than seven people will have been either strangled, stabbed or shot to death. If the given statistics hold true there will also have been more than 50 robberies, 110 cars stolen and 360 burglaries. Each year in the U.S. over 4 million women are victims of domestic violence, and in the same time period 550,000 women are raped.

We see only the tip, but the Bible says, "The eye of the Lord is in every place, beholding the evil and the good." Proverbs 15:26 tells us that even the thoughts of the ungodly are an abomination to the Lord. Jeremiah says, "The heart is deceitful above all things, and desperately wicked." If we don't embark upon desperate evangelism, using every means God has given us to convince, induce, persuade and compel them to come in, God will convince them on that Day when He comes "with ten thousands of His saints, to execute judgment on all, and to convince all that are ungodly . . . "—but then it will be too late.

David said in Psalms, "Their inward part is very wickedness," while Paul speaks of sin being "exceedingly sinful." He then gives God's view of humanity saying that "their throat is an open sepulchre; with their tongues they have used deceit; the poison of asps is under their lips: whose mouth is full of cursing and bitterness: their feet are swift to shed blood: destruction and misery are in their ways: and the way of peace have they not known: there is no fear of God before their eyes" (Romans 3:13-18).

Passion For Vengeance

In Arizona in 1981, two men offered to help a lady in distress. She had locked herself out of her car and they very kindly helped her open the car window. Now there's a point in favor of the goodness of man. How could this woman repay the men? They suggested a six pack of beer. She went into the store, bought the beer, but when she came back they abducted her in her own car. Both the men raped the young woman, then tied her hands and feet and went to her apartment. They ransacked it, stole her valuables and found to their delight, that she had a credit card with $8,000 in savings. Unfortunately for them, they were only able to withdraw $250 per day using the card, so it would take some time to get the whole $8,000. They both concluded that they couldn't let her live. They waited until dark, then took her, still bound hand and foot, up a mountain. They raped her again, then threw her off a cliff. She landed half way down, and they could hear by her groans that she wasn't dead, so they threw her off twice more. Despite this, she was still alive so they hit her head with rocks until she was unconscious, then buried her alive.

If you are anything like me, you will grapple with tears. That was somebody's daughter . . . someone's sister. If you are like me you will feel anger, shame, and a cry for justice for those men. This passion for just vengeance upon such wickedness is there despite our sinful nature. If the deeds of those men seem abominable even to us, the sinful offspring of Adam, how evil must they seem to a Holy, perfect and just Creator?

Unregenerate humanity is "found wanting" on the scales of God's Justice. Yet to speak of any thought of Judgment Day is offensive to them. They say within their sinful hearts, "God has forgotten: He hides His face; He will never see it" (Psalm 10:11). But as surely as God is faithful to all His promises of blessing for the obedient, so is He faithful to His promise of justice for the disobedient. He will fulfill His Word which He has magnified above His name. The Scriptures warn sinners that in accordance with their hardness and impenitent hearts they are treasuring up for themselves wrath "in the day of wrath and revelation of the righteous judgment of God, who will render to each one according to his deeds . . . to those who are self-seeking and do not obey the truth, but obey unrighteousness— indignation and wrath, tribulation and anguish, on every soul of man who does evil . . . " (Romans 2:5-9).

The Eye in the Sky

On October 6th, 1998, two men burst into the Foothill bank in Rowland Heights, California and robbed it. Unfortunately for them, a witness called the police and a car chase ensued for the next two hours. This was broadcast live over television during which time it was revealed how much money the robbers got. A cool $486. Despite the pathetic take, they were charged with armed robbery and felony invasion.

During the chase the newsreader said what all newsreaders seem to say during live car chases: "Why don't these guys just give up? They can't get away. Nobody ever gets away! Every time they break a law, they are getting further into trouble. The helicopter will track them wherever they try to hide. If the helicopter loses sight of them, the law will bring in police dogs . . . they can't get away. *Why don't they just give up?*"

The sinner is being chased by the Law of God. Every time he crosses the line of conscience, he stores up wrath that will be revealed on the Day of Wrath. *He can't get away.* The omniscient eye of a Holy God sees his every thought, word and deed. Why doesn't he just give up? They don't give up for the same reason criminals don't give up. They think that they will get away no matter how slim the chance. This is why they must be cornered by the law. They must be stopped in their tracks and made to look down the loaded barrel of a weapon. Then, if they know what's good for them, they will raise their hands in surrender.

Monastery Without Walls

The Bible says that the men of Sodom were "wicked and sinners before the Lord exceedingly." Among them lived righteous Lot. This man "vexed" (anguished, pained) his "righteous soul from day to day with their unlawful deeds." Are we also anguished by what we see in the world? Are we jealous for the honor of our God? Are we grieved beyond words to see His mercy despised and His Holy Name blasphemed? At the same time do we cringe in fear for the ungodly who walk after the flesh in the lust of uncleanness, full of presumption and self-will, with no fear of God before their eyes?

Jeremiah had this same conflict when he cried,

"Oh, that my head were waters, and mine eyes a fountain of tears, that I might weep day and night for . . . my people. Oh that . . . I might leave my people and go from them! For they are all adulterers, an assembly of treacherous men" (Jeremiah 9:1-2).

Many Christians aren't "vexed" because they either don't "know" the terror of the Lord, therefore they don't seek to "persuade men." Many are living in a monastery without walls. They have lost contact with the world. Life consists of Saturday night fellowship, Sunday services, Wednesday Bible study and a few other social activities. They are living in a Christian comfort zone, where little contact is made with the ungodly world.

Directly after the command to work out our salvation with fear and trembling we are told:

> "It is God who works in you both to will and to do of His good pleasure. Do all things without murmurings and disputings, that you may be blameless and harmless, the sons of God, without rebuke, in the midst of a crooked and perverse nation, among whom you shine as lights in the world, (then we are told what on earth we are supposed to be doing) holding forth the Word of life, that I may rejoice in the Day of Christ . . . " (Philippians 2:12-16).

Are we light among light, and salt among salt? Do we seek God for men in fervent prayer, then seek men for God in zealous evangelism? Paul charged Timothy to "preach the Word in season and out of season," and 2 Timothy 4:1-2 tells us why: " . . . The Lord Jesus Christ, who shall judge the living and the dead at His appearing and His Kingdom." Do we see Him as He is? Will we "love His appearing?"

The awe of that Day should cause an urgency to burn in our hearts.

CHAPTER FIFTEEN

THE URGENCY OF COMBAT

*"I must work the works of Him who sent Me while it
is yet day; the night is coming when no man can
work" (John 9:4).*

It is obvious throughout Scripture that God speaks
to humanity through dreams. He spoke in this way to
Joseph, Daniel and numbers of others. Joel Chapter 2
says that this will be one of the signs of the last days. I
don't know if some of my dreams have been God
speaking to me, but I do know that some have attributed
to my zeal for the lost.

I remember having a dream in which I was standing
at an outdoor restaurant. People were happily eating
and drinking. I distracted them by saying, "Excuse me,
may I have your attention for a moment. Last week I
came to this place and I was fearful to tell you something.
This week I want to tell you what I should have told you
then . . . unless you repent, you will perish!"

Some carried on eating, others looked angered,
while others looked down feeling conviction. Even
though many Christians would rather it not be so, this
is the simple message of the Gospel. Jesus told His
listeners that if they didn't repent, they would perish.

This is the message of John 3:16. The reason Jesus died, was so that those who believe "should not perish," but have everlasting life. God gave His only begotten Son, so that sinners wouldn't perish in Hell.

There *are* gentle ways to say harsh things. Only in a dream would I say outrightly, "Unless you repent, you shall perish." I once felt compelled to preach to sunbathers on Waikiki Beach in Hawaii. I stood among about 100 sun-worshipers who had prostrated themselves on the sand and said, "It must be like a dream to find yourself lying in the sun on beautiful Waikiki Beach. And it must be like a nightmare to have a preacher stand up and preach to you, but please bear with me, I have something very important to tell you. I won't be too long."

After about 20 minutes, a police officer approached me and said, "You had better stop soon. I waited until the eighth complaint before I decided to come over to you."

On another ministry trip to Hawaii (someone has to do it), I had a day off, so I went surfing at Waikiki. At one point the water went very calm for quite some time. I noticed that about 20 surfers were sitting 50 yards further out from me and my surfing companion. I was very aware of how water amplifies sound, so I called to my friend, "Have I ever told you how I became a Christian?" He called back that I hadn't, so I gave a loud, clear testimony, going through each the Commandments, Judgment Day, the Cross, faith and repentance. The water was calm, but with God's help, I preached up a storm. The Law rids the sinner of false peace and shows him that he is under God's wrath until he comes to the Cross.

Like Paul, we must reason of "sin, righteousness and judgment." Yet, this has been a glaring omission from the message of modern evangelism. We have failed to warn our hearers to flee from the wrath to come. Another Gospel has been preached, and another harvest has been reaped, leaving the Church impregnated with false converts.

John Wesley knew what it was to "save with fear." He said, "I desire to have both Heaven and Hell in my eye." In other words, he wasn't happy merely to get his ticket to Heaven without reaching out to those who were under the fire of the wrath of God. He caught a glimpse of the vision of John's words in the Book of Revelation:

"The heavens departed as a scroll when it is rolled together; and every mountain and island were moved out of their places. And the kings of the earth, and the great men, and the rich men, and the chief captains, and the mighty men, and every slave, and every free man, hid themselves in the dens and in the rocks of the mountains, and said to the mountains and rocks, fall on us and hide us from the face of Him that sits on the throne and from the wrath of the Lamb; for the great day of His wrath is come, and who shall be able to stand?" (Revelation 6:14-17).

The reason God anointed Jesus, was because He "loved righteousness and hated iniquity." Look at these verses that give us insight into God's character:

"Let not the wise man glory in his wisdom, let not the mighty man glory in his might; nor let the rich man glory in his riches. But let him who glories, glory in this, that he understands and knows Me, that I am the Lord, exercising lovingkindness, justice and righteousness in the earth. For in these things I delight, says the Lord" (Jeremiah 9:23-24).

177

If God gave us the wisdom of Solomon, we would have to give Him glory for the gift. If He gave us the strength of Samson, we would have to give Him glory for every muscle. If God gifted us with riches, we couldn't boast of them, for they came by the goodness of God. Our glorying should be confined to the fact that He is the "Lord." He is the Supreme Authority in the universe. From Him and through Him and to Him are all things. Every man will give an account of every idle word to Him. We understand that He not only exercises lovingkindness, justice and righteousness in the earth, but that He *delights* in these things. This is seen in no better place than on the Cross of Calvary. This is where there was a meeting of lovingkindness and justice. This is where righteousness and peace kissed each other. That's why the Apostle Paul said, "God forbid that I should glory, except in the Cross of our Lord Jesus Christ . . . "

It is in the Cross that we see the fearful Justice of our Divine Creator, as His wrath-filled fist came down upon the innocent Lamb of God. It is on the same Cross that we see infinite lovingkindness displayed, that we might live eternally.

The Pain of the Cane

When I was a teenager at school, we had a music teacher who lacked in the area of discipline. The poor man was also slightly deaf. Consequently, when he was playing the piano, chaos broke loose behind his back. During one of these lessons, I noticed a friend two rows from the front, trying to shake off a classmate who had grabbed his leg and was pulling him under the bench. I crawled under the seating in front of me and took hold of the culprit's leg. That's when I felt someone grab *my* leg. Without looking behind me, I used my free leg to kick off this leg-puller with a firm grip. It was then that I glanced behind me, and saw to my horror that it was the principal, who had come into the room to see what all the noise was about!

The three of us were sent to his office. Before we were given our punishment, we had a ten minute wait. When the principal finally arrived he picked up a three-foot piece of cane and gave us two painful swats in the area designed for the purpose.

It hurt. Man, *it hurt*. But the pain of waiting for the cane was just about as bad as the pain from the cane when it came.

Painful though the experience was, I would far rather receive 10,000 canes a day for 100 years, by the hand of the most robust football player, than be found in my sins on Judgment Day. *It is a fearful thing to fall into the hands of the living God.*

Knuckle Rap

America has lost sight of justice in so many areas. Take for instance the man who was caught drinking and driving for the 18th time. The judge ordered him to live closer to the liquor store so that he wouldn't have to drive there. Meanwhile, thousands of innocent people are being slaughtered on our roads by drunk drivers who know that if they get caught, they will only get a rap over the knuckles.

Some other countries have more respect for human life. If you are caught drinking and driving in South Africa you get a ten-year prison sentence and a $10,000 fine. Finland and Sweden will give you an automatic jail sentence and one year of hard labor. Bulgaria will execute you on your second offense. El Salvador will make sure you don't drink and drive again. They will execute you by firing squad on your first offense. I don't think there are too many drunk drivers in El Salvador.

When God came in Peace

Civil law has lost its bite because the Moral Law it is based on has been discarded. It may have been set aside by a sinful world, but it won't go away. When God gave His Law "so terrible was the sight, that Moses said, 'I exceedingly fear and quake!'" When God came in peace to give His Law, Moses was terrified. How fearful will it be when the fury-filled God of Vengeance comes to punish those who have deliberately transgressed that Law?

Do we care enough to pray? Do we care enough to preach . . . to warn, and to witness? God's Justice will be so thorough, that every sinner will be "ground to powder" by the stone of the wrath of God. They will drink the wine of His wrath. The Psalmist cried, "Horror has taken hold on me because of the wicked who forsake Your Law." J. Oswald Sanders pleaded in prayer, "Give us souls, lest we die!" Jeremiah cried, "My bowels, my bowels! I am pained at my very heart, my heart makes a noise in me, I cannot hold my peace, because you have heard. Oh my soul, the sound of the trumpet, the alarm of war" (Jeremiah 4:19). Listen to the "sowing in tears" spirit behind these words of C.H. Spurgeon: "When I've shot and spent all my Gospel bullets and have none left and little effect seems to be made upon my hearers, I then get in the gun and shoot myself at them." In other words, when he had preached the truth of God's Word, his burden was such that he opened his own heart and simply implored sinners to come to the Savior.

In reference to his passionate preaching to the lost, the Apostle Paul cried, "Necessity is laid upon me!" He was saying a "continual, intense distress" was laid upon him. He was no "happy-clappy" superficial Christian. When sinners conclude a time of witnessing with the unusual patronizing, "Well, I'm pleased you are happy," I tell them I'm not happy. Do you think "happy" would be the right word to use to describe the state of mind of the survivors of the Titanic, as they sat in lifeboats, with loved ones drowning all around them? They would have joy unspeakable that they were saved, but they would be grieved beyond words at what was happening around them.

The Bible says that Jesus had an "oil of joy above His fellows," but He was a "Man of sorrows, acquainted with grief." We are called to walk in His steps.

Joseph Alleine, a puritan of the 16th century, wrote a book called *Alarm to the Unconverted*. In it, his zeal for the unconverted is very evident. Listen to his heart as he prepares to plead with the sinner:

"But from whence shall I fetch my argument? With what shall I win them? Oh, that I could tell! I would write to them in tears, I would weep out every argument, I would empty my veins for ink, I would petition them on my knees. Oh how thankful I would be if they would be prevailed with to repent and turn?"

Look at his burden—"I would empty my veins for ink." How many of us would empty a pen of ink to warn a loved one or a friend to get right with God? Are we prepared to let God "lay necessity" upon us? Do we want the communication of our faith to become effectual?

Forget the Kids

Most of us are familiar with air travel. It is standard practice for airline attendants to stand in the aisle and draw our attention to the exits on the plane. Then, in a calm voice they say something like, "If an oxygen mask should appear in front of you, place it over your mouth and nose. Adjust the headband. Pull the pin out. Breathe normally. If you have children, attend to yourself first." Why do the airlines tell you to put yourself before your children? The answer is simply that if a parent has six young children and he tries to put a mask over their faces, by the time he reaches the last child he himself will probably be gasping for breath. The parent will be most effective if he attends to himself first.

In John 8:31-32, we see how a Christian can become most effective: "Then Jesus said to those Jews who believed on Him, If you abide in My word, you are My disciples indeed. And you shall know the truth, and the truth shall make you free." There we have the Biblical definition of a "disciple." He is one who has disciplined himself to abide in the Word of Christ. This results in freedom. This is freedom from sin, death and Judgment. It produces freedom to reach out to others and be effective in our witness to them. Sadly, many Christians are ineffective evangelistically, because they are still gasping for air—they have not attended to themselves first.

Stan's Dog

Many years ago, I had a friend named Stan who had a dog named "Circles." It was so named because it would walk forward two or three steps, and then do a complete circle. Then it would take another two or three steps forward, then another complete circle (it wasn't a trick, it was just the way the dog got around). As a puppy, it had been locked in a small shed for great lengths of time. It went around in circles seeking a way out, and when it came out, it couldn't stop.

Many Christians are just like "Circles." They continue to tread in circles. Each week, they go from the pew to altar to pew to the altar, then back to the pew . . . wearing out both the pastor and the carpet. If you are like Stan's dog, pay close attention because I am going to share the biblical key to get you out of the woodshed and onto the straight and narrow path where you are supposed to be walking.

Here is the key:

"Blessed is the man who walks not in the counsel of the ungodly, nor stands in the path of sinners, nor sits in the seat of the scornful; but his delight is in the Law of the Lord, and in His Law he meditates day and night. He shall be like a tree planted by the rivers of water, that brings forth its fruit in its season, whose leaf also shall not wither; and whatever he does shall prosper" (Psalm 1:1-3).

If we fulfill the stated requirements, the Bible promises we will stand tall and strong, like a tree planted by rivers of water. Our roots will grow deep, and we will produce fruit in season—love, joy, peace, patience, goodness, gentleness, faith, meekness and temperance. Also, whatsoever we do will prosper—our vocation, our marriage, our evangelistic endeavors.

I have saved myself hours in counseling time, by simply asking the problem-laden, defeated, joyless, circular professors of faith one question. This is the question: "Do you read God's Word every day, without fail?" The usual answer is "sometimes" or "sort of" or "most days." The truth is they are not continuing in the Word of Christ, they don't know the truth, and they are not free. They are not meditating on the Word "day and night," so they are therefore not like a tree planted by water. Their roots are shallow. When the winds of adversity blow, they topple over and need to seek the pastor to prop them up. Neither does their fruit remain. They lose their peace and joy and begin to wither at the first sign of adversity. Whatever they do, does not prosper.

These poor souls look at joyful Christians and say, "It's all right for them to be happy. They never have any problems." That isn't true. Ask around, and you will find that all Christians have trials, but the ones who keep their joy are the ones who fulfill the requirements of Psalm One. Their fruit remains. They stand tall and strong during the storms, because their roots go deep into God's Word. They are not blown away by trials or every wind of doctrine.

God gave a similar promise to Joshua. If he kept the Law, and if he would "meditate" on it "day and night," God said he would be "prosperous," and reaffirmed it with "and then you shall have good success" (Joshua 1:8). Do you read the Word every day without fail? Or do you skip a day here and there? Do you do that with your stomach? Do you forget to eat for a day or two?

So, for your own sake and for the sake of those around you who are still in their sins, discipline yourself daily to read and meditate on the Word. Put your Bible before your belly. Say to yourself, "No Bible, no breakfast. No read, no feed." The biblical priority is to put your spirit before your body (see 1 Thessalonians 5:23).

Jesus said "man shall not live by bread alone, but by every word of God." When Peter wrote his epistle and said "As newborn babes, desire the pure milk of the Word, that you may grow thereby," he wasn't particularly writing to babes in Christ. Newborn babies live to drink, because they drink to live. They have an inbuilt instinct to scream for dear life if they don't drink. We are commanded to do the same. Job summed up the necessity for feeding on the Word with, "I have not departed from the commandment of His lips; I have treasured the words of His mouth *more than my necessary food*" (Job 23:12, italics added).

Labor and Sorrow

Two drunks walked along a wharf one dark night, climbed into a small boat, and determined to row to the other side of the lake. The first drunk rowed for one and a half hours. Sweat poured from his brow, until he collapsed. The second drunk took the oars and rowed for three hours. He finally collapsed, exhausted. When they awoke at sunrise, they found that they had made only one mistake. *They were still tied to the wharf.*

Sadly, many professing Christians are still tied to the wharf of self-will. The yolk of Christ is not easy, and His burden is not light. The Christian life is one of labor and sorrow. It is one of struggle, sweat and misery. Their problem is that they have never cut the ropes from the wharf of self-will. They have never abandoned themselves to a faithful Creator. If they would feed daily on the Word, they would find that it produces faith (see Romans 10:17), and faith is what Satan hates. Faith moves mountains. I have seen the most miserable of Christians rise up in victory, *once they grasped the Psalm One principle of feeding daily on the Scriptures.*

The Bible is a supernatural book. When its pages are read with faith in the heart, that faith produces more faith, and from confidence issues joy. Joy yields a "continual feast" for the soul, so that the soldier of Christ can live in victory over every circumstance the enemy puts in front of him.

Don't wait any longer! Pull out the pin of self-will, then place yourself as a grenade into the Hand of Almighty God. Stand firmly on the blood-bought promises of God. If you have harkened diligently to the voice of the Lord—if you have presented your body as a living sacrifice, the promises of God are yours for the taking (see 2 Corinthians 1:20):

"The Lord shall cause thine enemies that rise up against thee to be smitten before thy face: they shall come out against thee one way, and flee before thee seven ways" (Deuteronomy 28:7).

CHAPTER SIXTEEN

PRINCIPLES FOR VICTORY, WEAPONS FOR WAR

*"Let us cast off the works of darkness, and let us put
on the armor of light" (Romans 13:12).*

In August of 1992, *Reader's Digest* published an
article called "How 'average' people excel." It related
how 'fast-trackers,' people who succeed in school, often
fizzle. Their main problem is that they are driven by
their own inflated ego, and they set goals too high for
themselves. They, more than anybody, understand how
clever they are, so they are never happy with playing
second fiddle to anyone. In other words, their pride is
their own downfall. The article, written from a purely
secular point of view, had some very relevant thoughts
that we may apply to the Kingdom of God. Here are
the keys found by a corporate consultant, who
interviewed over 190 men and women that one would
consider to be "ordinary" individuals who had achieved
secular success:

Learn self-discipline. This is the key to being
successful as a Christian. Of course, we don't
measure success in dollars as the world does, we
measure it in terms of our lifestyles pleasing God.

Self-discipline means discipline of self, and this in turn means discipline to Jesus. As we have seen in the previous chapter, it means that we read the Word daily, and obey what it says. Self-discipline means self-denial. It means listening to the voice of our conscience, and the voice of the Spirit. Consider Jesus in this respect. His ministry was a complete denial of self, from the temptation in the wilderness, to Calvary's terrible Cross. He denied His own will, and disciplined Himself to the will of the Father, for the sake of the Kingdom of God.

Bring out the best in people. There is nothing more pathetic than a selfish person. The Christian has crucified selfishness, and now lives to love his neighbor as much as he loves himself. The dividends are rich. He who loves others will be loved himself, and he who brings out the best in others will bring out the best in himself. Jesus lived and died for others. This is the key to successful relationships and to a good marriage.

Build a knowledge base. Think of Jesus when He sat as a twelve year-old at the feet of those who could give Him understanding of the Scriptures. He grew in grace and knowledge of the things of the Kingdom of God. We are commanded, "giving all diligence, add to your faith virtue, and to virtue knowledge . . ." To do so is to enrich the Christian life.

Develop special skills. Our skills are not in the natural realm. We seek skills that will save sinners from everlasting damnation. We long to be skillful by rightly dividing the Word of truth, a skillful soldier that needs not be ashamed. We develop dexterity that we might be sensitive to the voice of the Spirit, and so that we might speak a word in season to those who are weary.

Keep promises. A Christian would rather die than not keep his word. He "swears to his own hurt" (Psalm 15:4). If he says he will do something, he will do it if it is at all possible. In doing so, he is merely following after righteousness, and simply doing what is upright.

Bounce back from defeat. I have had many failures. I have begun writing books that I have abandoned. I have printed tracts that I have thrown into the trash. I have floundered while witnessing. I have wasted money on projects that have failed. I have preached dry sermons, prayed pathetic prayers, and made just about every blunder one can make. When our ministry first started back in 1974, we published a Christian paper called "Living Waters." On the back I ran a large advertisement headed with the words "Problems? Just call this number. You don't have to say a word . . . just listen." The number was for a local Dial-a-sermon, and I thought it would be a blessing to those who found themselves needing comfort. Unfortunately, I forgot to include the area code and some poor woman in another part of the country began getting calls with heavy breathing on the line. People with problems called her and they didn't say a word. They just listened.

I could write a book[6] solely on flops, washouts, mess-ups, blunders, botches, duds, bungles and failures, but who hasn't blown something in his life? Those who blunder the least are usually those who attempt the least. Steven Pile, the head of the "Not Terribly Good Club" of Great Britain was recently forced to resign from his

---

[6]I did. See, *Comfort, the Feeble-minded*

position when a book he wrote called, *The Book of Heroic Failures*, became a bestseller. He couldn't even succeed in his position as president! Albert Einstein said, "Anyone who has never made a mistake has never tried anything new."

Gathering Sticks

A young man once asked if I thought he should go to a mission school. I asked him how many people he witnessed to each day, and found that he actually spoke to 6 or 7 people daily about the things of God. His business was carpet-cleaning, and that gave him a personal contact with sinners from various walks of life. We looked at his future as a student. He would go to a Christian training school and spend six months solely with Christians. Then he would go out and do mission work . . . if he still had a mind to. Charles Spurgeon said, "Be careful when you are picking up sticks, that your fire doesn't go out."

If you don't witness and you feel you need training, go to a Bible school where you know they have a burden for the lost, so that you will end up with more zeal than when you went in. Or better still, get into a lifestyle where you rub shoulders with the world. I gained what knowledge I have through godly teaching, and from a number of years of open-air preaching.

A friend of mine was a very proficient "garbiologist." He collected the garbage for a local company. He said it wasn't too difficult, because you just picked it up as you went along. The same applies with evangelism. You will pick it up as you go along. It really isn't hard to witness, if you know what you want to achieve. It isn't the big deal the devil makes you think it is. Just find someone who is open to Christian things, take them through God's Law, then the Cross, repentance, and then faith. There's the skeleton. It's just a matter of putting the flesh on as you go. As you make witnessing a regular thing, it will come to you more naturally. In fact, it will come to you supernaturally, because you will have the help of God. The best way to learn to swim is to get into the water, then once you figure out that it isn't that difficult, you will get back into the water with less fear.

Think what a good soldier does when he isn't in engaged in combat. He cleans his weapon. He pulls it apart and puts it together again. He familiarizes himself with his implements of war. Learn the Commandments. Take each one apart and put it together again. Study the spiritual nature of the Law so that when a rebellious sinner says "I love God," or "I've never done anything wrong," you will know what to say.

For the Thinking Mind

I was sitting at the Long Beach airport feeling quite happy with myself. Good music was playing on the sound system, two people were tapping their feet and one was whistling along with the music. I had been upgraded to first class (because of frequent flying mileage), and was actually looking forward to boarding the plane. It means boarding the plane before the masses, and that takes the stress out of flying.

I had put "Ten Commandment pennies" into the coin returns of the telephones, and had placed Christian literature on a number of the seats. What's more, I had avoided the dreaded cleaning lady. More than once I have filled an airport with literature, and found to my dismay that the cleaning lady was dumping all the tracts in the trash.

If you want to see some action, go to an airport. Where else in today's busy world, can you find people sitting, and doing nothing? We have one tract which is excellent for airports. It is called the "Intelligence Test Bookmark," and has plenty of "get-away time." It doesn't look at all like a Christian tract, and gives you plenty of time to get away. Its heading boosts the ego by saying, "INTELLIGENCE TEST . . . for the thinking mind." Below the heading are eight brain-teasers. Number seven asks a question about a man who had broken the Ten Commandments. When he made it to the gates of Heaven, he found that God was "just," and had to, by His very nature punish sin. How could God let him into Heaven and still be just? On side two, it gives all the answers, including an explanation of how God did it through the Cross.

At larger city airports, you will find tens of thousands of people. What's more, many of them are from all around the world. This is your opportunity to begin an International Evangelistic Ministry. At Dallas airport for example, one airline has about 30 gates. Have someone drop you at gate one and pick you up an hour later at gate thirty. During that hour, you walk through, dropping these boredom-breakers on the empty seats as you go. I have done it hundreds of times, and never once have I been reprimanded, because what I am doing is totally permissible by law as a constitutional right according to a recent court case:

"The high court said airport authorities may prohibit repeated solicitation of money by political and religious groups. But the court also ruled that such organizations have a First Amendment right to distribute their literature in airports"[7] (*Wall Street Journal*, June 1992).

Maybe you have a personal library full of good Christian books. Take a handful, and leave one on the seat you've been sitting on. Just make sure you don't do this in an airport that is in a big mess, because the cleaning lady will come along and do her thing.

Are you grateful for Calvary? Then show God your gratitude. Have a gratitude attitude. Give Him the "widow's mite" of your witness. The incident of the widow giving her last two coins to God, shows us that only the gift that costs, counts. God knows that for you to slip a tract onto a seat may be equivalent, on a courage level to some other Christian standing up and preaching. *But you can do it.* Don't listen to your fears. Say, "If God is for me, nothing can be against me. I can do all things through Christ Who strengthens me." Then do it. Civil law is still on our side—you'll not be thrown to the lions. Let the devil eat dust.

A Powerful Weapon

I now want to show you how to pull the pin out of an effective little hand grenade. For me to do this, you will need a blank sheet of paper. So put this book down for a minute and go and get a sheet of paper . . . it will be well worth your while. Go on. If you haven't got access to one, you will probably find a blank page in the back of this book. This will be ideal for what I want to show you—you will have to trim the edge straight though (if you make a jagged edge while ripping it out).

Do exactly what I tell you (this may seem complex, but it is very simple). Fold the paper, from the top, down one third. You should now have a square piece in your hand. Fold the left top corner into the middle and crease

---

[7]You can download this document from our web site at www.raycomfort.com

it down. Fold the right corner down and crease it, as though you are making a paper plane. You should now have something that looks like a house with a pointed roof.

Continue making a plane by folding the paper in half. Crease it down the center.

You should now have something that looks like a paper plane before you fold the wings down. Now turn the point of the plane toward the ground, with the shorter edge to your left. Starting at the top left side, place your thumbs and fore-fingers a little more than a third across to the right, and carefully tear downwards in a straight line, until you have torn the piece off altogether.

Place the torn piece on a table where it won't blow away. Then rip off another (little more than a third), vertically (rip it as straight as you can). Place this piece with the other, then put the remaining (long) piece on the table, away from the other two strips. Now open the two pieces, and carefully make them into letters. You will find two "L's," and the other pieces of paper will form the letters "E" and "H." When you put them all together, you will have the word "HELL" (if you have been careful to do exactly as I said). The remaining long piece, when opened, will form a perfect cross.

Here is the story that goes with this: A Christian was once talking to an atheist and someone who went to church. The atheist said he didn't believe in God, Heaven, Hell, the Cross (as you are telling this story, begin folding the paper). The Christian warned him that he would have to face God whether he believed in Him or not. The church-goer said he believed everything the Bible said, but he hadn't repented as yet.

While the Christian pleaded with them both, a truck came around the corner, up onto the sidewalk and killed all three of them.

As they stood before the Judgment Throne of God, the ex-atheist looked down and saw a piece of paper in the Christian's hand. He said, "That's a ticket to get into Heaven, give it to me!" The Christian said, "I'll tell you what I will do. I will give a third of the ticket to each of you" (this is where you tear off the two strips, and place the longer one away from them. Then you pick up the two pieces) and say, "So they took their tickets, and gave them to God. He said, 'Let's see where the tickets say you are to go.'" As you open them, they spell the word "HELL."

Then you say, "The Christian walked up to the Throne and gave his one third of the ticket to God, Who said, "The only way to get in, is the way of the Cross," and you open the third piece, revealing the Cross.

This is an excellent way to conclude a time of witnessing to someone, as it sums up visually what you have been saying. If they die in their sins, and face the Law, God will give them Eternal Justice and they will end up in Hell. If they shelter in the Cross, He will give them mercy, and everlasting life.

Leave it All

A number of years ago, a movie was made called, "The Fourth Wise Man." It was a fictitious story, centered at the time of Christ, and was about a Magi who was hindered from travelling with the three wise men who took their gifts to Jesus. The man epitomized the spirit of the Law. When he and his servant came across a stricken stranger, they bathed his wounds, and when they had to leave, the Magi said to his servant, "Leave him with sufficient bread and water." When the servant protested, "There is hardly any left," the Magi said, "Leave all of it then."

The act so spoke to my heart. The servant was saying that there was barely enough to keep *them* alive, and was no doubt hoping his master would say not to leave any, or at least only leave the minimum. But this man did to others as he would have them do to him, fulfilling the Law and the prophets. Such acts of kindness don't come naturally to us, but with the help of God, we can express our love for the lost in that spirit.

If you have the Spirit of Christ, you will have what the Scriptures call "the wisdom that is from above." This is how the *Amplified Bible* renders James 3:17:

" . . . the wisdom from above is first of all pure (undefiled); then it is peace-loving, courteous (considerate, gentle). It is willing to yield to reason, full of compassion and good fruits; it is wholehearted and straight-forward, impartial and unfeigned—free from doubts, wavering and insincerity."

This is the spirit in which we should witness. It is something you already have in Jesus Christ. So don't be concerned that you aren't "gifted" as a speaker when it comes to reaching the lost. The Bible says of Moses, he "was learned in all the wisdom of the Egyptians, and was mighty in words, and deeds" (Acts 7:22), yet God didn't use him to deliver Israel until 40 years later. Instead, it took all that time of tending sheep to produce a meekness of character different from that which he had in Egypt. The Bible says, "the meek will He guide in judgment: and the meek will He teach His way" (Psalm 25:8-9). The wisdom that Moses gained from Egypt was not a wisdom from above. When he saw

196

injustice, he took the law into his own hands and committed murder (Acts 7:24). God doesn't need the wisdom of this world. He merely desires a pure, humble, peace-loving, compassionate soul to use as a mouth piece for the Gospel. He wants us to be a lighthouse of His love. The moment we receive the Spirit of Christ, we receive the gift of those virtues. We don't need to tend sheep for 40 years, when we have the character of the Good Shepherd manifesting through us.

If you want to see souls saved, witness whenever and wherever you can. In doing so, you will make sure you are in the perfect will of God. It is His Word that commands us to preach the word "in season and out of season." When I go out to witness and can't find someone to speak to, I sit down and pray that God will bring someone to me. I remember approaching three females once, and as I got closer, I noticed they were speaking in Spanish, so I sat down and prayed for someone to come to me, *knowing* that I was in God's will. Within 60 seconds, two young men sat right next to me. I overheard one of them say that they were stuck there until 9:00 a.m., so I knew I had at least 30 minutes to speak to them.

One of them came under conviction when I spoke of his personal sins and he glanced at his watch twice. I told him that he had until 9:00 a.m., so there was no need to worry about the time, and that it was his guilt that was making him feel uncomfortable. That made him smile. Sometimes people don't realize why they react the way they do. I prayed with them both individually, and for God to heal an injured arm of one of the men, and they seemed very appreciative.

In an earlier chapter, I mentioned how I often use "I.Q. tracts" when witnessing. These little cards make witnessing much easier. Probably the most difficult thing about sharing our faith is swinging from a conversation about the weather, to the subject of the things of God. At that point, our fear of rejection runs wild. These tracts make the swing from the natural to the spiritual, as smooth as soft butter. People do the test on side one, then go straight into the questions about God, almost always without offense. The best way to show you their potential, is to have you do the tests yourself:

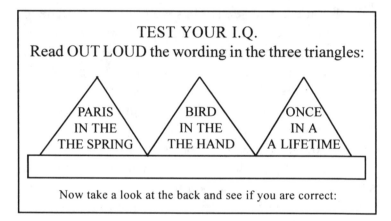

TEST YOUR I.Q.
Read OUT LOUD the wording in the three triangles:

PARIS IN THE THE SPRING

BIRD IN THE THE HAND

ONCE IN A A LIFETIME

Now take a look at the back and see if you are correct:

If you said, "Paris in the spring, Bird in the hand and Once in a lifetime," you got three wrong, try again. The word "the" and "a" are repeated. It's obvious, once you see it.

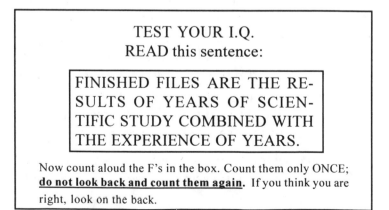

TEST YOUR I.Q.
READ this sentence:

FINISHED FILES ARE THE RE-SULTS OF YEARS OF SCIEN-TIFIC STUDY COMBINED WITH THE EXPERIENCE OF YEARS.

Now count aloud the F's in the box. Count them only ONCE; **do not look back and count them again.** If you think you are right, look on the back.

There are six; if you found three, you are normal. Usually seven out of ten people get three F's. If you found three, go back and check again. We have had people write to us and say, "There aren't six F's," and have had to send the card back with the "F's" circled. If you can't find them, write to us and we will circle the three "of's" that you missed.

Each of these tracts gives the answer on side two, where there are six questions about the things of God:

Here is another I.Q. Test; answer yes or no OUT LOUD: 1/ Is there a God? 2/ Does God care about right and wrong? 3/ Are God's standards the same as ours? 4/ Will God punish sin? 5/ Is there a Hell? 6/ Do you avoid Hell by living a good life? The answers are: 1/ Yes. 2/ Yes. 3/ No. 4/ Yes. 5/ Yes. 6/ No. You can't afford to be wrong; find out the truth— ask God to forgive your sins, then trust Jesus Christ Who took your punishment by dying on the Cross for you. Read the Bible daily and obey what you read . . . God will never let you down.

How to Use the Card

As I have said, probably the most difficult thing about witnessing, is bringing up the subject of the things of God. The Card does that for you, inoffensively. Another difficulty, is knowing what to say. The Card will help guide you through to the Gospel. Often people are self-confident and proud. The Card will almost always humble them. *Don't leave home without it.*

Often, you don't know if the person you are speaking to is trusting in Grace or in self-righteousness. This card will help find that out for you within two minutes of meeting him. In fact, it will also tell you his intimate beliefs about God, sin, Hell and judgment.

Since I was converted in 1972, I have given out 90,000 to 100,000 tracts (not to the same person). Over the years I have experimented different ways to get tracts into the hands of the unsaved. I've found that there is an effective and inoffensive way to get strangers to take a tract.

Keep the cards in your wallet or purse, then as you are taking one out (you will have their attention since you are giving them something out of your wallet—as it is of value), ask, "Did you get one of these?" [8]This question has a two-fold effect. It stimulates curiosity, as well as making them feel that they are missing out on something (which they are).

As they take it, they will usually ask, "One of what?" Smile and say, "It's an I.Q. test." Most people will also smile when they hear this (something to do with the human ego). It is so refreshing to have someone smile when given a tract. Many will try it straight away. As they read it, build a bridge by gently pointing out what they should do. If they fail the test, be sensitive that they may feel embarrassed when you point out their error. Take the opportunity to relate to them, saying that the majority fails it. Then say, "Now try the other side."

Don't worry if the person passes the test on Side One. Just say, "You did well . . . now try the other side, it's far more important."

So far you have had time to get to know the person (especially if they failed the test). Now comes the next benefit of this card. The majority of those who look at the second side, begin to "play the game" and actually do what the card says; they read OUT LOUD the answers to the six questions on Side Two—1/ Is there a God?

---

[8]If you are able to, greet the person first with "Good morning," or "How are you doing?" This will help break down barriers.

They say, "Yes" or "No." 2/ Does God care about right and wrong?, etc.

It is some consolation to know that in recent polls 96% of Americans believe in God; 82% believe in an after-life, and approximately 60% believe in Hell. So, few are offended by these questions. When they answer out loud, you have an excellent opportunity to ask why they think such a thing, and thus get to witness to them. When someone says they think God doesn't care about right and wrong, most can be reasoned with by appealing to civil law. Almost everyone thinks murderers should be punished (even if they can't agree on its form).

Then ask them if man, with all his evils, cares about right and wrong, how much more then will his Creator?

With this little card, in two or three minutes, you can build a bridge with a stranger. Then you can break down his confidence in his own judgments (eight out of ten times), find out his crucial beliefs, find out whether he is trusting in self-righteousness or Grace, as well as inoffensively witness to him. When he answers the six questions, you can say, "You did well . . . you got four out of six correct. The ones you slipped up on were number three, when you said that God's standards are the same as ours. The Bible says, 'His way is perfect'—'Who shall ascend the Hill of the Lord; He who has clean hands and a pure heart,' 'Blessed are the pure in heart,'" etc.

Digest the Commandments, so that you can go through them one by one, opening up each one to show that God requires truth in the inward parts.

Then, once you have clearly presented the Law, say, "And the other one you slipped up on, was where you said we avoid Hell by living a good life. The Bible tells us, 'It is not by works of righteousness that He saved us, but according to His mercy' (Titus 3:5)."

After you have thoroughly brought the knowledge of what sin is, using the Law of God, uphold the Cross in all its glory.

Other advantages of these cards are that they're low priced ($3 for one hundred), they are easy to distribute, and are extremely convenient (you can easily carry twenty in your wallet or purse). Keep a stack with you because you will often be asked for more. Don't feel as though you have to lead every person you witness to in a sinner's prayer. I pray with many people as I witness. If they are trembling, and saying something like, "What then should I do?" then I pray with them for salvation. If you lead someone in a prayer of repentance, and they haven't yet gained godly sorrow through conviction of the Holy Spirit, you may deliver them, but it will be a still-born, or it may be a premature delivery. If by chance they are genuine in their commitment, then you will have to incubate them and the odds are, like most premature babies that begin to grow, they will be sickly and weak. It is best to let them form in the womb of conviction, then in God's timing, they will be born again, and merely need to be fed the sincere milk of the Word. When fruit is ripe for the picking, it should fall into your hand, and when someone is ready for the Savior, you shouldn't have to pry them from the tree of the world. In fact, if someone is ready for salvation, you probably won't have to lead them in prayer, because the prayer will come from his own heart.

I once heard a respected pastor speak of being in an airport awaiting departure. He had trouble finding a seat, and after moving several times, found himself sitting next to a man whose wife had just died. Tears welled in the man's eyes as he spoke of the meaninglessness of life. The pastor was able to witness to the man about God's love for him. He even prayed with him, but he didn't lead him in a "decision." His reason was that when a person is in such a broken state, you can get him to pray anything. He gave him literature, put him in contact with a pastor in his area, but he left the man's salvation in the Hands of the Lord, that takes faith in God. It takes courage because the inclination in most of us is to get a decision for Jesus, and joyfully cut another notch into our evangelistic belt.

Did your parents ever make you kiss and hug your brother or sister to "make up," after a fight? Did it come from your heart, or did you grit your teeth, and make up for fear of wrath if you didn't? A sinner's repentant prayer should come from his own heart, and not because he feels compelled to, simply because of wrath. He should be sorry because he has sinned against the God of Heaven. It should come from his heart, as the words gushed from the heart of the prodigal son (see Luke 15:18). He should have "godly" sorrow, because he has transgressed the Law, and "repentance toward God," because he has "sinned against Heaven."

Sometimes when you are witnessing, you will meet people who think they know everything. One way to have a little fun and advance the cause of the Gospel at the same time is to inquire if you may ask them seven questions. I have often used these while witnessing, and even used one or two to humble arrogant hecklers in open air situations.

To see the power of these little "humblers," put this book down and have someone *verbally* ask you these questions and write down your answers. If you just read them yourself, you will fail to see their impact and not see their evangelistic potential:

1. How many of each animal did Moses take into the ark?

2. What is the name of the raised print that deaf people use?

3. Is it possible to end a sentence with the word "the"?

4. Spell the word "shop". What do you do when you come to a green light?

5. It is noon. You look at the clock. The big hand is on three, the small hand on five. What time is it?

6. Spell the word "silk." What do cows drink?

7. Listen carefully: You are the driver of a train. There are 30 people on board. At the first stop 10 people get off. At the next stop 5 people get on. Now for the question, what is the name of the train driver?

Answers to questions:

1. None, it was Noah.

2. Deaf people don't use raised print.

3. The question is an example of one.

4. Go.

5. Noon.

6. Water.

7. *You* are the driver of the train.

CHAPTER SEVENTEEN

FRONT LINE BATTLE

*"For by thee I have run through a troop: by my God
have I leaped over a wall" (Psalm 18:29).*

In January of 1993, I was invited to the Dallas area
by a pastor who asked me to speak at his Sunday church
services. He was a little disappointed, because he had
invited me to go out witnessing on Saturday night, and a
thunderstorm arrived about an hour after my plane landed.
I had never seen anything like it. Everything is bigger in
Texas. There was such intensity of lightning, that every
few seconds, the sky would light up like noonday. Then
it rained cats and dogs (they were everywhere). It looked
like we wouldn't have the opportunity to go outdoors,
so we decided that we would go witness at a mall.

The pastor was very gracious and gave me a choice
as to whether or not I wanted to go witnessing, saying
he would understand if I wanted to rest after the flight. I
could either rest up in my hotel, or with the help of God,
seek and save the lost. The temptation was there to rest,
but I of course chose the latter.

The words "lifestyle evangelism" have come to mean
to many that we merely *live* a Christian life, in the hope
that some day sinners will be drawn to us. I believe more

in "life-saving" evangelism. Who could stand passively on a river bank hoping a drowning person will be drawn to him so that he could then rescue him? The Scriptures use a more fearful analogy—fire rather than water (see Jude 1:23). The pastor in Dallas was putting legs to his prayers, and was wanting to go to the sinner.

It was dinner time, and he dropped me off at the entrance of a restaurant while he parked the car. A few minutes later, we were seated in a warm and dry atmosphere as a waitress made us feel at home. As she began to walk away, I said, "Here's a little gift for you," and handed her a glistening penny with the Ten Commandments pressed into it. She took the penny and, predictably, asked what it was. When I told her, she said a sincere, "Thank you very much."

When another waitress brought the menus to us, I gave her an I.Q. card, and said that she might like to try it when she had a moment to spare. A few minutes later, another waitress came and asked if she could buy a penny. I gave her one. The first waitress returned and said she had failed the I.Q. test. It was then that I saw another waitress standing behind the pastor. She smiled, so I gave her a penny. When she was very open to Christian things, I gave her a signed copy of one of my books, for which she seemed very grateful.

Notice that we didn't just sit there hoping that our light would draw sinners to us. We made an effort to reach out.

As we paid our bill in the lobby, four or five members of the staff stood around us and asked us questions as to who we were, etc. To let our light shine is merely a matter of letting the love of God flow through us, rather than stop in us.

When we came out of the restaurant, the storm had passed. So the pastor (Mike) gave me a choice as to where we could now go—either to the "cowboy" part of town, the "prostitute," or the "punk" area. Somehow I didn't feel like trying to witness to guys twice my size in high heel boots and ten gallon hats. The last place I want to visit when I am away from Sue would be a prostitute area (especially in the light of so many preachers around that time were falling, or should I say "diving" into sexual sin). I remember feeling unspiritual years ago, when I heard of a well-known preacher who would boldly go into brothels and witness to prostitutes (the Jesus loves you gospel). Here was one man who seemed to be able to keep the red blood in his veins cool. It turned out that he eventually fell sexually. He left his wife for another woman.

Moths should stay away from flames, so, without any hesitation, I chose Punksville. Punks are always a challenge. For some reason I feel safe with a woman who has tatoos, "hate" written on her cheeks, black lipstick, weird clothes, filthy language, semi-shaven scalp, a rooster hairstyle with orange hair and pins through her nose.

Unfortunately, we got lost and ended up in the Dallas "cowboy" area. As we made our way toward some very loud music, the wind blew something into the pastor's eye, and it lodged under his contact lens. It was so painful, we decided to go back to his car so that he could remove the contacts.

As we turned around, another gust of wind blew the hat off a man who was walking toward us. He was accompanied by a very pretty woman in her mid-twenties. As Mike and the man ran after the hat, the woman lunged at me and (to my unbelief), threw her arms around my neck and tried to force her lips onto mine. I screamed the pastor's name and pried the woman's arms from around my neck. Then I handed her a penny with the Ten Commandments pressed into it, and told her what it was. Mike and I witnessed briefly to both the man and Potiphar's wife, then we went back to the car and prayed for them. As we sat in the car I felt that I should say something about the woman trying to kiss me to the pastor. I widened my eyes and said, "That's the first time anything like that has ever happened to me." He looked back at me mournfully and said, with tongue in cheek, "It's *never* happened to me!"

We didn't find any punks that night, but we had a good time witnessing to a group of about a dozen youths. We entered a mall and gave I.Q. cards to two teenage boys. They did the tests, and couldn't believe they failed them. One ran off and returned with two friends so that they too could feel the humiliation of failure. When they blew it, I said, "You can't trust your eyes . . . watch this," and did some sleight-of-hand, which sent the same youth off with eyes like saucers, to get some more of his friends.

Suddenly, we had about a dozen young men watching my every move and listening to my every word. Even the security guard watched intently. When I told the young men I was a Christian and warned them that they had to face God on Judgment Day, they stayed and listened. We witnessed to them for a few minutes, shook their hands and moved to another part of the mall.

Perhaps you are thinking that you could never do such a thing. All you need is a little love to motivate you, and a little [1]knowledge to equip you. Anyone with half a brain and two hands can do these tricks, and they have so much evangelistic potential, because they will make

---

[9]We have a package which has two of the most incredible sleight-of-hand tricks, that will astound the person you are witnessing to. It is called the "Sleight-of-hand Pack".

your hearers respect you, and therefore listen to what you have to say.

Despite the loose woman, the lack of punks and the security guards who told me I needed a permit to do any more tricks or to even hand out tracts, we had a good time. That night as I lay my head on my pillow, I smiled a lot, thanked God that I broke out of the barracks of my comfort zone, and prayed for those who we had been privileged to witness to.

The Good Wine

One of the most fearful instances of someone breaking out of the barracks of his comfort zone, is Stephen. The Bible tells us that he was a man full of the Holy Spirit and faith. He was respected in his office as a minister of the Gospel of Salvation, was wise, had a good reputation, and could have therefore stayed in the security of worship and praise. He could have been satisfied with his waiting on tables ministry, but he wasn't. Stephen loved God. He loved the truth and he loved sinners enough to preach God's truth to them.

We pick up the story in Acts Chapter 6 when the twelve disciples decided that they didn't want to neglect prayer and the Word of God to serve tables. Therefore, they found seven men to do the job, one of whom was Stephen. The Scriptures tell us the "the number of the disciples multiplied greatly," because men like Stephen didn't confine their ministry to serving tables. They had their priorities sorted out, preached the Gospel, and God confirmed His Word with signs following (see verse 8).

This didn't please the enemy. Whenever a servant of God serves up truth in the court of the world, the devil is going to return the serve with a vengeance. When professing godly Jews couldn't resist the wisdom by which Stephen spoke, the father of lies provided some more of his children to distort Stephen's words, and say that he was speaking blasphemy.

Suddenly, Stephen found himself standing before the council and his slanderous accusers. All it took was one question, "Are these things so?" to push Stephen's evangelistic button. Beginning at Abraham, he recounted the history of Israel, saying nothing offensive to them until Acts 7:51. He saved the good wine for last. His sermon ended with a number of relevant points for his congregation to consider:

1. His hearers were stubborn

2. They were unholy

3. They were spiritually deaf

4. They and their fathers resisted the Holy Spirit

5. They were the sons of murderers

6. They were the betrayers and murderers of "the Just One."

Stephen disqualified himself from the "Popular Preacher of the Year" award. Then from his breast, he produced what Charles Spurgeon called his "ablest auxiliary," which was this soldier's greatest weapon—the Law of God. The Jews were proud of the thought that they had kept the Law, and by saying they had broken it, Stephen touched the apples of their evil eyes. He climaxed his sermon by saying that they "have received the Law by the direction of angels and have not kept it" (verse 53). He pointed to the Divine Plumline to show his hearers how crooked they were. This made them foam at the mouth like mad dogs. They were cut to the heart, then "gnashed at him with their teeth."

Their reaction didn't seem to worry Stephen too much. He was so full of the Holy Spirit, he was gazing at a vision of Jesus standing at the right hand of God, and said, "Look, I see the heavens opened and the Son of Man standing at the right hand of God" (Acts 7:56).

Another puissant poke in the apple of their anti-Christ eyes. They cried out with loud voices, stopped their ears, ran at him with one accord and dashed his body with great stones until he breathed the last breath of this contemptible world's air.

Stephen's sermon was a little different from that of the modern-day preacher. He failed to mention "Christ crucified," or of the fact that God loved them. He didn't even mention Grace. He didn't give that which is holy to the dogs. Neither did he woo his hearers with soft words, dim lights and soul-stirring music. If he had, he wouldn't have offended a soul, and could have remained in his comfort zone. Devil, demon, Jew and Gentile would all have smiled. Stephen's "decisions" were non-existent. By modern standards, he had failed to reap any souls. The only decision made by his listeners, was a unified decision to spill the preacher's blood.

Stephen's boldness so stirred one hearer that he reinforced a resolve that would change the course of Christian history. Saul of Tarsus was so offended by what he saw and heard, he decided he would wipe the Church off the face of the earth.

Stephen's precious blood was the first to be shed as groundwork for the Church that would follow. He knew from experience the truth of the hymn-writer that would be penned many centuries later, "Love so amazing, so divine, demands my life, my all."

Evangelical Utopia

Every time you open your mouth for God, you are breaking out of the barracks into frontline battle. You are taking a risk for the sake of the Kingdom. I was once sitting on a plane, relaxing and enjoying the flight. There were only a few people on board, so I had plenty of room to spread out and do some writing. I had good food, cool water, a pillow, and a tray for my computer—happiness. It was a relief when no one sat next to me, so instead of getting into the "battle of the fear of man," I could sit in comfort. There are no bees on planes.

After about three hours, I went for a walk to the rest room, and on the way back to my seat, I passed a man in his late twenties who looked a little bored, so I gave him an I.Q. card. When he failed two different tests, I sat down next to him and told him that we fail because our eyes are easily fooled. Then I did a sleight-of-hand trick that widened his eyes. He did the spiritual I.Q. test on side two of the tract, and proved to be very open to the things of God, so I spent about twenty minutes witnessing to him. Then I prayed with him, that his conscience would remind him of his past sins, that he would see the seriousness of his transgression, and that the Lord would grant him light until he came to a point of peace with God. I also prayed that God would bless him and his family and keep them in health. We parted with a handshake, and his other hand filled with literature.

When you step out of the warmth of the barracks, you risk being shot down in flames of rejection. But when you leave a warm room to venture into the cold, how nice and cozy it seems when you get back. When I sat back down in my seat, I had the heart-warming knowledge that I had pleased God and done what I should as a Christian.

If you have a good day for the Lord by being a true and faithful witness, when you go to bed at night, you will glow. You will know that this was a day of victory for you and defeat for the devil, because you broke free from the shackles of the fear of man.

The Stubborn King

Think of how many times Jeremiah warned King Zedekiah about the coming judgment of God upon Israel. The King was party to personal warnings, as well as public. I have never taken the time to count, but I wouldn't be surprised if he was warned over a dozen times. The batteries were removed from the smoke detector of the king's conscience, and one day, he was trapped by the fire.

Look at what happened when judgment came:

"Then the king of Babylon killed the sons of Zedekiah before his eyes in Riblah . . . moreover he put out Zedekiah's eyes, and bound him with bronze fetters to carry him off to Babylon. And the Chaldeans burned the king's house with fire and the houses of the people with fire, and broke down the walls of Jerusalem" (Jeremiah 39:6-8).

I wonder what the king thought about as he stumbled in darkness, bound with chains. Perhaps his thoughts were of the last thing he saw—the unspeakable agony of seeing his own beloved sons butchered before his eyes. Perhaps the words of Jeremiah flashed before his tormented mind, warning him that all of Israel (including his sons) could have been saved if had he obeyed the voice of the Lord. We can't begin to imagine the remorse that he felt.

How this must typify the ungodly who have been bound by the bronze fetters of sin, "taken captive by the devil to do his will." We warn that there is Judgment

213

coming (both temporal and eternal) to those who live for the devil, but most remain in unbelief. Their master is he who came to "kill, steal and destroy." He blinds the minds of those who don't believe. Like Zedekiah, so many see their own sons and daughters die before their very eyes. AIDS, and other sin-related diseases, as well as alcohol, drugs and suicide, kill many before their time. Multitudes give themselves to the burning fires of sexual lust, and so the devil breaks down the walls of entire nations.

Yet, there is still time to warn them. There is still time to pray that God will open their understanding. God told Jeremiah to tell an Ethiopian called Ebed-Melech, that He would deliver him from judgment. He said, "'For I will surely deliver you, and you shall not fall by the sword; but your life shall be as a prize to you, because you have put your trust in Me,' says the Lord" (Jeremiah 39:18).

This is the message we are to deliver. He who keeps his life will lose it, but those that trust in the Lord will be safe on that Day. On the Day of Judgment, the sword of the Word of God will not fall upon him, because it fell on the Savior two thousand years ago.

The name Ebed-Melech means "servant of a king." Those who are servants of the King will be true to the commission given to them and will carry out His every command.

CHAPTER EIGHTEEN

HAND TO HAND COMBAT

" . . . lo, I am with you alway, even unto the end of the world" (Matthew 28:20).

I was able to get a license to preach in Santa Monica in Southern California for a year. That was too long for one sermon, so I broke it up to just one night a week. Each Friday night I would take a team to the Third Street Promenade—three blocks filled with thousands of people in an open mall setting.

One problem with open-air speaking is crowd control. If hecklers get to close to the preacher, the crowd tends to follow them. Instead of speaking to 150 people, you suddenly find yourself being shouted down by a dozen or so vocal people who stand 5-6 feet away.

This was a big problem in Santa Monica . . . until we put in a "heckler's microphone" on a stand, about 15 feet in front of the preacher. If someone spoke, we would encourage them to use the microphone and their distance from the preacher determined the diameter of the crowd. I have a "kill switch" under my foot on my soapbox. If they curse or get too upset, I quietly cut off their volume with a press of my foot.

We had good nights and bad nights. A bad night was when we didn't get good hecklers. A good heckler is someone who speaks with conviction. Take for instance the cigar-smoking, tatooed, fouled-mouth lesbian who insisted that she was a Christian. She said that she had been part of a missionary organization. As she was about to go on the field, she disclosed that she was a lesbian, and they therefore wouldn't allow her to be a missionary. That made her mad. When I told her that they did the right thing, she went berserk. The crowd suddenly doubled and listened to the Gospel. She was a *good* heckler.

Some time before that a very angry man approached me while I was speaking, and screamed, "There is no Law! *I knocked the Law out of the hands of Moses!* I am God! I will prove it to you!" Then he showed me the letters "Ki" carved into the flesh of the back of one of his hands, and "ll" in the other. Being educated, I put the letters together and came up with the word "Kill." I thought, "I know how to speak to this man . . . very gently."

This man thought that he was God, so I decided to ask him for his name. That was what Moses did. His name was Larry. Interesting. He seemed to calm down after I asked him for his name, so I said, "That's interesting. Why don't you go back into the crowd and listen for a while, and let me know what you think afterward." He then quietly turned around, and went back into the crowd.

One Friday night, for some reason no one from the team could make it, so I decided to go alone. For the previous six months "The Light Show" had given an inroad for the Gospel via "entertainment." People would stop to watch the show, and then stay and listen to me speak. Without the lights, it was just straight Gospel. I drove the 30 miles by myself, then set up to speak. From the moment I opened my mouth, there was strong opposition. In fact, if there is such a thing as a spirit of "nasty," it was there that night.

The Bible makes it clear that when a nation gives itself to darkness, it hates the light. When Paul preached to the Thessalonians he said "We were bold in our God to speak unto you the Gospel of God with much contention . . . " (1 Thessalonians 2:2) There certainly was "much contention" that Friday night in Santa Monica. The crowd threw things at me, told me to shut up and go away. Twice they pulled the plug out of my amplifier, despite the fact that I had a permit to use it. Someone even ran off with it behind my back. I didn't realize it had been stolen until a Christian returned with it under his arm. He had chased the thief down, and retrieved it from him.

Numbers of professing Christians told me that I was wrong to speak about sin. They said that I should be preaching the Gospel *inside* the Church. Others passed me notes saying that Jesus' followers just preached "love." One angry man stood about ten feet in front of me with a very hard-looking lemon. He pulled his hand back, gritted his teeth and threatened to throw it at me if I dared mentioned Jesus. He was as bitter as the lemon he was holding! People in the crowd began urging him to throw it. He said that I could talk about God, but not about Jesus. I was standing on a soapbox and felt rather vulnerable, so I decided I could accommodate the man for a few minutes by saying that God gave the Ten Commandments to humanity. But there was no way I could get past the Seventh Commandment without mentioning Jesus. By the time

I got to the Cross, he had peeled half the lemon as he listened, which greatly pleased me as a semi-peeled lemon looks much more preacher-friendly than a whole one. He didn't throw it, but stepped forward and took his anger out on my amplifier. I was pleased that Santa Monica doesn't have loose rocks on the ground.

As I continued to speak, innocent-looking young girls shouted filthy obscenities. After some time, someone complained to the police about the preaching. I was told later that they had tested to see if I was speaking below the decibel limit. It seems that I was within the legal limit. Still, they made me switch locations.

For some reason, people in the crowd accused me of being a homosexual. One young man stormed off in anger because I had said that as a Christian I didn't lie or steal. Another older and very angry man screamed at me and insisted on giving me *his* version of the One Way sign. Another man, who was even angrier, didn't like that I said that Mother Theresa said that she needed Jesus as her Savior. He stood in front of me with his hand under his jacket and spitting out the usual colorful language, he accused me of blasphemy, and threatened to "blow" me away. He looked like he really meant what he said, so I said out loud that it was against the law to threaten to kill people, and that made him back off.

In all my years of open-air preaching, I have never encountered such concentrated hostility toward the Gospel. After I had finished speaking, a Christian excitedly asked if I would be back the next week. I said that I would, but I wasn't as enthusiastic as I could have been. After two hours of preaching, it is easy to become discouraged in the face of such focused and bitter opposition. I couldn't help but think of the scripture, "Marvel not if the world hates you," etc.

As I left, a man accompanied me back to my van. He said, "Not many people preach the whole counsel of God nowadays," and stuffed $500 in $20 bills into my hand. When I got home, I checked my shirt pocket and found that someone else had given me a $100 gift.

I am so pleased that we have passages such as Jeremiah chapter 9. The poor man was in the midst of a nation that had turned its back on God. Part of him wanted to run from such a sinful people, and part of him wept for them. He didn't run away and live a monistic existence. He stayed and warned them until the last minute, that God meant what He said.

Standing in the Gap

"You missed it. Arnold Schwarzenegger and his wife just walked by." As I stood in the Promenade, it was understandable that I had missed them, as hundreds of people walk by every few minutes. I said to the man that had just spoken to me, "I'm going to give them a tract." I grabbed a couple of our Titanic tracts (which always goes down well) and ran along the mall. I knew that it was biblical for wise men to follow stars.

As I stopped in the open mall, there was a sense of excitement among the people as they peered into the well-known "Gap" clothing store. I walked through the doorway and waited for a moment. There I was, *standing in the gap* for Arnold Schwarzenegger. Suddenly the couple appeared in front of me. I had given out thousands of tracts, so this would be a breeze. What an opportunity! I was about to give a Gospel tract to one of the biggest names in Hollywood

(Schwarzenegger). I reached out my experienced hand and used my line that never fails. I confidently asked, *"Did you get one of these?"*

As I reached out my hand, Arnold looked at me as though I was some kind of nut. Then he said in his deep, accented voice, "No!" I could tell by his hand gesture that I had struck an iceberg. My heart sank. I held back from saying, "Take it you wimp . . . " (I was in such a hurry, I forgot to take the time to greet him first).

Unbeknown to me, other members of our team were also involved in a star search. Rick had sat down at a computer that had been placed in the store for the customer's convenience. Suddenly, Arnold's wife, Maria Shriver, sat down next to him and asked what the computers were for. As Rick explained that they were for customers to look up merchandise, two other members of our team showed up and said, "We can't find Arnold Schwarzenegger anywhere!" Rick then told them that he was sitting next to Arnold's wife and said, "He'll be back."

Maria looked at Jordan, the eight year-old team member and said, "Who's this?" Rick said, "He's a young preacher who has just spoken in the promenade." For the previous two weeks, Jordan had been practicing a seven minute oration on the authenticity of the Bible, and that night, he had made his debut and spoken twice. Maria asked him what he talked about. It was fresh in his young mind, so for the next four minutes, Jordan spoke of the trustworthiness of the Bible, of its incredible continuity, its historical accuracy, etc. She was so impressed, when hubby did come back she said, "Listen to this, Babe," and had the eight year-old go through a summary of what he had just told her. Arnold too was very impressed. He said the equivalent of , "This has been a very interesting night."

Maria took one of our tracts, and carefully put it in her bag. As they left, Jordan called out "Hasta la vista baby," to which Arnold flinched . . . just a little. He had probably heard that line once or twice before.

Shortly after that incident, Terry, a member of our team was approached by a bearded gentleman, as he gave out the Titanic tract. The man then left with a smile on his face, clutching the "collectible" tract in his hand. His name was James Cameron, producer and director of the blockbuster movie "Titanic."

Eat at Al's?

There were two men who owned restaurants. The name of one of the men was Evan. His restaurant was situated at the top of a high hill. Admittedly, it was hard to get to, but the cuisine was well worth it. His customers were full of praise for him, even saying that his food was "divine." His promise was "good food for the hungry soul." There was one stipulation. His patrons had to wear clean clothing, such a demand was reasonable.

The second man's name was Al. It was easy to get to his restaurant. There was no high hill to climb. In fact, it was downhill all the way to his door. Neither did you have to change clothing in order to be served. It was "Come as you are."

Al boasted of infamous patrons such as Jack Kevorkian, Richard Ramirez and Jeffrey Dahmer, just to name a few. He insisted that he was the one who fed them their dreams.

His desserts were said to be delectable . . . temptations that overwhelmed his guests. His greatest dish was called "Eternity." Once his customers had tasted that dish, they were his forever. There were strong rumors from a reliable source that the restaurant was owned by the rich and powerful DeVille family.

The restaurant on the hill also had a famous dish. It was bitter at first taste, but then turned unspeakably sweet. It was called "Evan's gift." Those who tasted Evan's gift vowed that there was nothing on earth like it.

Anyone could eat at either restaurant, but there was one warning. Those who ate at Al's would forever have the bitter taste of remorse, those who ate at Evan's would never taste of death. Evan or Al, the choice was theirs.

CHAPTER NINETEEN

THE BATTLE OF EXHALATION

"Who shall separate us from the love of Christ? Shall tribulation, or distress, or persecution, or famine, or nakedness, or peril, or sword?" (Romans 8:35).

As I flew over the city of Des Moines in Iowa, I could see snow on the ground, something fascinating for someone coming directly from the Southern Californian climate. As soon as I arrived at Teen Challenge in the city of Colfax, I sent a cold fax to Sue, saying it was a cool 31 degrees. Freezing though it was, I was ushered into a warm guest room. In fact, my room was so warm I awoke in the night with intense thirst. Fortunately, I had opened the first of the double windows and placed a bottle of sparkling, "natural" flavored mineral water in the cooler air for such a time as this.

I reached out into the blackness of the night, and unscrewed the lid. Suddenly, I found myself beneath a fountain of cool mineral water, as it burst from the bottle. The cold weather plus the movement of my hand picking up the bottle, had been enough to stir the contents to a frenzy. It was quite an outburst.

God sometimes puts His children out in the cold for a reason. Moses had great desire to be a deliverer, but

God put him on the shelf for forty years. He knows that the pressure of desire is building within the vessel of those that love Him. All it will take is for Him to shake the Christian, just a little, then release the cap of that which is hindering the living waters from flowing out into this dark world.

Never be discouraged by the thought that God has put you on the shelf for no reason. If you love God and are called according to His purposes, then whatever is happening to you, is happening for your good (see Romans 8:28). He is working in you to will and do of His good pleasure.

I once spoke at a church where the pastor was very zealous for the lost. A year later, I returned to the area to find out that the man's wife had run off with a lesbian who had been fellowshiping at a local church. She had also taken most of their household contents as well as his credit cards, running them to the limit, and leaving him $15,000 in debt. As if that wasn't enough, a few members of his church didn't like the fact that this had happened, and began murmuring to a point where he was forced to resign from his office. He found himself out in the cold.

It seemed God had put him on the shelf, but within one year, God had taken him in His Hand and released him back into ministry. He was part of a new work in another state.

The time will come when God will fully release the restraint. At that time I'm sure that many will be showered in times of refreshing from the presence of the Lord, because of the result of the pressure that dear brother went through. God only shakes the Christian for the furtherance of His purposes. The world suffers in vain, we suffer for our own profit and for the profit of the world—if we are "exercised" by whatever experience God takes us through. When the devil seeks to sour our hearts by putting bitterness in our minds, faith will not let that happen. The man who trusts in God says, "Though He slay me, yet will I praise Him."

I once finished ministering, and longing for a place to rest, could see only one chair at the back of the church. It was blocking the entrance of the recording booth and had a sign draped over it saying, "Do not enter." Of course no one in his right mind would sit on a chair with a sign on it.

As I stood up after about five minutes of resting my weary body in the chair, a young man (very apologetically) said, "You have the words 'Do not enter' written on your back." The sign had been written in eye-liner and was now embedded in black on my white shirt.

One fiery dart that Satan loves to discharge at the Christian, is the dart of bitterness. The pastor who found himself seemingly stripped of everything, still has on the armor of God. No one could take away his shield of faith from him—he could stand, and having done all, continue to stand. However, it has been pointed out that there is no provision for the back of the Christian. The enemy needs to know that he will find the shield of faith in the way of a direct frontal attack, and a 'Do not enter' notice, if he tries to enter subtly through some back door. God left Joseph simmering in a prison for thirteen years. He was bound in chains, and it seemed he would have had every right to become bitter toward Potiphar and his sex-starved wife, and his brothers, as well as toward God. But faith wouldn't let that happen. Bitterness didn't find an entry into his heart, even through the rear door.

Joseph's life has great lessons for the Christian. Not only is it a hidden type of the life of Jesus, but it carries within it instruction, direction, and encouragement.

I have often wondered if Joseph did the right thing in telling his brothers of his dreams. Even his father was upset upon hearing them. Human nature is such an unstable thing, it doesn't take much to stir jealousy within the heart. Knowing my own heart, I am careful to whom I boast of some of the good things God does for me. I would hate to cause another Christian to stumble in any way, because of unwise words on my part. But young Joseph insisted on telling his brothers, and it stirred a unified murderous spirit that almost cost him his life.

Sometimes we have no choice. When we come to a knowledge of salvation, we must speak that which we know to be true. To our friends and family, we sound as though we have had but idle dreams. They, like the brothers of Joseph become stirred by the god of this world, and because of the reproach of Christ and the offense of the Cross, direct hatred at us. God however, moves in the life of the Christian, as He did in the life of Joseph. We find ourselves being lifted to places of responsibility. He found himself as a trusted servant in the household of Potiphar. When things were going good for Joseph, one lusty lady enters the scene. This was a sinner's dream, contrived in the cunning minds of Hell's residents. She whispered, "Stolen water is sweet, and bread eaten in secret is pleasant." She personifies the seduction of sin as it whispers into the mind of the Christian. Don't listen to her voice! Cry out to God to uncover her wickedness. Plead for Him to make her sweet lips odious to your ears. Ask the Father to make the candy-coated taste of lust, bitter to your pallet. Resist sin, and be steadfast in the faith. Say with Joseph, to the seductive voice of lust, "How could I do this thing and sin against God!"

Look at the spirit that motivated Potiphar's wife. When Joseph didn't yield, she showed how much she really cared, unleashing her acidic heart when he rejected her advances. It was the same spirit that used Judas for its insidious purpose. Once it had used him, it cast him aside.

So Joseph found himself in prison because he chose to do the right thing. In a world that loves sin, those who stand for righteousness will suffer. In doing so, they may receive a frown from the world, but they have the smile of God. "Blessed are those who are persecuted for righteousness' sake, for theirs is the Kingdom of Heaven."

If you are faithful in small things, God will trust you with bigger things. Late in 1992, I received a call from a pastor in Texas, in whose church I was to speak. He had been trying to get me into a large Bible school called "Christ For The Nations," with whom I had had no previous contact. They were booked up with speakers for the next two years, and it didn't seem very hopeful. I called them and found out who was in charge. The top man, Dennis Lindsey was on vacation and his mother whose name was Freda, was in charge. I found their fax number and began writing a letter to fax to them, stressing the importance of the teaching I wished to share.

I had written "Dear Freda," and three paragraphs, when the phone rang. A voice said: "Hello, I'm calling from Israel. I have just heard your 'Hell's Best Kept Secret' teaching on tape. My name is Shira, my mother and father's names are Gordon and Freda Lindsey, and my mother runs *Christ For The Nations* in Dallas, Texas. This teaching is so vital, I am going to send my mother a fax and ask her to have you speak there."

I couldn't believe it. I had the fax on the screen in front of me, with her mother's name already written. God's timing was perfect for me, and His timing will be perfect for you . . . all in His time. In the meantime, don't sit and do nothing. Prove your worth. If you go out to witness and you come back miserable because nobody listened or things didn't go the way you planned, you haven't failed. You are proving that you do care. Look on tough times as "attitude tests."

In the mid-80's I flew from New Zealand to spend a few days in Los Angeles. I knew that God wanted me to share the teaching in the U.S., and here I was. I organized a meeting, did some publicity and showed up with another brother at the church in which I was to hold the Saturday morning seminar. See if you can guess how many people showed up? No one. *Not a soul.* Zilch. If a handful had shown up, I would have been disappointed. When *no one* came I knew God's hand was in it. We quickly shut the doors and left, rejoicing in the knowledge that God had given me direction. I had the right message, *but the wrong timing.* God's timing came about five years later. When it came, I didn't have to *push* open doors. He opened them for me.

Fighting Prejudice

A friend once called and asked if I would be interested in getting into a business selling "high tech" personal alarms. He sent me the literature, an alarm, and tapes showing the company's credibility. I was convinced that it could be a way for my eldest son to make a living, but to make sure, I decided to test the product myself. I put on some dressy clothes, a striking tie, and began to beat the sidewalk of our local boulevard.

The experience was horrible. Almost everyone, as soon as they saw I was selling a product, took that as a license to treat me as if I was a con-man. If I was buying something, then I deserved courtesy, but because I was selling, there was immediate impatience, intolerance and prejudice. Almost every manager with whom I spoke had the presupposition that I was out to hoodwink them. The experience reminded me of the fact that most of us are very prejudiced. We judge people on how they look, the clothes they wear, the style of their hair, and even by the car they drive. Even as Christians, we can be prejudiced. I heard of a pastor of a large church, who sat down with his staff and said, "We are going to watch a video I disagree with," as he switched on our *"Hell's Best Kept Secret"* teaching. After the screening, he said, "I would just like to say, that I agree with everything on that video." His limited and second-hand knowledge had shaped prejudice in his heart. Once he understood the basis of the teaching, he was able to accept it as legitimate.

Unregenerate contemporary humanity is bent on prejudice when it comes to the things of God. Their limited knowledge leaves them with a prejudicial attitude. They have been programmed into thinking that we are fanatical, religious "fundamentalists." However, if they only knew what we have in Christ, if they could only have the light of understanding about the issues of eternity, they would listen with bated breath. This is why our first contact with an unsaved person is so important. We can't let them justify their prejudice. While we speak to them on a natural level, they should be feeling the warmth of a genuine sincere heart. Then, when they find that we are Christians, they should be saying within their minds, "This person is different." These first few minutes are a time to establish basics in both speaking and listening.

The following are listed by a group called Media Management as the ten most annoying mistakes made while listening. For business, it can mean a loss of money, but in the Kingdom of God, it can mean that we are not as good a witness as we could be. We should strive not to fall into these errors and confirm their prejudice:

1. Lack of eye contact.
2. Disagreeing with everything said.
3. Holding side conversations.
4. Correcting grammar or word choices.
5. Answering before the question is finished.
6. Not responding.
7. Bad breath or sitting too close.
8. Completing speaker's sentences.
9. Coughing or clearing throat.
10. Interrupting.

Most of us don't listen very carefully. Take for instance the camera crew who took a camera to the streets and asked a number of people what they would do if they found that their best friend was a "homosapian." A number of people said, they "would never speak to him again!"

Notice also that the first thing on the list is "eye contact." Of all the people on the earth who should be able to look the world in the eye, it is Christians, because we are speaking the Gospel truth. There is no ulterior motive—we are not selling anything, all we are "after" is the person's eternal well-being.

For some time, I was a regular guest on an interesting radio talkshow called "Religion on the Line." The two-hour show had a Catholic priest, a Protestant minister, and a Rabbi as guests each week.

Once Sue and I arrived at the studio, we were let in by the security guard, and as we signed the necessary

230

forms, he asked, "How was church today?" I told him it was good, and asked if he was a Christian. He said he was one once, but had fallen away from his faith. I told him that the thing to get him back to the faith was a look at the Ten Commandments. I asked him if he had lied. He had, so I said, "What does that make you?" He hedged by saying, "A story-teller." I smiled and said, "Come on . . . what does that make you?" He said, "A liar." He had also stolen, and was therefore a thief. But when I asked him if he had ever broken the Seventh Commandment by lusting after a woman, he said he had never done it. I didn't believe him, so when his eyes looked down in conviction, I put my hand on his to get back his eye contact and said, "Now be honest." His eyes then sparkled, and he said, "I'm gay." It was then that *I* lost eye contact. *I was holding his hand!* Sometimes things don't go the way you planned.

That incident reminded me of a time I was in the heart of San Francisco. As I sat down and opened up my lunch, I smiled and said to the gentleman a few feet away from me, "Would you like a sandwich?" He smiled back, conveyed that he didn't, but said, "I'd like to buy *you* something though." I smiled and said, "No thanks." Then he said, "I *really* would like to buy you something." I stopped smiling and firmly said, "No thanks." Then he stood up, left and returned a few minutes later with some food for me. I didn't feel like eating anymore.

I'm not homophobic. Someone who is homo-*phobic* is *scared* of homosexuals. I'm not scared *of* them, I'm scared *for* them, that's why I take the time to witness to them and warn them that they, as well as all humanity, need to flee from the wrath to come.

The other annoyances on the Media Management list are reasonably obvious, except number seven. Ask any preacher who has had to endure a time of counseling at an altar call, and he will confirm that when Adam fell, so did his breath. I have had to counsel people while standing sideways as though I wanted them to speak into my ear, when I was really hiding my nose. I have even rubbed my nose while listening to people in an effort to protect the delicate instrument. It should be the sinner of whom it is written "Their throat is an open sepulcher," not the Christian. People shouldn't think of Lazarus when the Christian opens his mouth.

I remember sitting in a plane listening to a man give his life story. His breath made an open sepulcher seem like the fragile scent of a rose. Time seemed to stand still. He had morning breath in the afternoon. I kept eyeing the emergency door, and fully expected the other passengers in the plane to have pulled down their oxygen masks to get relief. *Pointing out the breath-taking view didn't even help.* This man was a walking insect repellant. When he bit into an apple, I thought there would be a burst of applause from the captain, the crew and all those on board. In my heart I was saying, "Thank you Lord, O thank you Lord."

CHAPTER TWENTY

BATTLE-READY

"But sanctify the Lord God in your hearts: and be ready always to give an answer to every man that asketh you a reason of the hope that is in you with meekness and fear" (1 Peter 3:15).

It was early in the new year of 1993, and the mall in which Sue and I strolled was comparatively quiet after the busy Christmas rush. So when we entered a store, a young man said, "Hi folks. How are you doing?" The cynical thought entered my mind, "You really mean—'Hi folks, I couldn't care less how you're doing. All I want from you is your money.'" Then he said, "If you have any questions, feel free to ask them."

I waited for about ten seconds, strolled across to the counter and said, "I have a question. What is the meaning of life?" He didn't hesitate for a second, but said, "The meaning of life, is to live it to the fullest." I said, "That's what you *do* with life, but what is its *purpose*?" He was stumped, so I said, "If you are not a Christian, life is utterly futile, because death will take your life from you, no matter how full it is." He agreed, and said, "That's true, death is the only sure thing in this life."

God has given all of us a will to live. The Bible lets us know that all of us are under the power of the fear of death, until we come to the Savior (Hebrews 2:15). The human heart longs for immortality, or at least longevity.

I told the man in the store that the only two things that are sure in life, are death and Judgment Day, and gave him a penny with the Ten Commandments stamped onto it. I then said that the Law was the standard of judgment, that we've all broken it, and that we all need the Savior. He agreed, and we parted in good spirits. That three-minute conversation put the "eternal" into a transitory stroll through the mall. I didn't go out especially to witness, I was just ready for any opportunity if it came along. My mind was programmed to stay battle-ready.

In recent years I have made sure that I have the attitude that I don't go to the mall to buy clothes. I go to give out tracts, and I get some clothes while I'm there. I don't go to the supermarket to buy food. I go to give out some tracts, and while I'm there I get some food. This is true "life-style" evangelism.

The Found "Link"

A friend who works as an animal control officer, came by my home for a visit. As we were talking, he said he had an animal in the back of his truck that would be an excellent evangelistic tool for me. My mind rushed through a jungle of animals in anticipation. Was it a snake, to illustrate the subtleties of the devil? Was it an elephant to portray the weight of God's Law? I hoped it would be a monkey, something I have wanted for years. Sue says we have had three children, and that should keep me happy, but a monkey would have so much potential for open-air preaching. I would dress him in blue shorts with suspenders, a red shirt, white socks and sneakers. I would train him to give out tracts to the crowd, springboarding off him into Darwin's theory-tale. I would name the chimp "Link." I could say that I finally found what evolution called the "missing link."

As Steve opened up the side of his truck, suddenly I saw the animal he had in mind. It was a skunk! I jumped back, then immediately ran inside to get Sue. Perhaps if I said I wanted a skunk, she would lean more easily toward a chimp. I used a similar principle to get our first bird. I went into a pet store and suggested we buy a big fat white rabbit. She said, "What do you want that for!" So I said, "How about a little bird then?" and she said, "Alright, just a little bird." If you want a dog, first propose getting a horse. If you want a horse—an elephant, etc.

When Sue came out to the truck with me, I saw something I hadn't seen before. The skunk was stuffed. It looked alive, but it was as dead as a dead door-knob. I felt a little stupid, but quickly picked it up and ran to show my daughter Rachel, who was on the phone. She thought it was real and screamed. In fact, she almost lifted the roof off the house. It seemed the deceased skunk could raise as much, if not more of a stink, dead, than it did alive.

When Jesus lay in the tomb, He was dead. Death had laid its icecold hand upon His body. His skin was drained of color. His heart sat like a cold rock within His breast. His cold fingers lay still and stiff. Suddenly, deep within the heart of the Son of God came a beat...one beat whose implications resounded blessed hope throughout the whole earth. Another heart beat followed, and then another. Within seconds, color began to return to the flesh of the Messiah. His stiffened fingers began to move, His chest raised as He breathed air into His still lungs. *Life broke the steel bands of death from the body of the Son of the Living God.* Just as four words from the mouth of the Creator had caused light to flood the universe in the beginning, so, in this new beginning, light had flooded the dark tomb. *It was not possible that death could hold Him!*

Death, the stinking skunk that it was, is now dead. In fact, it is more than dead. Its very guts were torn from its body. Now, death is but a stuffed beast, and like Steve's skunk, can only scare those who lack the understanding that it is lifeless:

"Death is swallowed up in victory. O Death, where is your sting? O Hades, where is your victory? The sting of death is sin, and the strength of sin is the Law" (1 Corinthians 15:54-55).

The wages of sin is death. Jesus paid the full wages of the Law's demands on the Cross. He "redeemed us from the curse of the Law, being made a curse for us." He satisfied the Court of Eternal Justice, now the prison doors swing wide open for those held captive by Satan to do his will.

I was preaching at a fabricated funeral in Colorado. As I stood on a soapbox in front of six pallbearers and a (living) corpse, which (who) was covered by a white sheet, about 150 people stood and listened to the good news that death had been conquered in Christ. Suddenly, the crowd began laughing. I turned around and saw a very small child sitting on the corpse! While most who watched the funeral stood wide-eyed in the face of death, this toddler rested himself on the corpse, as though it were nothing but another of life's everyday experiences.

Those who fully understand the victory wrought on the Cross, and the triumph of the resurrection, refuse to fear death. They, like the child, see no threat. It is but an empty hand grenade, a defused bomb, a stuffed skunk. It is no threat to them, nor does it have any power over them. Death is under their feet through faith in Jesus Christ. It is but a dark door with a golden handle, that opens to the pure and brilliant light of eternal joy.

How unspeakably tragic that the world doesn't know what we have found in Jesus Christ. God forbid that life should pass us by while we are building a Kingdom that *can* be moved. If the Lord tarries, we will find that old age will hinder us from doing exploits for God that are a breeze to the young. It is fine for the elderly to be young at heart, but the heart needs a body that can move. May He use our eyes to see the harvest, while we can still see. May He use our ears to hear the cries of the lost, while we can still hear. May He use our mouths while we can still speak, our hands to reach out to the unsaved, and our feet to carry to them the Gospel of peace.

You Snooze, You Lose

The early Church had a shortage of people to wait on tables. That legitimate ministry was being neglected, so they had to *commission* people to do so. Stephen was one that was hand-picked to wait on tables, but he couldn't remain serving within the confines of the Church. His fire couldn't be contained. Stephen was full of the Holy Spirit. The Zeal of God's House had eaten him up. He had food to eat that most of us don't know of. He had to preach in the open air.

Nowadays we have many who kindly wait on tables. Nowadays it is the Great Commission that is being neglected. When the fire of the Holy Spirit moves on the Church, it must go open-air. Our Father's business is to seek and save that which is lost. A church on fire cannot stay in the Upper Room, even if it does so under the guise of legitimate "Church business".

The Bible tells us that there was a young man named Eutychus. He had the privilege of hearing the Apostle Paul expound the Word of God. He was in an "upper room" where we are told that there were many lights. It was near midnight. As the young man sat in a window, sleep fell upon him and he fell down from the third story and was killed. He was gone—dead. He probably broke his neck, which was not a problem. Paul raised him from the dead, then carried on teaching.

Eutychus had some good excuses for snoozing off:

1. Paul's sermon was long.
2. The "lights" no doubt made the room hot.
3. He was a young man up until midnight.
4. He was "overcome" by sleep.

It is the midnight hour. We sit on the window of eternity. We can fall into eternity in a heartbeat. If the stale air of this world's influence makes us sink into a sleep of apathy, we must seek refreshing from the presence of the Lord. When our Christian life seems to be a dry and lifeless sermon without end, and the joy of feeding on God's Word is no longer in our hearts, we must get on our knees and return to our first love.

Jesus found his disciples "sleeping for sorrow" when they should have been praying (see Luke 22:45). That was before the fire of God's spirit made them new creatures in Christ. That was before they understood the reason for Gethsemany and Calvary. They slept in ignorance. We have no excuse! We know why Jesus had to suffer! We know that there is a gospel to preach!

Just a Comic

I can recall speaking to a man who totally rejected the Bible as having any worth. Besides that, he was sure that it was not possible that any human being could understand its message. He told me that monks had been studying it for hundreds of years, and not even their learned minds could interpret its words, so how could any man "off the street" understand the Scriptures? When I informed him that that was why he needed the Holy Spirit to lead him into all truth, he said he didn't believe in the Holy Spirit—"just in God."

As he puffed on his cigarette, he spoke of the sins of other Christians, used God's name in vain, and told me that he went to church every week and confessed his sins. Then he said that all we need to do was follow the Ten Commandments. So, we went through the Law. He admitted that he had stolen ("just a comic" when he was young). He also acknowledged that he had lied (when he was young), but when I said that God considered lust to be the same as adultery, he recoiled. It was one sin he didn't confine to his youth. That touched a raw nerve. He said there is nothing wrong with lust . . . if "you don't dwell on it for too long." Now here is a strange thing. Lust is OK for a time, but the duration of time in which a man lusts, turns it from purity to iniquity. The god he believed in was obviously not the God of the Bible. When I asked him what his name was, he told me it was "Art." Suddenly it made sense. Here was another case of idolatry. His was another god, "graven by art and man's device."

Of course the Bible is a hard book to understand . . . until we are born of the Spirit. There are many passages in Scripture that don't make any sense at all to the unregenerate. If a sinner is seeking salvation, he may read the words of Jesus to the rich young ruler and end up in error:

> "If you want to be perfect, go, sell what you have and give to the poor, and you shall have treasure in Heaven; and come, follow Me" (Matthew 19:21).

It seems clear—straight from the mouth of the Master. To get to Heaven all a man has to do is sell what he has, give to the poor and then "follow" Jesus. But then he turns to Ephesians 2:8-9 and reads:

"For by Grace you have been saved through faith, and that not of yourselves, it is the gift of God, not of works, lest anyone should boast."

Those who are not born of the Spirit will understandably end up in the State of Confusion. The Chinese language sounds very strange to me. I don't know how it can make sense to anyone. Yet a four-year old Chinese child can understand it completely. Why? Because he has been born into a Chinese family. The Chinese language is not darkness, but light to him. The language of scripture will be nothing but babble to those who are not born into the family of God. The natural man receives not the things of the Spirit of God, neither can he know them, they are foolishness to him, because they are spiritually understood. He must be born of the Spirit, into the family of God, to understand spiritual things.

Nobody Understands

A pastor friend of mine often takes teams to rock concerts to give out tracts. He designs literature with the group's lyrics on the front. He then uses them as a springboard to answer the questions on the inside, then moves through the Law into Grace.

In April of 1993, he took a team to a "Guns 'n' Roses" concert, and handed out a tract with the lyrics from their hit "Dead Horse" on the front:

"Nobody understands, quite why we're here, we're searching for answers that never appear . . . "

He and his team walked the long lines of people boldly saying what the authorities at the concert were saying: "No alcohol, no drugs, no cans or bottles." As they did so, they gave out tracts.

When the pastor arrived home, he found a message on his answering machine. It was from Mr. Rose, and he was blooming red-faced mad. He introduced himself and then said:

"How dare you blankity-blanks give out your blankity-blank, blankity-blank at my blankity-blank concert. You have a blankity-blank nerve using my blankity-blank lyrics on your blankity-blank!" Click!

Had he dropped his four letter words, his message would have been two-seconds long.

The next day, the pastor found another message on his machine. This one was much longer, and it was from a young lady at the concert who had come to the Lord directly as a result of the tract. Her voice was soft and sincere as she spoke words of appreciation, that they cared enough to break away from their barracks to go to the front line of the concert to reach out to the lost. I'm sure the pastor would gladly face the thorny rebuke of ten thousand roses, if it meant the salvation of even a single soul.

In 1993, I was invited to speak at Yale University. I was excited because of the opportunity to speak at a university with such a reputation, and, I learned, a godly heritage. I found out that 78% of the first graduates went into the ministry, and that famous Christians of the last century, such as David Brainard and Jonathan Edwards, who preached America's most famous sermon, "Sinners in the Hands of an Angry God" were students there.

When we arrived, a zealous young man named Brian gave me a tour. He showed me the poster advertising homosexual activities, on the chaplain's door of the divinity school. He pointed out that of the 240 students in the "divinity" school, only about 10% were Christians. I saw drinking fountains with "If any man thirst, let him come to me and drink" engraved into them, and doors with Bible verses cut into the wood. Posters advertised student orgies in the "Brainard underground," and others announced homosexual activities on campus, all with the chaplain's blessing. Divinity professors put themselves above Holy Scripture as they sat in cynical judgment over it, rather than letting Scripture judge them.

As we looked at the heritage of the university, I noticed a party of children, all around 11 years old, standing in the grounds of the university. They seemed to be a tour party who were having a break from the tour. I approached them with one of our I.Q. test tracts, then did some sleight-of-hand. Before I knew it, I was surrounded by 80 children, and preached to them for 10-15 minutes. When one of them recited most of the Ten Commandments by memory, I gave him a few dollars as a reward. This seemed to get the attention of the rest, who not only listened, but almost fought over tracts when I finished speaking to them.

That afternoon, I set up a soapbox in front of about 20 students who were lazing on the grass, studying. Most of them didn't appreciate my presence, and a few began heckling with conviction enough to enlarge the crowd to about 80 students. I was thrilled because I had heard that, even though 96% of mainstream America believes

---

[10]Many times I have seen the Commandments slam a hardened rebel against the wall and point their great cannons at his face. I have seen his reaction as he feels the cold steel of the pistol of conscience against the warm flesh of his head. His mouth is stopped by the Law and he

in God, this is down to 65% at "ivy league" universities such as Yale. When an atheist denied God's existence, I began to reason with him about how I could prove His existence. As he listened, it was as though a light came on in his eyes.

How to Speak With an Atheist

It is important to take someone who professes to be an atheist through the Commandments, *before* you mention the things of God. When you ask him if he has kept the Ten Commandments, you are not asking for his belief in God, or of the existence of Hell, so initially, the subject of his beliefs probably won't arise. When you give him a tract, a penny pressed with the Commandments, or mention something to do with spiritual things, just ask,[10] "Do you think that you have kept the Ten Commandments?" Most think that they have, and will say something like, "Pretty much. I haven't killed anyone." Then say, "Let's go through them." Don't ask if you may, just quickly follow with, "Have you ever told a lie?" Most will admit to telling a lie—or a fib, or a "white lie." Then ask, "What does that make you?" If they have trouble saying the word *liar*, help them by gently saying "What would you call *me* if I told lies?" They will usually say, "A liar." Smile and say "That's it!"

Ask now if they have ever stolen anything. If they say "No," smile and say, "Come on . . . you've just admitted to me that you are a liar. Have you ever stolen something . . . *even if it's small*." Most will then say, "Yes." Then say, "Jesus said that if you look with lust,

---

listens to his only hope of salvation. For years I longed for other Christians to somehow be able to witness the power of the Law. Early in 1997, God gave me my heart's desire. We captured a powerful sequence on camera in an interview with a young man in Seal Beach, California. The video is called, "The Hollywood Perspective."

you commit adultery in your heart. Have you ever done that?" When the answer is "Yes," say, "By your own admission, you are a lying, thieving, adulterer-at-heart—and we've only looked at three of the Ten Commandments. There's another seven we haven't even looked at."

Then say "On Judgment Day, when God judges you by the standard of His Law, do you think that you will be innocent or guilty?" Most will say, "Guilty," but when you ask if he thinks he will go to Heaven or Hell, he will more than likely grab his most powerful weapon and confidently say, "I don't believe in God, or Hell." That's when you say, "That doesn't matter. You still have to face God on Judgment Day *whether you believe in Him or not.* If I step onto the freeway and there is a massive truck heading for me, and I say, *I don't believe in trucks,* my lack of belief isn't going to change realities." His most powerful weapon has no ammunition.

Then tell him that he has *already* admitted to you that he is a lying, thieving, adulterer-at-heart, and that God gave him a conscience so that he would know right from wrong. His conscience and the conviction of the Holy Spirit will do the rest.

That's why it is essential to draw out an admission of guilt *before* you mention God, Judgment Day or the existence of Hell.

Why There are no True Atheists

"There is no God!" as an *absolute* statement. For an absolute statement to be true, I need absolute knowledge. For example, if I said, "There is no gold in China," for the statement to be true, I need to *know* that there is no gold in China. I must have knowledge as to what is in every rock, what's under the soil, in every riverbed, because if there is a speck of gold, my statement is untrue.

If I say, "There is no God!" I need *absolute* knowledge for the statement to be true. I need to *know* that there is no God. I need to be omniscient.

How to Make an Atheist "Backslide"

Ask your listener if he professes to be omniscient—if he has "all knowledge." If he is reasonable, he will say "No." Then draw a circle and say, "Let's say that this circle represents all the knowledge in the universe. Let's imagine that you possess and incredible one percent of all the knowledge in the universe. Is it possible, in the ninety-nine percent of the knowledge you haven't yet come across, that there is ample evidence to prove that God does exist?" Again, if he is reasonable he will be forced to say, "With the limited knowledge I have at present, I have come to the conclusion that there is no God, but I really don't know." Therefore, he is not an "atheist," but an "agnostic." He doesn't know if there is a God.

How to *Prove* the Existence of God

When I look at a building, how do I know that there was a builder? I can't see him, hear him, touch, taste, or smell him. What *proof* is there that the builder did exist? If the person you are speaking to has a working brain he will say something like, "The *building* is obvious proof that there was a builder." You couldn't want better proof that there was a builder, than to have the building in front of you! (This same deep, rich, intellectual, scientific principle can be used with paintings and painters. When I look at a painting, how can I be sure that there was a painter? The paint*ing* is absolute proof that there was a paint*er*. I couldn't want better proof that there was a painter, than to have the painting in front of me!).

I don't need faith to believe in a builder, all I need is eyes that can see and a brain that works—"For every house is builded by some man; But He that built all things is God" (Hebrews 4:3). Exactly the same applies with the existence of God. I don't need faith to believe in a Creator, all I need is eyes that can see and a brain that works: "For the invisible things of Him from the creation of the world *are clearly seen*, being *understood* by the things that are made, even His eternal power and Godhead; so that they are without excuse" (Romans 1:20, italics added).

If I want to approach the builder to do something for me, then I need to have faith in him. In the same way, the Bible says that without faith it is impossible to please Him. He that comes to God must first believe that He exists and that He is the rewarder of those that diligently seek Him (see Hebrews 11:6). If I come to God denying His very existence—something that is self-evident, then I am obviously in rebellion and cannot please Him.

God-given common sense tells us that everything made has a maker. Can you think of anything you own that wasn't "made?" You car, belt, shoes, socks, TV, radio, house, etc. Everything *made* must have a maker. Look around you. There are flowers, birds, trees, the sun, the moon, the stars, etc., every one of which is far more complex than anything that man has made.

Actually, man hasn't really "made" anything. Ask our most intelligent scientist if he can make you something from nothing. Just a flower. Maybe a bird—from nothing. We don't know how to "make" a grain of sand. We can recreate, but we have no idea how to create. So, if modern man, with all his genius cannot create a grain of sand from nothing, how dare he imagine in his wildest dreams that this incredibly complex creation of which we are a part, came into being without a Maker. Such thoughts are intellectual suicide.

The dictionary says that *proof* is "evidence and argument sufficient to induce belief." Every man and woman has enough evidence in creation alone to give belief that there is a Creator. This is why the Bible says, "The fool has said in his heart 'There is no God.'"

Trainee Preachers

Back to Yale University—the next day. Brian took me into the heart of New York by train, and we preached at Washington Square in Greenich Village. As I broke the ice, the place reminded me of the square in which I spoke for many years, but there were a lot more people, and a lot more drugs. When we spoke, we had much opposition (it was hand-to-hand combat). One woman fumed because I said that abortion was wrong. When I asked her if her baby was born a month premature, if she would cut its throat herself if she didn't want it, she said she would.

As we were leaving the area, Brian said, "We will preach on the train going back through the Bronx." I remember thinking, "You've got to be kidding! *Are you nuts?* The Bronx has a murderous reputation at the best of times. If people were offended in the open (from which they could leave), how much more angered would they be if they couldn't get away?" He couldn't see my thoughts, so I said, "Let's do it!"

As the train went through the Bronx, it was packed to capacity. Brian broke the ice this time. He made his way into the middle of the carriage of 90 people, introduced himself and began preaching. Not one soul objected. They just sat there and listened. I felt so proud of this new friend of mine as he boldly warned them of Judgment Day, and preached the Cross of Calvary. In fact, I became so encouraged, I tapped him on the shoulder and whispered, "I want to preach." It showed me how you and I can give courage to others by paving the way.

We both preached, gave out over 300 tracts, and felt so excited, we could hardly sleep that night.

When I told a friend in California that we had preached on the trains in New York, he widened his eyes and said, *"What about the conductor?"* I smiled and said, "Oh, we didn't have any music . . . we just went straight into the preaching."

CHAPTER TWENTY-ONE

AWAKEN A SLEEPING ARMY

"But His word was in mine heart as a burning fire
shut up in my bones, and I was weary with
forbearing, and I could not stay"
(Jeremiah 20:9).

Venice Beach is famous. It's also weird. In fact, there are so many strange things going on at any given time in the renowned Southern California tourist spot, I could carry Lazarus over my shoulder, and not get too many strange looks. He was just one among fire-eaters, sword-swallowers, palm-readers, armless and legless break-dancing dwarfs, and turban-wearing roller-bladers.

Lazarus is our corpse. He doesn't say much, but he sure helps draw a crowd. He gives people a reason to stop and listen to a preacher, in a Gospel-hardened nation. Sometimes he lies on the ground with a sheet over him, other times he lies across the arms of two undertakers in top hats and tails. Next to the undertakers, stands my waiter. He is also dressed in tails, but with no top hat, and he carries a silver platter on one hand. "What," you ask, "is a waiter doing standing next to a preacher, two undertakers, and a corpse? And what does he have under the platter?" That's the same question people ask as they stroll by, and some are even curious enough to stop for a moment, and listen to the preacher.

Under the platter are some props. A rubber brain, a rubber eye, and a few other essentials for an open-air preacher in the last days. When I refer to the human brain, the waiter (with great poise), lifts the lid. I take the brain in hand and say, "This is a brain. It makes you think, doesn't it? It's basically meat. Throw it to a dog, and he will probably eat it. Yet, all the sophisticated computers in the world combined cannot do what this brain can. It can think on its own . . . yours may be doing that right now." Then I speak about the difference between mankind and animals.

After speaking for a while, I look toward my son-in-law EZ, and nod. This is what we call tag-preaching. He jumps on to the soapbox, and opens up some more interesting thoughts, until a crowd gathers. Then he too preaches the Gospel of salvation.

It was a Saturday in September 1996. It was hard work, but overall, it had been a good day. Two lesbians from a second-story window had heckled us. A crazed woman had screamed at me from a distance of six inches. It looked as though she would rearrange my face, but she didn't. In fact, she helped draw a larger crowd.

On the way home, EZ raved about Venice Beach. We had preached at a number of different places along the coast of Southern California, and had mostly been greeted by apathy. He raves about anything to do with the Lord. He is always pestering me to go open-air preaching. When the Apostle Paul wrote to the Corinthians, he said, "Your zeal has provoked very many," and EZ's zeal provoked me. That's why I was pleased that an organization in New Zealand had invited him and my daughter Rachel to minister, in the land of new zeal. It would be an opportunity for EZ to not only see my old preaching haunt in the city of Christchurch, but to also preach there.

Oops!

It was early November 1996. We had only been in New Zealand for an hour, and I was already speaking to a crowd in "Speaker's Corner," in Christchurch, New Zealand. As I spoke, someone was throwing banana peels at me. I could see out the corner of my eye, that whoever it was, had short dark hair, and was wearing blue jeans and boots. As I turned to the crowd and said "Perhaps you feel like this man here . . ." I heard a loud, "*I'm not a man!*" Then this distraught lady, screamed something at me, and stormed off, much to the amusement of the crowd.

After I apologized to the woman as she stormed off, someone gave me a bear hug from behind, then walked into the crowd and began to heckle me. It was Tom. He was a gentleman who heckled me almost daily for three years. He used to spit at me or on me, depending on the wind direction. It was so good to see him—after eight years. Suddenly Steve showed up. Steve also heckled me for years. He had a most sincere, heartfelt, deep-rooted, genuine caustic hatred for the Gospel. He was a homosexual, and a "backslider," who never slid forward in the first place. He was Mr. Bitterness, and he was letting his venom out once again . . . and helping to draw a goodsized crowd. He was even better than Lazarus–which is quite a compliment.

A year earlier, I hadn't had such a good day there. While I had been speaking, Bill the Buddhist showed up in the crowd. Bill was a product of the modern Gospel. He had given his heart to Jesus many years before. His claims to have had Jesus appear to him in the form of light, had never impressed me. But as he stood in front of me and yelled abuses, he looked radically different from the Bill I had known over the prior years. His face looked gaunt. His skeletal body was dressed in female clothing, and he was as bitter as an unripe (unpeeled) lemon.

As he bellowed at me, I began speaking on the subject of homosexuality. This didn't bother him, until I referred to him as "homosexual." The lemon exploded. He rushed out of the crowd, pulled me off my soapbox and dragged me from the scene. I couldn't help but feel humiliated. In the past, when I had been slapped in the face, I was able to turn the other cheek. This time I had no choice. Bill, who was taller than me, pulled my shirt up over my head, and dragged me from the scene across the square to the local police station.

He was furious because I had called him a "homosexual," when he maintained that he was a "transsexual." He intended to press charges against me for such an insult to his integrity, but changed his mind when he cooled down. When I made it back to the crowd ten minutes later, they were waiting to see the outcome. I gathered what dignity I had left, stood on my box and said, "Sorry about that. I often get 'carried away' when I'm speaking." They laughed, then clapped, which was some consolation for my humiliation.

However, the day EZ and Rachel were in the Square, things were humming. I was pleased that Bill hadn't made an appearance.

More Plane Speaking

Three days later, I was on a plane sitting next a friend who loved our "curved illusion" tracts. These tracts fooled the human eye into seeing something that wasn't true. When a curved pink and blue card were held together, one looked larger than the other. But they were identical in size. People found them fascinating. In fact, when I gave them and our "Wallet"[11] tract to flight attendants at one airport, they were so impressed, they upgraded me to first class.

As we sat on the plane, my friend Julian was so enthusiastic about the tracts, he said, "Let's show them to the passengers!" I wasn't *that* excited. I wanted to encourage his zeal, so I didn't betray my thoughts.

We decided to try the cards on the stewardess before he spoke to the passengers. When her reaction was very positive, he asked if he could show the passengers. She hesitated, then said, "O.K., but be quick." To my delight, Julian then stood to his feet, looked down the aisle and said, "Excuse me. We have, with permission of the airline, a little on-board entertainment . . . which one looks bigger, pink or blue?" Then I handed him a pile of tracts, as he gave them out to the passengers.

As he sat down, he then confided in me that it was the first time he had done such a thing. Eternity will show if God used those tracts to speak to one of those passengers, but it was a blessing to see such a concern for the eternal welfare of sinners. God bless this faithful soldier of the Lord. His zeal provoked me.

---

[11]Don't leave the Wallet in sight within your car. We have had a number of people tell us that their car was broken into, and only the tract stolen.

Putting Your Life on the Line

Let me ask you a few questions. Would you find it difficult to give out tracts on a plane? Could you preach in the open air? Could you give a tract to the person behind you in a supermarket line? Do you have a fight with fear? I certainly do. The thought of frontline (or even backline) battle paralyzes us.

Here are some more questions. Would you like to try bungie jumping? Many Christians would. I know this because I often ask congregations these questions. I ask how many would like to try sky diving. Hands shoot up. How many like roller coasters? Most *love* them. Then I ask them what it is that they like. It's the fear. It's the adrenaline rush. I tell them that I saw a man bungie jump and the bungie cord came untied. A teenager from our youth group tried the thrill of sky diving, and her parachute twisted. *She fell to her death at the age of 17 years.* I guess she was the one in every 100,000 who fall to their deaths. You may have seen an incident on television, where a 13-year old boy tried sky diving. He became so paralyzed by fear that he didn't pull the ripcord, and for some unknown reason, his automatic emergency shoot didn't open. He fell 2,000 feet to his death. I also inform congregations that between 1973 and 1996 there were 45 deaths in the U.S. from roller-coaster-type rides, and over 6,000 injuries.

Think of it. We are prepared to put our lives on the line—*to risk death*, for the love of fear. But for the *fear* of fear, we are prepared to let sinners go the Hell forever.

What then is the difference between the two fears? One we love, one we hate. One is a thrill, the other a torment. The tormenting fear we feel is *very* real, yet the reason for this fear is irrational. I have experienced it thousands of times when I give out a tract, or when I strike up a conversation with a stranger with the objective of sharing my faith. Yet when I rationalize the feeling, it was totally *unfounded* fear. There was nothing to fear, but the next time it manifests, it is just as strong.

How then do we overcome it? Simply by realizing that the fear I feel in my heart, is a barometer of the truth that I hold in my hand. God has not given us the spirit of fear, so it is obvious where the "tormenting" fear is coming from. *It is enemy propaganda.* We wrestle not against flesh and blood, but against spiritual wickedness (see Ephesians 6:12-18). The origin of our fear is not from within our hearts, it is from the hosts of Hell.

Why Do You Ask?

A few days after the good day in the Square, I was on another plane with Rachel and EZ. A rather large man was sitting next to me reading a book. When I inquired if it was a good book, he said that it was interesting. I gave him a few minutes, then asked what he did for a living. Most people don't mind being asked that question, but this man looked at me and abruptly said, "Why do you ask?"[12] I answered that I was just being friendly, and asked if he was a cop. He said that he wasn't. There was silence for a moment, then he said, "I am the Dean of Saint Paul's Cathedral."

When I asked if he had been born again, he said that he didn't embrace that slant of "evangelical language." When I said that it wasn't "evangelical"

---

[12]I found out later that the man was guarded toward me because he had seen me giving out tracts at the airport.

255

language but the words of Jesus, stated in John Chapter Three, he piously said, "I can accept that." He had the warmth of dry ice.

There were a couple sitting across the aisle. I turned toward them and asked where they were from. They didn't speak English, so I asked, "United States? New Zealand?" and lifted my shoulders in a questioning gesture. Their eyes lit up and they said, "Barcelona!"

This was my chance to see if our two optical illusion tracts had the ability to transcend the language barrier. I held up the two cards, then swapped them over. It worked! They opened their eyes wide with amazement, so I passed them the cards. It was then that I found that they were a part of a 40 strong tourist party, so I passed the tracts to each of them. Then I gave them our wallet tracts. They loved that, so I gave out our pennies with the Ten Commandments pressed into them. They didn't know what I had given them, so I said, "The Ten Commandments!" They remained puzzled. I said "Moses!" and gestured a "beard" on my chin. I then reached into my bag, grabbed my Bible and held it in the air. They yelled, "Biblia! Biblia!" It was then that I heard the sound of melting ice. The Very Reverend was laughing.

I was on a roll. I did a sleight-of-hand trick for the crowd, and they laughed with delight, calling "Bravo! Bravo!" I was now standing in the aisle and did another trick. More "Bravo's!" then spontaneous applause. I bowed, and for some reason, felt like a bullfighter.

That's what we are—bull fighters. A great beast called "fear" stands before us. If we don't overcome it, it will overcome us. We must take hold of the red cape of the blood of the Savior, and bring it into submission. The Bible says, "They overcame him with the word of their testimony and the blood of the Lamb." Then we must kill the beast with the two-edged sword of the Word of God—"I can do all things through Christ who strengthens me."

EZ's zeal had provoked me. Julian's zeal had provoked me, and I pray that what zeal I have will provoke you. If you have never given someone a tract, maybe you will say to yourself, "I could never stand in the aisle of a plane and give out tracts, but I think I could drop one in a shopping cart as I'm leaving a supermarket." Or maybe you could ask someone, "Did you get one of these?" and pass them a tract. Perhaps a Christian friend will see you do that, and your zeal will provoke him.

My enthusiasm even had an effect on my cool religious friend. Afterward, he smiled and became very friendly toward me. A little boldness had not only put a pile of Christian literature into the hands of a party of Barcelonian tourists, but it had warmed his heart. He even took one of my books, saying that he would read it, and he sought me out later to give me one of his business cards.

It was Charles Spurgeon who gently reminded his hearers on the importance of enthusiasm. He said, "When you speak of Heaven, let you face light up, let it be irradiated with heavenly gleam, let your eyes shine with reflected glory. But when you speak of Hell, well, then your ordinary face will do."

CHAPTER TWENTY-TWO

THE ENEMY'S DEVICES

"Lest Satan should get an advantage of us: for we
are not ignorant of his devices"
(2 Corinthians 2:11).

Since the time of Christ, there has been continual opposition to the Gospel of Salvation. Jesus said, "You shall be hated of all men for My sake." Isaiah said, " . . . he that departs from evil makes himself a prey." Anyone who repents of sin will become a target for the anti-Christ spirit which rules the world (see Ephesians 6:12, 2 Corinthians 4:4). From the time of Nero, when Christians were set on fire as torches to illuminate the darkness of his gardens, until the present day, Satan has sought to come against the Gospel with every possible means.

As the world throws itself blindly into sin, the more it will hate righteousness. When I first started preaching back in 1974, there was a semblance of opposition, but as time has passed, the antagonism has become more intense. I remember open-air preaching once when a woman began accusing me of the usual "judge not least you be judged" thing. Suddenly, the whole crowd of about 200 people, in one great wave of the anti-Christ spirit became a vast lynching mob. The incident gave me some understanding of what Stephen came up against when his listeners were offended by his words. Humanity seethes with hatred for the truth, and all it takes is a little stirring for that enmity to boil over. The enemy has millions of more-than-willing soldiers who are longing to unleash a barrage of malice against the ambassadors of the God they hate. Many a Christian would have followed in the bloody steps of Stephen had not civil law restrained the ungodly.

Some weeks after the "judge not" crowd, an angry young man who looked like the type who came out of the tombs, picked up a large wooden cross, which a Christian had leaned up against my preaching-ladder. He then used it as a hammer to smash it into a thousand pieces in a fit of demonic rage. I stood back and thanked God that the ladder was bearing the reproach, and not me.

A few days later, a well-dressed plump woman in her early thirties came out of the crowd, yelled at me in the most obscene language, slapped my face, then punched me in the mouth. A few weeks after that a rather heavy gentleman, who said that he had "been sent into the local square to stop the preaching," made me want to do what Jesus said, and flee into another city when persecuted.

I repented of fear, but the next time he was in the crowd, he had a can of gasoline in his hands. I remember thinking as he listened to me preach, "I want to be 'on fire' for God, but not like this!"

The following day he stood in front of me again. In a fit of rage, he screamed out obscenities as I preached. This time I was not at all fearful. There were two reasons for this. The first was because God was with me, and the second (unbeknown to the man), two policemen were standing directly behind him.

Suddenly, he stopped the obscenities and began to, in a deep powerful voice yell, "Get out of my way! Get out of my way! Get out of my way!" He bellowed this about twenty times. Then the police made their move. It took them more than twenty minutes to arrest him and put him in the squad car that was right behind them. I watched fear come on the faces of the non-Christians, who could hear animal-like screams coming from his mouth as demons manifested themselves through him.

Rarely is there freedom from opposition to the Gospel when it is preached in truth. Sometimes it's blatant, other times it is very subtle. Many times I have been criticized by professing Christians who tell me that I should preach about the love of God, rather than talk of sin and judgment. I usually coax them onto my soapbox and ask them to show me what they mean. One thing I have noticed is that when they speak about love, God's goodness, and God's wonderful plan for humanity, etc., the crowd is passive. There isn't a word of opposition. But as soon as sin, its fearful consequences, God's holiness and the Cross are mentioned, they become offended and oftentimes angry.

One of the Eight

I remember once watching in disbelief as a woman dressed in black, stood in front of my crowd as a self-proclaimed prophet to the nation. She looked the part, holding a wooden staff in one hand. She pulled a diamond ring off her finger and threw it at the crowd, saying that it was symbolic that God was divorcing the nation. Then she smashed a bottle on the ground, saying that He would destroy the nation for its iniquity. She claimed that she was alive 2,000 years ago, and helped Paul write the Epistles. She also said just as in the days of Noah, only eight would be saved. She was one of the eight, and she determined the other seven. She also maintained that my spirit visited her in the night (it did not). Four-letter filth words would spill out of her mouth as she brought God's reproofs to the nation, in perfect King James English of course.

These few incidents, plus a number of others have ingrained in me knowledge of the truth that we don't wrestle against flesh and blood, but against hateful spirits, who "work in the children of disobedience" (Ephesians 2:2). Believe me, your struggle as a soldier of Christ to do battle is more than a mere fear of man. Jesus called Satan the "father of lies," and the lies come thick and fast into the ears of those who want to fight the good fight of faith. The Bible tells us that when "the enemy shall come in like a flood, the Spirit of the Lord shall lift up a standard against him" (Isaiah 59:19). We are seeing the tide of occult activity gush upon this world. Satan is walking about as a roaring lion a little faster than in times past, because his time is short. He is seeking whom he may devour. At the moment he may devour many, because many are in his territory.

The subtlety of the spiritual occult realm is its guise of harmlessness. This was epitomized in the following letter I received from the manager of a large book publisher:

"Mr. Comfort, it may be of interest to you that I specialize in writing books on the occult, and you would probably find some in your local library (occult source-book, other temples, other gods, inner visions, etc., etc). My experience of Christian evaluations of the occult is that they are invariably shallow and misinformed and worse than that, extremely intolerant. How the Hare Krishna, Mormons, J.W.'s, 'The Occult,' E.S.P. and T.M. can be classified together, let alone dismissed out of hand, is beyond me. Isn't Christ Himself a mediator who has E.S.P. and healing gifts? P.S. I once had a vision of Christ while on an LSD trip and it was very awe-inspiring. How do you explain that? Was I possessed by the devil?"

Years ago, my children attended a school where the principal confided in me that the occult did have a fascination. He said that the school now "studied the occult domain each year at Halloween as it studied Christianity at Christmas and Easter" (Halloween is an ancient Druid celebration of death, honoring the god of the dead). He even shared how a ten-year-old had asked him about ectoplasm, which the dictionary says is the "viscous substance exuding from the body of a spiritualistic medium during a trance." My eldest boy came out of class the same day I spoke to the principal and said, "They're still doing it Dad . . . today we learned about yoga and levitation." I took my kids out of the school that same day and put them into a Christian school.

All around us we are seeing fascination for the occult. Psychic hotlines and other demonic activities are being endorsed by celebrities. One magazine carried a real deal for just two dollars: "Yes! Here is the biggest bargain of the decade for the millions of men and women just like you who understand the importance of astrology and luck in your lives."

The advertisement continued to say that this Astro-luck package will bring the greatest love, joy and happiness in your life. Along with a special chart came a "Maya cross." This little symbol of good fortune was said to bring love and wealth, and was referred to as an "ancient talisman." It continued with the words, "obey that impulse . . . order now," and asks the very relevant question, "Will this cross transform your life?"

The word "Maya" comes from Hindu philosophy and means "illusion." The word "illusion," according to the dictionary means "deception."

What's in a Trinket Anyway?

Some years ago, two teenage girls approached me to see if they could talk to me about the demonic realm. They were both non-Christians and didn't know how to express their concern. I arranged to speak with them the following day. To cut a long story short one of the girls[13] manifested demons on the floor of my office. After she regained consciousness from a time of exorcising prayer, and I counseled her to commit her life to Christ and also make a complete break of all occult practices, which included getting rid of a small trinket which she wore around her neck. Two weeks later, I received a phone call from her friend to say that she was still having blackouts. Once again all sorts of demonic manifestations came through this quiet young girl as she laid on my office floor in a blacked-out state.

As she lay on the floor, I noticed she was gripping something around her neck so tightly that all the blood had drained out of her hand. I pried back the fingers of her now white hand to find the trinket I had told her to get rid of. It looked like "Tinkerbell" from Peter Pan, and was made of silver. I felt it was probably a goddess of fertility, or something similar. I took it from her hand, walked to the other side of my office and hit it with a hammer. She remained blacked-out in the far corner of the room. Two of my friends were praying for her. I had my back to her, and yet every time I hit that trinket with the hammer, demons in her screamed. I must have hit it

---

[13]This incident is related in depth in our book, *The Power of Darkness.*

five or six times and each time I hit it, they screamed. It was like something out of a horror movie.

This is the Age

The first book of Timothy 4:1 warns: "Now the Spirit speaks expressly that, in latter times, some shall depart from the faith, giving heed to seducing spirits, and doctrines of devils." That is the age in which we are now living. I read an article recently where psychologists related a case of one man having 26 different personalities. The newspaper stated that each personality had a complete and separate identity. One psychologist said it was "just like a scene from *The Exorcist*."

After I had spoken at a young people's camp, a seventeen year-old asked for counsel. His complaint was that he had an inferiority complex. As I quietly prayed for him he blacked out, slumped onto the floor, with his back arched, and screamed as demons began to manifest.[14] Using the authority of the name of Jesus I commanded the spirits to tell me the area of stronghold in the young man's life. The word "Bitterness!" came from the youth's mouth.

When he regained consciousness, I counseled him to let go of any bitterness he held against anybody, justified or unjustified (see 2 Corinthians 2:10-11). I then asked him to tell me what areas of occult activity he had been involved in. He listed a number, including ouija boards, LSD, Satanic praise, drinking blood (under the influence of marijuana) and of course, rock music.

What would cause a young man to drink blood? He was deeply into the ancient rock group AC/DC, and had been influenced by their album, "You Want Blood? You've Got It!" Other tracks on their album were, "Hell

---

[14]Obviously, an inferiority complex doesn't mean automatic demonic possession. Most of us have some sort of inferiority complex.

Ain't Such a Bad Place to Be," "Rock and Roll Damnation" and "Sin City."

This incident happened way back in the eighties. Not long after the incident, I did an indepth study of the rock world. Bear in mind that it has gone further downhill since that time. Many of these musicians are now dead. But their music is still popular (they being dead, yet speak), and it will be around for many years to come. Let me share what I found with you.

One very popular artist of that time was Alice Cooper. In real life he was known as "Vincent." Vincent, who was the son of a Baptist preacher, revealed in an interview in a secular magazine that he was once in a seance when a spirit manifested itself. It promised him that if he would allow it to inhabit his body, it would make him and his group world famous. Vincent then named himself and his group after the demon spirit "Alice Cooper."

Alice sang about necrophilia (the joy of having sex with a corpse). On stage, he jumped in and out of coffins, and even hung himself, and had the rope cut just before he was about to die. He also had a preoccupation with snakes. On one of his albums, he was pictured urinating on the back cover, with a smear of blood across the front cover. He sang, "So pray for him father, you need not bother! 'cause I am the fox and I go where I want . . . if Heaven ignores me, the devil adores me."

Another group that our young friend was into was Iron Maiden. They derived their name from a horrific medieval torture instrument, and called their third album (a million albums sold), "The Number of the Beast." Many other groups showed obvious links with the demonic world. The Plasmatics, who took their name from blood plasma, had tracks "Butcher Baby," "Living Dead" and

"New Hope For The Wretched." Judas Priest sang, "Sin After Sin," while Ozzie Osbourne was well known for chewing the heads off bats and doves on stage. His albums were aptly named, "Diary of a Madman" and "Paranoid." Cossy Powell, originally known as The Sorcerers, sang their top hit "Dance With The Devil." Led Zeppelin, who have been heralded "a deity," didn't bother to hide the fact of demonic involvement: "The mystery of the world's most exciting band was heightened by Jimmy Page's well-publicized flirtation with the occult and black magic ceremonies . . . the mysterious death of drummer John Bonham in late 1979, effectively drew their eleven year chapter to a close."

Jim Steimer, the lead singer of Meat Loaf said, "When I go on stage . . . I get possessed!" KISS, who incidentally sold well over 30,000,000 albums said, "We are members of the Satanic brotherhood of America first and musicians second!" As usual, with rock stars, the lead singer Gene Simmons revealed his likes and dislikes to the fans, "I've always been interested in what human flesh tastes like." The lead singer of the group was compelled to see the movie, *The Exorcist,* 26 times! Blue Oyster Cult called one of their songs, "Don't Fear The Reaper," on which they sang of suicide, referred to Beelzebub, and stated the truth when they sing, "Our father is not in Heaven!" The Eagles released an album called "A Day In Hell." They also sang about "Witchie Woman," and had a track called, "They Just Can't Kill The Beast." They were all members of the first Church of Satan, in fact their biggest hit was about that church, and was called "Hotel California." The geriatric Rolling Stones, who signed the biggest recording contract in history released an album entitled, "The Satanic Majesties' Request" and sang, "Sympathy for the devil," while "Queen" sang, "Beelzebub has a demon set aside for me" . . . the list goes on and on.

Jimi Hendrix said back in the sixties:

"Atmospheres are going to come through music because the music is in a spiritual thing of its own; you can hypnotize people with music and when you get them to the weakest point you can preach in the subconscious what you want to say. The music flows from the air so that's why I connect it with the spirit."

I preached once in open air about occult-rock and was afterward approached by a non-Christian teenager. He said how he had gotten high while listening to a song called, "Stairway To Heaven." He was standing directly in front of the stereo listening, when suddenly he "fell backward and went into a fit." Obviously, at that point a spirit entered him.

One of the groups I looked at was "The Dead Kennedys." On the front cover of their album called, "In God We Trust" they had a picture of Jesus crucified on a dollar bill. Four-letter words were common with their song called "Religious Vomit," referring to the president of the United States of that time, as being "Born-again with a fascist craving." Catch the words of one of their songs with a message:

"God told me to skin you alive . . . I kill children . . . love to watch them die . . . I kill children . . . make their mommies cry. Crush them under my car . . . I love to hear them scream . . . feed them poison candy . . . spoil their Halloween."

Around the time I was studying this music, I was driving in my car when I saw a group of people in the middle of the road. As I approached, it was obvious that a child had been knocked off his bike a few minutes earlier.

I drove past and saw a sight that I will never forget. The child was dead because his head had been crushed under a car. I wept all the way home. It turned out that five doped youths had been trying to scare kids on bikes with their car and on this occasion they had gotten one. The spirit that permeates through many of those into this music, is written backward on their T-shirts . . . "REDRUM" . . . MURDER.

The Enemy Hates Light

A Christian friend pulled into a fast food restaurant and heard a local Christian radio station on full volume. He remarked that it was good to hear it. The woman attendant replied, "I only have it on that station to keep the punk-rockers away. They don't come near this place when that station is playing."

If there is one thing that rock music has in common, it is the spirit of rebellion. The word rebellion is from a root word meaning "bitterness." It means "to be disobedient, to provoke and to rebel." Rebellion in the heart of man is an open invitation for demonic possession. The Scriptures warn that "an evil man seeks only rebellion; therefore, a cruel messenger shall be sent against him" (Proverbs 17:11). The word "against" comes from a Hebrew word which is always used in relationship to a downward aspect. This was evident in the life of King Saul who was rebuked by Samuel with the words, "Rebellion is as the sin of witchcraft," and Saul followed that downward trend of being tormented by a demonic spirit.

Sin says, "Not Your will, but mine!" Psalm 10:4 tells us that "the wicked, through the pride of his countenance, will not seek after God." It is not that the ungodly cannot seek God, it is that he *will* not. The rebellion of the will is clearly evident in the fall of Lucifer:

"How you are fallen from Heaven, Oh Lucifer, son of the morning! How you are cut down to the ground, you who weakened the nations! For you have said in your heart: *I will* ascend into Heaven, *I will* exalt my throne above the stars of God; *I will* also sit on the mound of the congregation on the farthest sides of the north; *I will* ascend above the heights of the clouds, *I will* be like the Most High" (Isaiah 14:12-14, italics added).

A young punk-rocker once manifested demons after I had spoken at the church he was attending. The strongholds in his life were, sex, vanity and rock music. I sat the youth down, gave him a drink of water and said, "I want you to pray about your sex life, your musical tastes and do a study on humility." The next evening I received a phone call from him saying that he had taped over all his rock cassettes with Christian music. He also decided to stop frequenting bars (as he had done in the past as a professing Christian), and he was also going to tell his girlfriend that he now loved God, and their sex life was over.

He found complete freedom from the demonic realm *because he closed the door by an act of his own will.* Any professing Christian who has continued difficulties with the demonic realm more than likely has given an open door to the enemy. The Bible says, "Give no place to the devil." If he "has a place" it's because it is being given to him.

Many Christians live in a world of naiveté when it comes to the demonic world. We once had a meal with a Christian family, and during the meal the mother got up from the table to turn up the volume on the television so that her son could listen to his favorite heavy rock music.

On one of the most popular children's programs on television, I watched in unbelief, as they introduced the program with a group similar to KISS (the SS is shaped like the SS on the Nazi police uniform). The rock group on this program was called "Molech." Molech was the name of the Ammorite idol of the Old Testament, which sat upright with arms outstretched. The arms were heated until they were white hot. Children were placed into its arms as a sacrificial ritual. Drums were constantly played to drown out the screams of the child.

To encourage children into rock music is to place them into the white hot arms of Molech, and the beat and power behind the music will drown out the cries of the child as occult powers envelop him and take him into the fires of Hell.

I received the following letter from a young girl:

"Some time ago, I had a rather frightening experience through listening to rock music (before I was born-again). I've been a Christian since I was about ten years old (I am now fifteen), but I never walked in the light until now.

"My girlfriend and her boyfriend were in the dining room while I was in the lounge dancing to some rock music. While I was dancing something made me turn off the light. Suddenly, my body seemed possessed by some kind of spirit (something like the Holy Spirit, but instead of peace it made me terrified), but I was sort of fascinated. I danced for about one hour not knowing which direction I was facing, moving with the music. When the tape ended I was able to find my way to the switch and turn the light back on. My friends had come into the room and were watching me, I walked over to them and sat down. I couldn't even speak. My friend said to me, 'Don't look at me like that Tracy.' I managed to speak by now and asked, 'Like what?' She replied: 'You've got the devil in you!'"

When someone gives themselves over to heavy rock music, they don't get into the spirit . . . it gets into them.

The word 'wiles' used in Ephesians 6:11 to describe "the wiles of the devil," comes from a Greek word *methodieas.* It is the word from which we derive our English word 'method.' One of Satan's major methods of snaring this generation has been the international method of music. Maybe you are ignorant of this fact, but ancient rocker David Bowie wasn't. He said, "Rock and roll has always been the devil's music—you can't convince me it isn't."

Wired for Sound

I heard about a young girl who saw a wire hanging from the top of her house. She grabbed the wire with one hand and was fascinated to find that as she moved its raw end across the concrete, sparks began to fly. She then gripped it with both hands, and began to wave it back and forth across the concrete with sheer delight as sparks flashed like sparkling fireworks. Unfortunately, her hand touched a piece of broken wire and a mass of electricity began to flow through her little body. She screamed, 'Mommy, Mommy . . . *my hands are on fire!'*

Her mother rushed out of the house, but was flung away by the power when she touched her child. It was then that a passerby ran into the garage, grabbed an axe and cut the wire.

That action saved the little girl's life, but not before she had been severely burned. That story is a graphic illustration of the occult. Satan attracts the mind through fascination, but waits until he has your will—until he has both hands on the wire before he pours on the heat. Those who escape with severe burns are fortunate compared to the many who don't. The only answer is to sever all connections with the sharp axe of renunciation. Paul speaks of this in 2 Corinthians 4:2: "We have renounced (disowned) the hidden things of dishonesty (Greek—*shame*)."

What Should We Then Do?

There is no doubt that the enemy is coming in like a flood, but the question is what should God's people do about it? First, I believe that we should 'sanctify the Lord God in our hearts,' and our homes. Do we have any idols sitting in our homes in the form of statues, pictures, paperweights, souvenir masks, occult books, tarot cards, etc.? If you are not sure about a certain item, pray about it and if you have no peace, destroy it. If you have a fascination for the mystics, repent of it. The fascination means that the door is slightly open, even if it is only for you to peep through. Desire to look into the mystics is a work of the flesh (see Galatians 5:20) which, for a Christian must be reckoned dead. Those who practice such things will not enter the Kingdom of Heaven (verse 21), so you don't even want to be tempted.

Satan has many ways and means by which he is attacking this generation. As we have seen in this chapter, rock music is one of them. The Bible warns us that the enemy is very subtle and will often resort to camouflage. The dictionary meaning of camouflage is a "disguise of guns, ships, etc.; affected by obscuring outline with splashes of various colors; use of smoke screens, boughs, etc. for the same purpose; means of throwing people off the scent."

Let's look closely at a few camouflaged items. If you have had any dealings with the occult; if you've been harboring bitterness; or if you've been into Dungeons & Dragons, ouija boards, seances, heavy metal rock music, L.S.D., color therapy, fortune-telling, horoscopes, hypnotism, E.S.P., psychic powers, levitation, good luck charms, astro-projection, transcendental meditation, etc., you need to renounce it or them from the heart. That means you pray a prayer of abandonment. Pray something like this:

"Satan, I totally renounce you and (name the area of the occult you were into). I disclaim it! I don't want it in my life! In Jesus' name, I submit to God and resist you and all your works. I am cleansed by the blood of Jesus. I close the door to Satan and open myself to be completely possessed by the Holy Spirit. In Jesus Name I pray, Amen."

Real-life Drama

I was waiting to minister to a gathering of about 300 youths. Most of them were Christians. Just before I was about to speak, the local youth group performed a drama. To create the "atmosphere," they turned down the lights and played some heavy rock music. It worked. The air was electric. A spotlight flashed onto an obvious prostitute, a drug addict . . . suddenly in the darkness a scream came from the congregation. Then there was more screaming. *This wasn't part of the drama.*

A young man who had been into the rock scene began to manifest demons. As the lights were switched on, the youth, in a demonic fit flung himself across a table where my publications were on display, then rolled onto the floor, where he screamed and writhed.

The pastor asked what he should do. I told him, then changed my message to the "power of rock music."

I was told some months later that many of the "Christians" there that day, had their jackets zipped up to hide rock music T-shirts.

If you find yourself counseling someone who has been into the occult, be wary of prolonged demonic manifestations. When someone begins to manifest demons, I pray against the spirit, in Jesus' name; command it to tell the area of stronghold, then have the person pray a prayer of renunciation. Often one can determine the area of stronghold through a few questions before prayer, i.e., "Do you honor your parents, have you been into the occult? etc." If there has been a resentment, bitterness or some area of sin that would allow a foothold for the enemy, there may be a scream or some sort of manifestation, but don't get caught up for hours praying for or arguing with the spirits. They are seeking to wear you down. More than once, Jesus told demons, "Hold your peace, and come out of him!" Just get straight into the prayer of renunciation.

Some time ago, a clean-cut, well-dressed Malaysian student asked me why his hands contorted when he went to prayer. I asked him if he had been into Buddhism and he said that as a child he had bowed to his grandmother's altars. As I began to pray his hands twisted and contorted, then he began to choke.

I led him in a prayer of renunciation, renouncing Buddhism, and Satan. The moment he prayed, his hands went back to normal and peace came to his mind, because *he* closed the door. You can pray for someone until you are blue in the face (literally), and it will do no good if that person will not submit to God. That submission is what makes the enemy flee.

I was ministering at a camp when a girl in her late teens approached me, and asked whether or not I thought she should get rid of a rabbit's foot key ring she had been given as a gift. I said that she should pray about it and come to her own decision about destroying it. I had made my mind obvious through the message I had given that morning. She came back the same afternoon and told me that after praying about it she felt the Lord said that it was "O.K. to keep it." That night she manifested demons at the altar.

In another incident, I went to visit a woman who had been having oppressive problems and I was amazed to see a 4 to 5 foot carved idol in her living room! It was a gift from her husband, and she felt that as a Christian she should do all that she could to keep peace in the home. I directed her attention to Deuteronomy 7:25-26:

"You shall burn the carved images of their gods with fire; you shall not covet the silver or gold that is on them, nor take it for yourselves, lest you be snared by it; for it is an abomination to the Lord your God. Nor shall you bring an abomination in your house, lest you be doomed to destruction like it; but you shall utterly detest it and utterly abhor it, for it is an accursed thing."

Her attitude was a little short of what it should have been. In fact, she had nicknamed the thing "Charlie." She also manifested demons at an altar some time later.

Other things on the list which should be renounced are witchcraft, astroprojection, Masonic Lodge, numerology, wearing an Ankh cross (similar to the Christian cross but with a loop at the top), practicing yoga or practicing martial arts such as karate, etc., (some of these things are harmless to begin with but have ties with idolatry or the mystics), practicing automatic writing, taking LSD, or being involved with or practicing anything which is of the mystics. If you have prayed to idols or statues of Jesus or Mary, there also needs to be a total renunciation (see Exodus 20:4-5).

This one is my personal conviction (so please bear with me if it seems petty). I am also convinced that men wearing earrings has adverse spiritual connotations. Earrings on men speaks of rebellion. In the past they have been very prevalent among homosexuals, punk-rockers, gypsies and pirates. Notice in Israel's rebellion of Exodus Chapter 32, that the people "broke off the golden earrings," which speaks of some sort of bondage to Egypt. A young man told me that he was about to preach the Gospel on a street corner, and God spoke to his heart and said, "You are not preaching My Gospel with that thing in your ear." Another Christian was saved out of a rebellious lifestyle. The moment he was saved he removed the earrings from his ear. Then he was drawn into a group who began murmuring about the pastor. Back in went the earrings. When he understood from scripture that he was not "murmuring against Moses, but against God," he repented, and immediately took the earrings out again.

They were in themselves harmless, but were outward indicators of inward rebellion. *I have no right to tell another Christian that he shouldn't wear earrings.* That's between him and God, but he should understand that jewelry carries tremendous power in the spiritual domain.

Listen to these words of a converted witch, relating about suicidal thoughts she had:

"Because I still wore the rings that had been given to me on the night of my initiation, I still had contact, and they (those in the witches coven) were able to contact me through my mind."

Those who feel that the International Peace Movement is a worthy cause, should take the time to study the origin of the "Peace Symbol." According to the historian, Nestorius, it is an inverted and broken cross. Titus' legions bore it on their shields when they destroyed Jerusalem in 70AD and it then became known as the "broken Jew." It has been used by Arab commandos of the Palestinian Liberation Front. Bolsheviks painted it on the doors of the church buildings they closed in the revolution, and it was branded on the bodies of Jews killed by communists during the Spanish Civil War.

If you have had any involvement in any of these things listed you need to not only renounce involvement, but you need to destroy the object. Don't sell your rock albums, destroy them, preferably in fire (see Acts 19:19, Deuteronomy 7:25).

CHAPTER TWENTY-THREE

BUILDING THE SOLDIER'S COURAGE

"I beseech you therefore, brethren, by the mercies of God, that ye present your bodies as a living sacrifice, holy, acceptable unto God, which is your reasonable service" (Romans 12:1).

The Scriptures tell us in the Book of Chronicles that Amaziah, King of Judah did that which "was right in the sight of the Lord, but not with a perfect heart" (2 Chronicles 25:2). How could someone do something which is "right" in the sight of a perfect God, with an attitude that is less than perfect? The word "perfect" in this case doesn't mean sinless perfection, but comes from a Hebrew word *shalem*, meaning "made ready." It means serving God with a wholeheartedness, with a "Here I am Lord, send me" attitude. I certainly don't want Sue doing that which is right in my sight "but not with a perfect heart." I don't want her to hand me my slippers saying, "Dinner is served Sir," like a well-trained housemaid. No, like every husband, I want my wife to be devoted to me with her whole heart. I know that she feels the same about me.

Sadly, much of the contemporary Church is in the state of doing that which is right, without the perfect heart God desires. We pray, fellowship, give our money, read the Word, yet so few are prepared to take the Gospel to every creature, to be "fishers of men," to preach the Word in season and out of season . . . to say, "Here I am Lord, send me."

If we want to see this world reached with the Gospel, we must also have a fire in our soul. Late in 1996, I was making my daughter a cup of tea at 6:00 in the morning, dressed in a white robe (which is scriptural). As I reached out to lift to the boiling kettle off the stove, I heard a curious sound. It was a "whoosh" noise. I looked at my left sleeve and noticed that it was on fire. Then I heard another similar sound, this time around my back. Then I heard a third "whoosh" as my right sleeve burst into flames. I said to myself, "Ray . . . you have a problem." I also remembered that I had placed a fire extinguisher in the kitchen for such a time as this. Its instructions said something like: "Stand about six feet from the fire, and aim the nozzle at the base of the flame." I did have a problem.

I decided that I would take the burning robe off. As I disrobed, and threw the garment to the ground, I heard another "whoosh," as the whole thing burst into flames. It was then that I realized that the robe's manufacturers had soaked it in gasoline to make life more interesting for those who purchased it.

I learned two things from the incident. One: Don't lean over a naked flame in a white bathrobe, and Two: A man on fire moves rather quickly.

When you look at the soldiers of *The Book of Acts*, they moved rather quickly. That's because they were on fire for God. The zeal of God's House had eaten them up. They were about their Father's business. They were whole heartedly sold out for the Kingdom of God. That's the key to the power of God being manifest in the Church. The Bible says that "the eyes of the Lord run to and fro throughout the whole earth, to show himself strong on behalf of them whose heart is perfect toward Him" (2 Chronicles 16:9). That's the same word—"perfect." Many Christians are living in defeat because they are not serving God with a "perfect heart." The Lord is not showing Himself "strong" on their behalf. We need to be "willing in the day of (His) power."

Harry Houdini was undoubtedly the most famous escape artist to ever live. Even though he defied death so many times, he didn't die trying to escape from some death-defying feat. A young man who had heard about Houdini's incredibly strong stomach muscles, approached him backstage and struck him a blow to the stomach. Unfortunately, Houdini was caught off guard and received a ruptured appendix. Seven days later he died of peritonitis.

Satan knows that the Christian can sometimes be caught backstage, off guard. That's why there are so many warnings in Scripture about "watching" and being "sober and vigilant," because your adversary the devil walks about seeking whom he may strike in the stomach. Each of us needs to have the strong muscle of a holy lifestyle pulled tight to resist the blows of the devil. None of us want to be caught off guard.

Fresh Water Surfing

For years I was hooked on surfing. I don't surf now for a number of reasons. There are too many sharks off the coast of southern California seeking that delicious, saltwater delicacy, soft surfer's leg[15]. Besides, if I go for a summer surf and get caught in the freeway traffic, I don't get back until winter. But I will definitely take it up in the millennium when the sharks are friendly, and the water is warm. We will have 1,000 years before God does away with the sea, then it's freshwater surfing for eternity.

Before surfboards became smaller and lighter, we didn't even think of tying them to the leg, as they do nowadays. If you fell off, every instinct within you would tell you to seize the board, because if you didn't, you would have a long swim to the shore to retrieve it. I had no idea how strong this instinct was, until I tried water skiing.

I took off after the boat, and things were fine for about ten seconds. Suddenly, I fell, and found myself being dragged under the water for about thirty feet. My impulse was to hang onto the rope even though I was under the water. Dummy! I ended up with a head full of saltwater.

When we come to Christ, our sinful nature doesn't want to let go of the ropes of our pet sins. Habitual sin is ingrained in our nature, but if we have any sense, we will let go because sin will do nothing but drag us down.

A 20 year-old man was on a snowmobile in Colfax, Iowa in the late seventies. He was having a ball, racing around on the glistening white snow. He swung the machine around and sped between two wooden posts at about thirty miles an hour. That was the last thing he did. A thin, almost invisible wire between the posts, decapitated him.

Satan will let you have a ball. He will let you race around and enjoy the pleasures of sin for a season. You

---

[15]I did get some satisfaction recently when I had lunch at a pastor's house. He had his TV on during our Sunday meal. The movie "Jaws" was on, so I watched it while I ate shark for lunch.

are in his territory, so you therefore give him permission to devour you. His will is only to "kill, steal and destroy," and somewhere he has a wire strung at just the right height for your neck. All he needs is a little cooperation. He wants you to put your foot on the accelerator and get up a little speed.

How to Succeed as a Thief

A popular magazine once ran an article by an ex-cat burglar. He didn't steal cats, he preyed on the homes of those of us who are ignorant of his ways. Most of us, because of a lack of knowledge, virtually put up a sign saying, "Thieves, I'm outta town, so come in and steal what you want."

This is how we do it. We have unlit rear entrances which are enshrouded by trees and hedges. They act as a magnet for the burglar. The ex-thief said that a loud air conditioner was an open invitation. If people could sleep through its noise, they weren't going to hear him breaking into their home.

He would even masquerade as a newspaper subscription salesman, knocking on doors, ready to do a phony sales pitch if anyone answered. Then he would leave a card on the door handle, if no one answered. If it was still there the next day, it was a sure sign that the family was away.

A name on the mail box gives the burglar all the information he needs to find your phone number and call to see if you are home. Even alarms don't guarantee security. Often people put the alarm sticker on the front of their house to scare away would-be burglars. All the burglars do is write a letter to the company and say they are wanting to purchase an alarm system. They then study the literature to become familiar with it so they can easily disarm it. Exterior alarms can be filled with shaving cream to silence them, while most locks can be simply picked. Windows can be silently broken by applying a sheet of paper covered with Vaseline, so that when they break, they do so silently.

He says that most people lay out their houses like a candy store. They place their jewelry, wallet, etc., in the bedroom or by the kitchen sink, and if he needs a car, the keys are on the end of the counter. The man's best advice to stop burglars: "Get two dogs, and make sure they bark." He said that even a house guarded by a Chihuahua is well protected, because people wake up when the dog barks. He advises that if you hear a burglar in the house, not to confront him. If he has a gun, he will probably shoot you and even all the family, rather than go to prison. His advice, and the advice of the law, is to call the police.

Satan knows what he is doing. He is an expert in his field. He sees many signs that tell him he is safe to make entrance. A dusty Bible is an open invitation. Lack of the light of good understanding is another open attraction. He wants us to be in the dark—to be "ignorant of his devices." He wants a sleeping Christian, someone not watching and praying, as Jesus told us to.

Don't confront the devil, call upon God for backup. If you have a problem with lust, realize that it is a weapon of darkness that will be the death of you. Call upon the Lord. Tell Him to disarm the devil. Tell Him that you don't want that creep creeping around in your property. He only comes in the dark, and you need to walk in the light to keep him away. Have the guard dog of a good conscience, and listen when he barks. He is there to protect you.

Dogmatic Resistance

Even before I was converted, I stumbled upon a major Scriptural principle. I was riding my motorbike home from work, when a rather large, vicious German shepherd rushed out of a driveway and began to snap at my back tire. As I was about to pour the power on (it was a Honda 50) and leave the animal in the dust, I had a thought: "Wait a minute! Greater is that which I am sitting on than that which is chasing me!" I then stopped the bike, much to the bewilderment of the dog, turned it around and chased that animal up the street.

If Satan is chasing you, slam on the brakes and say, "Greater is He that is in me, than he that is in the world," then submit afresh to God, resist the devil, and he will flee from you. You have God's promise on that (see James 4:7).

I once showed up in the local square to find that one of my preaching buddies was being hampered by peace protesters. They were holding a rally on the other side of the square and had come across to ask him to stop preaching. Their argument was "We are all on the same side; both standing for peace." I gently told them that we preach peace *with* God while the peace movement preached peace *without* God.

I then told my friend to keep preaching. That upset the peace people, to a point where they purposely and persistently pushed, pulled and poked at the poor preacher. When they stopped him, I felt something erupt within me, and immediately began preaching about 20 feet away. They ran toward me to stop my speaking. When they stopped me, my friend burst into flames, and so it went on until they gave up.

If you have never felt the wind of persecution blow upon the fire of the Holy Spirit within you, you are

285

missing out on something amazing. You don't know what power dwells in you until that fan fuels the flame and sparks a boldness in your spirit. We have tapped into the supernatural realm. The Bible tells us, "that when Saul made havoc of the Church" the disciples were scattered abroad and went everywhere preaching the Word (see Acts 8:3-4). Saul merely stirred the winds of persecution. When Paul was placed in prison, he wrote that "many of the brethren in the Lord, waxing confident in my bonds, are much more bold to speak the Word without fear" (Philippians 1:14). Others took up the mantle of Saul of Tarsus, and now persecution against Paul stirred the fire in his brethren. He went on to write " . . . in nothing (be) terrified by your adversaries."

The Battle of Fear

As I have mentioned before, if you are like me, *every time you venture out of the barracks to do battle, you will first battle with fear.* When you size up someone before you approach them to give them a tract or witness to them you will hear a voice say, "Are you kidding! Look at the guy . . . *and you think you are going to give him a tract?* He's an obvious Christian-hater if ever I saw one. Look at his Christian-hating jaw and his Christian-strangling hands. He's praying for some self-righteous fundamental fanatic to try to ram religion down his throat. As soon as you open your mouth, he's going to rip your ears off. He will humiliate you. No, you shouldn't do this. Don't be a fool, go back to the barracks where you will be safe."

I remember once going down to the local municipal courts and waiting to witness to anyone who would listen. There was hardly a soul in sight so I said, "Lord, I will wait here for five minutes, and if no one comes I will go home."

Three minutes later, I watched a couple in their 20's sit down about 50 feet from me. I said, "No Lord, I want people to be by themselves. People are more open when they are alone." I was about to go back to the Comfort Zone (we have a sign on our house saying "The Comfort Zone"), but I felt so guilty, I reluctantly walked across, sat down beside them and gave them both an IQ tract. They said that they had "Charismatic" Christian backgrounds, but I felt that they weren't right with God. I said to the young lady, "Do you think you have obeyed the Ten Commandments?" When I asked her if she had ever told a lie, she said she had. I asked, "What does that make you?" She said, "A sinner." When I said, " . . . a *liar*," her mouth dropped open in shock. It was obvious that she had never thought of herself as a liar, but I told her that is how God sees her. When I reasoned with her about it she nodded in agreement. She also admitted that she had broken the other Commandments and agreed that if she died in the state she was in she would go to Hell.

Then I turned to both of them and said, "No fornicator will enter Heaven. If you have sex before marriage that is breaking the 7th Commandment also. God sees everything you do; He even knows how many hairs are on your head!"

The young man looked at me in unbelief and said, "That's weird. *I was just reading that this morning!*" He then brought out a pocket book of God's promises and said that he was in bed with his girlfriend reading about the fact that no fornicator would enter God's Kingdom, and that He knew how many hairs were on his head. *He was reading Scriptures until 4:00 a.m. and was so stirred that his girlfriend thought he was on drugs.*

I told them that they needed to repent, put their faith in Jesus and live according to His Word. That meant they must stop having sex and get married, if they loved each other, *then* they could enjoy the pleasures of sex. I said, "Imagine if you had $20 that you were going to give to your son as a surprise, but an hour before you were to give it to him he stole it out of your wallet. That's what you have done with the gift of sex." They both nodded, and we prayed together. Thank God I didn't go back home. The devil's a liar and if the fears come thick and strong, you can be sure God wants to use you for His purpose.

The Will and Conscience

If you use the Law in this way—reasoning with sinners with love and gentleness, you will deal directly with the will and conscience. Many Christians instead deal with the intellect. Rather than seeing conviction of sin, they find themselves in a discussion about evolution, the validity of Scripture, or hypocrites in the Church. Rarely do those subjects even come up when you use the Law. When a man is looking down the barrels of Ten Great Cannons, he becomes more concerned about his own survival rather than issues that suddenly seems irrelevant. If side issues do come up, deal with them as quickly as possible, then do what Jesus did in Luke 13:1-5. Bring the sinner right back to his personal responsibility before God on Judgment Day.

Here's some ammunition I have found helpful in the battle for sinners: Imagine if I said to you that I was working for the UCLA Medical Institute, and that our scientists, due to recent changes in the law, can now pay big money for human eyeballs. Not only could your eye give sight to a blind person, but you would walk away with one million dollars in cool, tax-free cash. What's more, the operation would be totally painless, take less than one hour, and the fake eye would look as good as the authentic one. You will look the same; but you won't *look* the same . . . one eye will be blind. *Would you sell me one of your eyes for a million dollars?*

Perhaps you would sell just one eye for a million dollars. *How about selling both for fifteen million?* Think for a moment what you would do with all that money— you could see the world. Not quite. You could sit at home in the blackness of blindness and count it. I'm sure no one in their right mind would consider selling his or her eyesight for *fifty* million dollars!

Perhaps you have never given it any deep thought, but your eyes are priceless, and yet they are merely the windows of the soul—the "life" that peers through the shutters of your eyes. If your eyes are without price, *what must your life be worth?* In fact, Jesus said that your life is so valuable, you are to actually *despise* your eyes in comparison to the worth of your soul. He said that if your right eye causes you to sin, you are to pluck it out and cast it from you, for it would be better to go to Heaven without an eye than to go to Hell blind, where the "worm never dies and the fire is never quenched." He said that the combined riches of this entire world are not worth losing your soul—"What shall it profit a man if he gains the whole world and loses his soul?"

Of all the things you should prioritize in your life, it's your eternal salvation. The most important thing in your life is not your health, your marriage, your vocation, your ministry, etc. It is the salvation of your soul. These things are merely temporal. Your salvation is eternal.

I was sitting on a plane once and noticed that the young man next to me had consumed three cans of beer on the flight. After I had witnessed to him, I said, "Be careful of that stuff. Any doctor will tell you that it will make you impotent by the time you are 45 years old . . . know what I mean?"

He suddenly looked *very* sober. Out the corner of my eye, I could see him biting the top of the can thoughtfully. From then on he ordered sodas. I remember thinking "If only he was as concerned about his soul as he was about is his body."

Since then, I have found that the selling of the eye offer helps sinners see the value of their soul. I have heard many people I have shared it with say, "I've never thought of it like that. Wow!"

CHAPTER TWENTY-FOUR

CHARACTER OF THE ENEMY

"...that you may be able to successfully stand up against all the strategies and deceits of the devil"
(Ephesians 6:11).

One of the most vital keys in a war, is to know your enemy—his strengths, his weaknesses, his weapons, etc. Thank God, the work has already been done in this area for us. We need not send out reconnaissance. Reconnaissance is "a military examination of tract by detachment to locate the enemy or ascertain strategic features." The Word of God exposes every strength, weapon and weakness of the enemy.

In this chapter, we will further study the methods of the dark side. We will do this so that we know how to attack, and how to defend ourselves when attacks come. To understand the full nature of our enemy, we will look at his name and his activities according to the Scriptures.

First, he is called an accuser and a slanderer:

" . . . for the accuser of our brethren, he who keeps bringing before our God charges against them day and night, has been cast out!" (Revelation 12:10, *Amplified Bible*)

This is clearly illustrated in Job 1:9-11:

"So Satan answered the Lord and said, 'Does Job fear God for nothing?' Have You not made a hedge around him, around his household, and around all that he has on every side? You have blessed the work of his hands, and his possessions have increased in the land. But now, stretch out Your hand and touch all that he has, and he will surely curse You to Your face!"

Satan is an accuser by nature. The word "devil" means accuser. This was epitomized once just after I had finished preaching in the open air. For nearly two years, a young lady heckled me. This woman was so demonically controlled, I was able to use her as a spiritual barometer to gauge the depth of the anointing on the preaching. When I could feel the energy[16] of the Holy Spirit—a confidence, a clarity of thought, a knowledge that something is happening in the hearts of the hearers, I would notice that she became very agitated. Ninety percent of the time she did nothing else but accuse.

I had just disembarked from my preaching ladder when a woman handed me a carnation. I felt stupid standing there holding it. I passed it to a beer-drinking, tattooed young lady who was standing beside me and looked as though no one had ever given her flowers. The whole incident, from my receiving the flower, to passing it on, took about ten seconds. As the first lady handed it to me, my heckling lady friend shouted, "Aha, receiving flowers from strange women!" As I passed the flower onto Miss Tattoos, she yelled "*Ungrateful!*"

---

[16]This is difficult to explain unless you have experienced it.

[17]It's interesting to note that the world hates hypocrisy in the Church. They detest the "pretender." Does that mean that they *want* the Christian to be genuine? Do they *want* us to be true and faithful in our witness and therefore

There was no way I could win. That incident epitomizes the accusations of the devil. ²He will hate you if you do, and he will hate you if you don't.

A phrase that you may have heard in Christian circles is, "pleading the blood." This is a legitimate and effective weapon against the accuser. In a sense we are standing in the eternal court of Almighty God. Satan is the prosecutor (accuser). God is the Judge. Jesus is the counsel for our defense (Advocate). We are the accused. Satan points his accusing finger toward us and calls for retribution. He wants us damned. What do we plead . . . innocent or guilty? The answer is neither. We are neither innocent, for we have transgressed the Law of God, nor are we guilty, for the blood of Jesus has washed our sins away. So, we plead "the blood." What we are doing in pleading the blood is saying, "Satan, the blood of Christ hasn't just covered the evidence of our sins, it has completely washed them away—our sins no longer exist. Our case will be dismissed for a lack of evidence!" We are able to say, ". . . for the prince of this world comes, and has nothing in me."

As long as we remain free from sin, Satan has no grounds to accuse—we need never to feel guilty: "There is therefore now no condemnation to them which are in Christ Jesus, who walk not after the flesh, but after the spirit" (Romans 8:1).

If Satan isn't busy accusing you in your own mind, you can be sure that he's busy slandering your name elsewhere . . . that's if you are "living godly in Christ Jesus." Jesus said, "Blessed are you, when men shall revile you and persecute you, and shall say all manner of evil against you falsely, for My sake."

---

speak of sin, righteousness and Judgment? Do they want us to live in holiness rather than in compromise? Does the world really want us to speak up against pornography, greed, adultery, abortion, homosexuality, fornication, and other sins they so love? In their eyes we are damned if we do, and damned if we don't.

I find it hard to keep up with the enemy's lies. Years ago I was involved in drug prevention work, and heard that I was "Mr. Big" in the drug world. I was also surprised to hear that I had done six years in prison, that I smoked dope, that I owned two properties, that I owned a very expensive car and that I had terminal cancer.

Our attitude to all these things is to "rejoice and be exceedingly glad." The enemy only shoots for those soldiers who are a threat to him.

If you hear a rumor about a brother or sister, defuse it if you can. Say to the person who is firing the bullet, that you will do your best to find out the truth. You don't want to be an instrument of Satan to discredit a fellow soldier of Christ.

Satan is also the blinder of the minds of men:

"And even if our Gospel is veiled, it is veiled to those who are perishing. The god of this age has blinded the minds of unbelievers, so that they cannot see the light of the Gospel of the glory of Christ, who is the image of God" (2 Corinthians 4:3,4).

Notice that the Scriptures speak of the Gospel as being light, and the sinner as being in darkness. This darkness of the mind is also substantiated by Ephesians 4:18, ". . . having the understanding darkened, being alienated from the life of God through the ignorance that is in them, because of the blindness of their heart."

This is why it is so vital to use the Law of God when witnessing to a sinner, "For by the Law is the knowledge of sin." Remember that Paul said, "I had not known sin, but by the Law." As the sinner begins to see himself according to the Law of God, it gives him something to measure himself by. He begins to understand what sin is. He will only call for mercy when he understands that he needs to call for mercy. Satan hates Christians grasping the reason why God gave His Law. He knows that when they work with the Holy Spirit and use the Law to convince and convict men of sin, there will be more soldiers enlisted in the Army of God. The decision to follow Jesus is not made in blindness, nor from an emotive response, but from a clear understanding of the issues of salvation.

Those who preach judgment, but fail to use the Law to give the sinner something to measure himself by, will either produce a spurious conversion or one who lacks gratitude. If Hell alone is preached, those who come to a decision do so solely out of fear, and not out of repentance. He flees from the wrath to come but deep in his heart he considers God to be unjust. He doesn't see himself worthy of Hell because he hasn't seen sin as being "exceedingly sinful," which comes only by the Commandment (see Romans 7:13). This state of deception hides from him the true nature of Calvary's cross. He fails to truly see it as an expression of God's love for undeserving sinners.

Satan is also a counterfeiter. He has created a massive religious system which masquerades as God's representative on earth:

"For such men are false apostles, deceitful workman, masquerading as apostles of Christ. And no wonder, for Satan himself masquerades as an angel of light. It is not surprising, then, if his servants masquerade as servants of righteousness. Their end will be what their actions deserve" (2 Corinthians 11:13-15).

Satan can disguise himself as an angel of light. This is why it is vital for us to exercise godly discernment.

We are to judge prophecy, test the spirits, walk in wisdom, watch for wolves, mark those who cause division in the ranks, and to look for the fruit of genuine conversion.

As we have seen, our enemy is as a roaring (noisy) lion. He is called an adversary. The Greek word used is *antidikos*, which primarily means an appointment in a law suit (accuser). We are exhorted to resist him steadfast in the faith, taking consolation that other Christians are involved in the very same battle we are involved in.

Another enemy tactic is to bring division into the ranks by creating false impressions, and bringing about misunderstandings (see 2 Thessalonians 2:9-11). The way to deal with this is to have good lines of communication with each other.

Friendly Fire

"Friendly fire" is the army's way of saying that they killed their own troops. It's an absurd expression. There is nothing "friendly" about being shot in the back by your own side. "Stupid," "tragic" or "betrayal" are far more applicable. Whatever it's called, to kill someone in your own army is to do the work of the enemy.

Early in 1997, a 26-year old man was the subject of much gossip in his church in Costa Mesa, California. He was said to be a nice young man with a friendly disposition, but the incessant gossip was too much for him. He hung himself. His suicide note merely said "Gossip kills." He was a victim of friendly fire. Think of his parent's pain. Think of the testimony of a church who kills its own. Think before you lend your tongue to demons!

Be careful to keep unity within the ranks of the Army. Some years ago at the Seattle Special Olympics, nine contestants, all physically or mentally disabled, lined up for the 100-yard race. When the starting gun fired, they took off, not exactly in a dash, but with a relish to run the race to the finish and win. All, that is, except for one boy who stumbled on the asphalt, fell over and began to cry. The other eight heard the boy cry, slowed down and looked back. They all turned around and went back. *Every one of them.*

One girl with Down's Syndrome bent down and kissed him and said, "This will make it better." All nine linked arms and walked across the finish line together. Everyone in the stadium stood, and the cheering went on for several minutes.

Unity in the Body of Christ receives Heaven's acclamation.

A Land Mine

In 1 Timothy Chapter 3, Paul speaks of the enemy laying "snares." These land mines often lie hidden beneath the surface of the ground. To tread on one can be extremely injurious and can even destroy one's ministry. Paul's words to Timothy were, "He must also have a good reputation with outsiders, so that he will not fall into disgrace and into the devil's trap."

Some years ago, I fell right into one of these snares. Sue and I were invited to do a series of meetings and speak in a number of schools in a certain district. In those days, I would use the subject of drug abuse as a springboard to the Gospel by making out a list of questions such as, "Have you ever used drugs?", "Do you think Christianity is a legitimate answer to the drug problem?" There were about fifteen questions in all.

At the end of the week, a newspaper reporter interviewed me regarding my activites. I told him that I had visited five schools and spoke on the subject of drug abuse. I named the schools that had kindly allowed me to speak to their students. At the end of the interview, the subject of the survey arose. The reporter suggested that we count how many students had actually experimented with marijuana. I was amazed to find that one in four had used the drug at one time or another. We parted with a friendly handshake, then Sue and I left for our flight home.

The day after arriving home, I received a long distance call from the area in which I had ministered. It was a radio reporter, who opened the conversation with "We would be interested in asking you a few questions . . . you've made headlines up here!"

It turned out that the reporter had entitled his story, "ONE IN FOUR IN SCHOOLS USE DRUGS!" Anti-drug campaigner, Ray Comfort stated today that one in four students used marijuana . . ." *Then he named the schools I had visited.* The article gave the distinct impression that I had left the schools who let me speak, and betrayed their trust by going straight to the newspapers. The story was also run on network radio and nation-wide television.

Over the next few days I received a stream of letters from principals and Christians who spoke of things such as prudence and ethics. I ended up writing a mass of apology letters in an attempt to clean up the mess I had made. I had stepped onto a well-camouflaged land mine.

The U.S. Army now has something to combat land mines. It is call "The Grizzly." It looks like a tank with a v-shaped plough attached to its front. This machine is so powerful that it cuts through the soil at 15 inches below the surface, cutting a 15 foot wide pathway of safety for the ground troops. That's what "grizzly" prayer does for the soldier of Christ—"acknowledge Him in all your ways, and He shall direct your paths." As we commit our way to God through prayer, He plows a way of safety for our feet to tread.

How to Beat a Bout of Depression

Perhaps the most common weapon in the enemy's arsenal is depression. He is trying to put de-pressure-on. Paul spoke of being "pressed out of measure" (see 2 Corinthians 1:8). Such pressure can surround a soldier like a high barbed-wire fence. Sometimes depression can come because of circumstances, and sometimes we can find ourselves depressed for no apparent reason. Whatever the case, whether natural or spiritual, the depressed soldier is a weak soldier. The joy of the Lord is his strength and when there is no joy, there is no strength. There are times when, as with David, we find ourselves talking to our souls and asking why are we cast down. We know that we should rejoice, yet the wall of depression seems to stop us. For such a condition, I believe I have a sharp pair of wirecutters.

More than likely, the "natural" circumstance which has caused us to be in a state of despondency, has a "spiritual" origin. The Scriptures tell us that we "wrestle not against flesh and blood." Satan wants to render us ineffective.

Let's say that someone has told me that "Brother Smith" has been offended by me. It's nothing I've said or done. He just doesn't like me. But because I work with him I have to rub shoulders with him every day. Suddenly, I find that I am thinking negative thoughts about this man. In fact, I can't stop thinking about it. I seem to be trapped by my thought-life. I say, "I will not think anymore about the situation!" Then before I know it, I am chewing the whole bitter thing over again. The more I say, "I will not think about it," the more it plagues me. I become depressed and lose my joy, and the last thing I feel like is doing battle.

If you have had such an experience, take heart. This remedy works. When the enemy hurls the grenade of depression at you, throw it back at him with one of your own. Turn a negative into a positive.

This is how to prepare the explosive. Take a pen and paper and write down what you hope to achieve in God. Write down everything you think God would like to see happen in your life. Then write down everything you think Satan would not like to see happen in your Christian walk.

Now shape those things into a positive prayer/confession. This will be mine for the Brother Smith situation:

"Satan, every time you come at me with negative thoughts, I am going to pray this positive prayer: Greater is He that is in me than he that is in the world. No weapon that is formed against me shall prosper and every tongue that shall rise against me in judgment, I shall condemn. This is the heritage of the servants of the Lord. I have the righteousness of Christ, and because God is for me, nothing can be against me. I can boldly approach the throne of Almighty God and ask what I will, knowing that it shall be done for me. Thank you Lord for Your faithfulness. Right now, I ask in Jesus' name, that You make me an effective soldier for the Kingdom of God. Open doors that I might take ground for the Kingdom. Make me a prayer warrior. Grant me a greater burden for the lost. Fill me with Your love, give me wisdom, and let my life glorify You in every way. I ask You to forgive me for my bad attitude toward Brother Smith. I pray that You will richly bless him and his family. Give me a special love for him. Show me what I can do to express my love for this brother. Thank you Lord that these things will surely come to pass because You have said, 'All things whatsoever you ask in prayer, believing, you shall receive.' In Jesus' Mighty Name I pray, Amen."

Type or write down that prayer of affirmation, and appropriate it to your particular situation. Have it photocopied three or four times, and keep one in your pocket, one by your bed and one in your car or at work. Read it aloud *every* time your negative thought comes. *The negative thought will remind you to pray that prayer.* Every time that negative thought comes, it will be like a ringing bell saying, "How about praying that prayer of positive confession?" Instead of wearing you down, he will be building you up. You will be turning a negative into a positive.

This works, but you must be diligent. If you find yourself thinking negatives straight after you have prayed the prayer, say, "So it's going to be hand-to-hand combat is it?" Grit your teeth and pray it again, and again. Soon you won't have to look at the paper. You will find yourself automatically praying the second that negative thought comes. And by the way, expect the answer to that prayer.

How to Lift Yourself Above the Battle

I often use the following principle to help me endure the pains of everyday warfare. Arrows of self-pity and ingratitude can pierce the flesh and grievously wound us. It is a prayer I call "I have a problem..." It also works:

"Father . . . I have a problem. It's weighing heavy on me. It's all I can think about, night and day. Before I bring it to you in prayer, I suppose I should pray for those who are less fortunate than me—those in this world who have hardly enough food for this day, and for those who don't have a roof over their heads at night. I also pray for families who have lost loved ones in sudden death, for parents whose children have leukemia, for the many people who are dying of brain tumors, for the hundreds of thousands who are laid waste with other terrible cancers, for people whose bodies have been suddenly shattered in car wrecks, for those who are lying in a hospital with agonizing burns over their bodies, whose faces have been burned beyond recognition. I pray for people with emphysema, whose eyes fill with terror as they struggle for every breath merely to live, for those who are tormented beyond words by irrational fears, for the elderly who are wracked with the pains of aging, whose only "escape" is death.

"I pray for people who are watching their loved ones fade before their eyes through the grief of Alzheimer's disease, for the many thousands who are suffering the agony of AIDS, for those who are in such despair they are about to commit suicide, for people who are tormented by the demons of alcoholism, and drug addiction. I pray for children that have been abandoned by their parents, for those who are sexually abused, for wives held in quiet despair, beaten and abused by cruel and drunken husbands, for people whose minds have been destroyed by mental disorders, for those who have lost everything in floods, tornadoes, hurricanes, and earthquakes. I pray for the blind, who never see the faces of the ones they love, or the beauty of a sunrise, for those whose bodies are horribly deformed by painful arthritis, for the many whose lives will be taken from them today by murderers, for those wasting away on their death-beds in hospitals.

"Most of all, I cry out for the millions who don't know the forgiveness that is in Jesus Christ...for those who in a moment of time will be swept into Hell by the cold hand of death, and find to their utter horror the unspeakable vengeance of eternal fire. They will be eternally damned to everlasting punishment. O God, I pray for them.

"Strange. I can't seem to remember what my problem was. In Jesus' name I pray. Amen."

In closing this chapter, let's briefly look at other names and titles of the enemy. He is called the god and prince of this world (2 Corinthians 4:4, John 12:31). He seeks to hinder the work of God (1 Thessalonians 2:18). He is a liar, the father thereof and the instigator of lies (John 8:44, 1 Peter 5:8). He is a murderer and a devourer (1 Peter 5:8, John 8:44). He is the promoter of pride (Genesis 3:5, 1 Timothy 3:6). He is the ruler of darkness (Acts 26:18, 2 Corinthians 6:14, 1 John 2:9-11). He is the stimulator of lust (Ephesians 2:2-3). He is the suppressor of the Word of God (Matthew 13:38-39), and he is the tempter (Luke 4:1-13).

Thank God for His Word! Can you imagine trying to fight the enemy without God's War Manual to expose Satan's strategies?

Let any attempts by the enemy to discourage you, encourage you. They are actually a compliment to your potential in God. Early in 1984, God directed me to withdraw from street preaching to encourage evangelistic outreach within the Body of Christ. After nearly a year without the expression of open-air evangelism, I felt that I was beginning to dry up. I decided to spend lunch times on Thursdays back on my ladder. As I embarked upon my inaugural oratory, a woman in her mid-sixties approached me. She reached up, grasped my arm and asked, "What does it say in Hebrews 12 about chastening?" I quoted the requested portion of Holy Writ. She then asked, "What comes after that?" I said that I didn't know. Then in an angry tone, she spat out, "If ye be without chastisement, *then ye are bas—rds!*" As she did so, she began to hit me furiously. I grabbed her arm and said, "If you keep hitting me like this, it will draw me a big crowd!" That disgusted her so much, she walked away . . . it was so good to be back.

"KILL, STEAL AND DESTROY!"

*"Lest Satan should get an advantage of us; for we
are not ignorant of his devices"
(2 Corinthians 2:11).*

Some Christians don't like Christmas. They see
Santa Claus as a disguise for Satan's Claws. Perhaps
they are right. However, instead of getting upset by
Christmas, we should use it to breach the advances of
the enemy.

I once got hold of a flat-decked truck, a pot-bellied
Christian, a Santa Claus suit from a hire service, a large
bag full of candy, some musical instruments, carol
songbooks and a megaphone. On Christmas Eve, we
drove around the street, parked on street corners, and
sang Christmas carols. When adults came out with their
kids to listen and the kids packed around to get candy,
I preached the Gospel on the megaphone using
Christmas as a springboard. The words of some of the
carols are pleading for comment:

"Mild He lay His glory by, born that man no
more may die. Born to raise the sons of earth, born
to give them second birth . . . "

We parked outside bars and watched delighted smiling, beer drinkers come outside to hear carols at Christmas. It was fascinating to see their changes of expression as the subject moved from Christmas to Christ. I will never forget the sight of a red-faced gentleman struggling to lift a large container of alcohol into the trunk of his car, while trying to keep *both* hands cupped over his ears.

We also put together a tract, with Santa "Ho ho ho-ing" on the front, bringing out the meaning of the birth of Jesus.

For years we withdrew from Halloween. There are not too many nice hymns about Halloween. As far as we were concerned, we didn't want to have anything to do with it . . . until one year when we turned this curse into a great blessing. We put tracts and candy into Zip-lock bags, switched on the outside lights, and put a sign up saying "We welcome trick-or-treaters."

Over 100 people came to our door for tracts! It was the easiest door-to-door ministry I have ever been involved in. Now I look forward to Halloween each year as an advance rather than a retreat for the Army of the Lord.

A Cut Above

Some of the proudest hecklers I get are university students. The little knowledge they have puffs them up like a bullfrog doing a midnight mating call. They are also very prejudiced. They see someone speaking on a soapbox and conclude that the preacher is a simpleminded, uneducated, brainwashed fanatic who chooses blind faith in a fairy tale book, rather than to accept the unquestionable wisdom of modern science.

That's why I enjoy taking a friend named Steve with me when I open-air preach. Steve is a thoracic surgeon.

We were street preaching in Santa Monica, when a university student named Ben came up and commented on a plastic brain I have as a sermon prop, to illustrate the ultimate brainless thought—that brains just occur by accident.

As he picked the gray matter up, with an air of educated hauteur he said, "The left side is not anatomically correct." When Steve asked him why he believed that, he revealed the source of his faith: "My instructor told me the left side is larger." Steve then made the comment: "I believe they're both roughly the same size, but there are some neurologic diseases that can cause some change in size and certainly some decrease in size is seen with age."

Ben croaked condescendingly, "What would you know about it?" After all, Steve was one among the groups of simpleton fanatics. Steve replied that he did general, vascular, and thoracic surgery for a living.

Ben smugly picked up the plastic brain and said, "What's this part called?" Steve frowned thoughtfully. "Well, that's called Broca's area of the brain which is responsible for speech. It's located on the left hemisphere of the brain, the right and the left of the brain being divided by the longitudinal fissure, the central sulcus is here with parietal, temporal, and occipital lobes here, here, and here, with the majority of the cranial nerves located here. Is that what you wanted to know?"

Ben mumbled, "Just testing . . . " He didn't pick up the brain again.

Mr. Nasty

Jesus said that no man could serve two masters. We will either love God or we will love money. The one we beckon to is the one we bow to. This was clearly illustrated recently when I went to the local court to share my faith, a place I regularly go to witness. One man who was paying off court fines by working in the parking lot, proved to be very anti-Christian, so I was polite to him but gave him a wide berth each time I saw him.

I spoke to a couple of people and noticed that Mr. Nasty was also talking to his friends, no doubt warning them about me. As usual, I went to slip tracts under the windshield wipers of cars as I was leaving. I have done this with thousands of cars, with never one complaint from a soul.

As I lifted the wiper on the first vehicle, I heard one of Mr. Nasty's friends holler, "Don't put one of those #!@!!** things on my @!**$% truck." I immediately lifted the wiper, took back the tract and smiled at the guy. Then I got my wallet out, and as I did so I heard, "I said, 'Don't !#$!!* put any of that !$!!+*% stuff on my @!$*!* truck!'" I ignored him, got some money out of the wallet and slipped it under his windshield wiper. The tone of his voice altered completely, and he called a friendly, *"Hey, thanks!"*

It was the change from my hand that produced the change in his heart, and revealed the god to whom he immediately bowed.

While We Are On the Subject

While we are on the subject of tracts, here are ten reasons why we should use them:

1. A tract can get inside a house and stay there.
2. It always catches people in the right mood because it speaks to them only when they read it.
3. It sticks to what it has to say and never argues back.
4. It never flinches or shows cowardice.
5. It is never tempted to compromise.
6. It never gets tired, discouraged or gives up.
7. It is very economical.
8. It can present the Gospel when we don't have time to do so.
9. It works while we sleep.
10. It can be mailed to places we can't go.

(Adapted from, *Soul Winning with Tracts,* by Dr. Curtis Hutson)

The days of boring tracts are over. One of our titles is called *The Wallet.* It is so realistic, I have seen non-Christians steal it. One man purchased 35,000 copies of the tract. He liked it. We have one title with a ten minute "getaway time." That means the tract is so well-disguised that you have ten minutes to get away before they even know that it's a Christian tract. As I have mentioned, we also have (among many others) a Titanic tract. I don't think that I have ever had such a good response to any tract. It is such a blessing to see non-Christians smile and say things like "This is wonderful. Thank you very much." I have given out one hundred at a "swap meet" with only one rejection. If you have never used this tract, give it a try.

Here is my approach: "Did you get one of these? It's a "Titanic collectible." As people take it, their faces light up with gratitude, and often they say, "I saw the movie." Then I say, "That will be worth a lot of money in about a hundred years." Often they say, "I'll be dead in one hundred years . . . " and I answer, "Well read the back then, it will tell you what to do." When I have given them out in restaurants, I have had customers and staff come to our table and ask for them. Three months after the movie was released, we were already on our third printing (100,000). It was then that I realized that we were only touching the tip of the iceberg.[18]

Billy Graham said, 'Nothing surpasses a tract for sowing the seed of the Good News.' Why should Christians use tracts? Simply because God uses them. He used a tract to save the great missionary Hudson Taylor, as well as many, many others. That fact alone should be enough incentive for every Christian to use tracts to reach the lost. One lady found one of our tracts at the bottom of a sealed 24-pack of Pepsi. It seems we have a brave soldier at the Pepsi packing plant.

I believe in the ministry of tracts. In fact, if you ever find me in public without a tract, I will give you $20. On two occasions Christians have found me in swimming pools and said, "Aha!" *Aha nothing.* I have tracts on me in swimming pools. If you ever see me, try for $20. I bet you miss out. That offer keeps me laden with tracts, so that when I see someone waiting somewhere, I'm always armed with ammunition. Why don't you do the same?

Spiritual CPR

In mid-1993, a 4-year old girl became sick with what her parents thought was merely a virus. As time passed, she became so ill that they rushed her to the nearby hospital. By the time she arrived, she was clinically dead. Doctors and staff immediately began

---

[18] For details on how to obtain our tracts, see the back of this publication.

emergency procedures on her now ceased heart. After 20 minutes, a special emergency team of ten people were called in and began a procedure where they put so much pressure with CPR on the child's flexible rib cage, it would have crushed that of an adult. After an incredible 41 minutes, the little girl's heart began beating again, making this the longest time in modern history that someone survived heart cessation, without brain damage. The reason the doctors did not give up when others thought the child was dead, was simply because they could see that the child's pupil's were still responding to light. That meant that the brain was not yet dead.

Death has seized upon the sinner. It has justly claimed him. He is without hope, without God, and without light. But never give up on witnessing to him. Make it second nature to apply the pressure of the Law upon his ceased heart. You are working with a team of ten. Remember that "the Commandment is a lamp and the Law is light" (Proverbs 6:23), so watch the pupils to see if there is response to the light. Let that give you hope. The Ten Commandments are working together to bring the dead sinner to a point where he will breathe in the life of the Gospel.

The Honor Roll

We have a multitude of soldiers who have courageously run into battle before us. We need the initiative of Jonathan, who said to his armor bearer: "Come, and let us go over to the garrison of these uncircumcised: it may be that the Lord will work for us: for there is no restraint to the Lord to save by many or by few."

We need the courage of David, who *ran* toward Goliath saying, "You come to me with a sword, a spear and with a shield. But I come to you in the name of the Lord of Hosts, the God of the armies of Israel, whom you have defied!"

We need the insight of Elisha who saw the chariots of fire round about him, and the confidence of Joshua, who knew that God would not fail nor forsake him. The angel of the Lord encamps round about those that fear Him, to deliver them.

We have been called into active service, but in the past we have been more concerned about the *order of* service, than our *orders for* service. God forgive us. We have been given battle orders from Headquarters to seek out those who are enemies of God in their minds through wicked works. We are to persuade and compel them to desert their sin. They must defect before the Great Day of Battle, when the Ultimate Weapon of Eternal Justice will be unleashed against sinful mankind. On that Day there will be no neutral ground . . . they will suffer the vengeance of eternal fire. On whosoever the stone shall fall, it shall grind him to powder. God's justice will be thorough. Our message is "Surrender or be damned. Become a citizen of the Kingdom of Heaven or forever be banished from its gates by the King of Kings, into everlasting fire prepared for the devil and his angels."

We have been sent as an emissary of peace to diplomatically plead with the ungodly to lay down their weapons. But in a world that hates its Creator, we are forced to precede the offer of peace with the threat of war. We must therefore mobilize as a mighty, militant, aggressive army, spearheading attacks through the power of prayer. We must ransack the barracks of Hell

312

and penetrate the territories of the devil with the flag of righteousness and the trumpet of victory resounding.

Retreat is not an option. If we fall back in battle, it is merely to muster forces and gain our spirit. We know that our strengths are the enemy's weaknesses. He crumbles before the powers of holiness, righteousness, justice, virtue, morality and truth.

Unending celestial rations of pure living waters and the bread from Heaven fuel our fighting spirit. Our prayer life energizes our evangelism. We know that we mustn't be casual in prayer, or we will be casualties in war. We give no place to the devil.

It is God Who teaches our hands to war. THE WEAPONS OF OUR WARFARE ARE NOT CARNAL, BUT MIGHTY THROUGH GOD TO THE PULLING DOWN OF STRONGHOLDS. The very finger of God has issued us with the Ten Great Cannons of His Law. The ground troops lie low in humility while the cannons blast over their heads into the soul of the enemy. There is no greater artillery in our arsenal to break the spirit of the adversary, to weaken his lines of defense, or to send terror into his heart. Their very presence generates strong confidence among the troops. As each cannon is discharged, it sends a message of fear and trembling, and the smoke of the wrath of Almighty God.

"No fear!" is our battle cry, and boldness our battering ram. We have been called into combat. We will have no draft dodgers, no cowards, no AWOL, no withdrawal, no cease fire, and *no* surrender! If God is for us, *nothing* can be against us. We are more than conquerors through Him that loved us, and though a host shall encamp against us, we shall not be afraid.

Silence is the enemy we will not let into our ranks. The walls of Jericho have been encompassed. We have been silent too long—it is time to shout down the strongholds of the enemy.

With honor, we will prevail. By the Grace of our God, we will triumph over evil, for when the smoke of battle clears, that is the struggle for which we contest. We fight the *good* fight of faith, so muster your courage, lift up hands that hang down and strengthen feeble knees. Call on the reserve of your valor, and thoroughly grasp the gravity of the cause for which you do battle— for the salvation of the sons and daughters of Adam.

We are not alone. Throughout the world is a loyal infantry made up of men and women who are strategically placed by God. They are unseen through the fog of distance, but they are unified in purpose. Veteran soldiers who have died before us surround us as a crowd of witnesses to applaud our every advance. Don't break ranks. Strive for the unity of the Gospel, following the Captain of the Lord of Hosts who is leading the charge. Through our God we shall do valiantly, for it is He who shall tread down our enemies. Let the trumpet make a certain sound! Hear its soul-stirring sound, and let the stirred soul lift up the flaming sword! The high praises of God are in our mouths. The two-edged Sword of God's Word is in our hands. Cry, "Give me liberty to preach, or give me death! For me to live is Christ; to die is gain!"

We only enlist those who will fling caution to the wind, and who will join an invasion of tooth-gritting, uncompromising, unyielding, relentless, evangelism. We must assault the enemy with spiritual snipers, godly guerrillas, soul-loving storm troopers, counterattacking on the right hand and on the left. Our weapons are love, faith, goodness, mercy, gentleness, and if the world spurns us, if our blood is spilled on the soil of this sinful world for the cause of the Gospel, so be it. If our Commander catches our tears in a bottle, how much more will He value our blood poured out on the earth? The foundation of the Church was laid in the soil of a bloody hill, and soaked with the blood of Stephen and a multitude who 'waxed valiant in fight." If we have also been crucified with Christ it is no great thing to give the supreme sacrifice.

We crave soldiers who will lunge at the devil, who will let him feel the heat of the sharp two-edged Sword and free those who are "taken captive to do his will." We want chivalrous, undaunted, valiant, noble warriors—loyalists, patriots, advocates of righteousness, defenders of the faith, upholders of the truth within our garrisons to force back Satan and his hellish hordes. We must have soul-thirsty soldiers, self-sacrificial "kamikaze" Christians. We ache for twenty-first century soldiers, who are not afraid to bear the scars and stripes of the Lord Jesus.

May God gives us those who will give themselves in the final battle for the souls of men and women, without reserve, to radical, revolutionary, God-pleasing militant evangelism. May He help us be wise and win souls . . . and radically influence this world for Jesus Christ.

"A thousand shall fall at your side, and ten thousand at your right hand; but it shall not come near you. Only with your eyes shall you look and see the reward of the wicked. Because you have made the Lord, who is my refuge, even the Most High, your habitation" (Psalm 91:7-9).

How to Draw a Crowd

Perhaps you are considering doing some open-air preaching. One of the most difficult things to do nowadays is draw a crowd. Today's society has been programmed to want immediate action, and open-air preaching isn't too attractive to guilty sinners. Therefore we have to be as wise as serpents and as gentle as doves. A serpent gets its heart's desire subtly. My (and no doubt your) heart's desire is for sinners to gather under the sound of the Gospel.

This is what I have learned to do: I ask passersby, what they think is the greatest killer of drivers in the U.S. which stirs their curiosity. Some begin calling out "Alcohol!" or "Falling asleeping at the wheel!" I smile and say "No." I repeat the question a few more times, asking those who have stopped that they will never guess what it is that kills more drivers than anything else in America. A few more shouts emit from the crowd. We now have people waiting around for the answer. What is it that kills more drivers than anything else in the United States? What is it that could be the death of you and me? You won't believe this . . . trees! Millions of them line our highways, waiting for a driver to kill. When one is struck, the tree stays still, sending the driver into eternity.

Then I tell the crowd that I have another question for them. I ask what is the most common food people choke to death on in U.S. restaurants? Over the next few minutes, we go through the same scenario. People call out "Steak!" "Chicken bones!" Believe it or not, the answer is "hard boiled egg yoke."

By now we have a small crowd. I ask them what they think is the most dangerous job in America? Someone calls out "Cop." I say it's not. Someone else may say another dangerous profession like "Fire fighter." I say, "Good one, but wrong." I give out a suggestion by saying, "Why doesn't someone say, "Electrician!" Someone takes my suggestion and says, "Electrician!" I say, "Sorry, it's not 'Electrician.'" The most dangerous job in the United States is to be the President. Out of 40 or so, four have been murdered while on the job.

I say I have another question. Does anyone in the crowd consider themselves to be a "good person?" By now I have noted who in the crowd has the self-confidence to speak out. I point to one or two and ask, "Sir, do you consider yourself to be a good person?" The Bible tells us that "every man will proclaim his own goodness," and he does. He smiles and says, "Yes. I do consider myself to be a good person." That's when I ask him if he has ever told a lie. Has he stolen, lusted, blasphemed, etc.? That's when all Heaven breaks loose. There is conviction of sin. Sinners hear the Gospel, and angels rejoice.

Try this way, and with the help of God, you can do it. For further instructions, see our book, *Springboards for Effective Evangelism*, or the video "Open-Air Preaching: New York."

* * *

We have many unique tracts, books, and tapes by Ray Comfort to help you be more effective in your witnessing. We even have a special video series to set you or your church on fire for God—call for a price list, or purchase materials directly with your credit card. This book is available at low bulk copy prices—call us for details. Feel free to check out all of our products on our web site at: www.raycomfort.com

Living Waters Publications,
P.O. Box 1172,
Bellflower, CA 90706.
Credit Cards (800) 437-1893